Wings of Judgm

THE TOKYO INCENDIARY RAID
MARCH 9-10, 1945

North

ARAKAWA CANAL

JOBAN LINE

Ueno Park

SHITAYA

ASAKUSA

SUMIDA RIVER

Honjo Fire Station

HONJO

Kanda Fire Station

RYOGOKU

Ryogoku Bridge

KANDA

FUKAGAWA

Imperial Palace

Tokyo Station

FUKUGAWA

Bombed Area
Fire Stations
Bombing Target Points

0   .5   1 mi.
0   .5   1 km.

EarthSurface Graphics

Wings of Judgment

American Bombing in World War II

Ronald Schaffer

Oxford University Press
New York   Oxford

Oxford University Pressn
Oxford New York Toronto
Delhi Bombay Calcutta Madras Karachi
Petaling Jaya Singapore Hong Kong Tokyo
Nairobi Dar es Salaam Cape Town
Melbourne Auckland

and associated companies in
Berlin Ibadan

Library of Congress Cataloging in Publication Data
Schaffer, Ronald.
Wings of judgment.
Bibliography: p.
Includes index.
1. World War, 1939–1945—Aerial operations, American.
2. Bombing, Aerial. 3. World War, 1939–1945—Moral and
ethical aspects. 4. World War, 1939–1945—Psychological
aspects. 5. United States. Army Air Forces—History—
World War, 1939–1945. 6. Strategy. I. Title.
D790.S33 1985   940.54'4973   85-4861
ISBN 0-19-503629-8
ISBN 0-19-505640-x (PBK.)

3 4 5 6 7 8 9 10
Printed in the Unitetd States of America

To
Robbie, Jenny,
and Dan

Acknowledgments

It is a pleasure to give thanks to the people and organizations who made this book possible. My colleagues, John Broesamle, Ronald Davis, Paul Koistinen, James A. McMartin, and Leonard Pitt provided thoughtful comments on various drafts of the manuscript. Robert Dallek of the UCLA history department offered indispensable advice about this project at a crucial stage in its development. His colleague F.ter Loewenberg led me to the psychological studies consulted for Chapter 9. It should be noted that only I am responsible for errors of fact and interpretation.

I owe many debts to the librarians of California State University, Northridge, UCLA, and the University of Southern California and to archivists, librarians, and historians in several other parts of the United States. I wish especially to thank C. E. Dewing, Edwin Coffee, William H. Cunliffe, Gerald K. Haines, Edward J. Reese, and John E. Taylor of the National Archives and Records Service in Washington, D.C.; John C. Broderick, Chief of the Manuscript Division of the Library of Congress; Dean C. Allard, Head of the Operational Branch, Navy Historical Center in Washington; Judy G. Endicott and Gerard E. Hasselwander of the Albert F. Simpson Historical Research Center; Duane J. Reed of the Special Collections Branch of the USAF Academy Library; Elizabeth B. Mason of the Columbia University Oral History Research Office; Charles G. Palm of the Hoover Institution Archives; Forrest C. Pogue of the George C. Marshall Foundation; Raymond Teichman of the Franklin D. Roosevelt Library; John Wickman of the Eisenhower Library; General John W. Huston, then Chief of the Office of Air Force

History and two of the chief historians who have served in that office, Stanley L. Falk and Richard H. Kohn.

Marcia Dunnicliffe of the California State University, Northridge History Department, typed several chapters and improved the entire manuscript with her keen editorial eye. Dale Pitt provided invaluable suggestions. David L. Fuller of Earthsurface Graphics prepared the map of the Tokyo fire raid. I wish to thank several students who helped sort materials and proofread the text: Christine Stueve, Stephen M. Acheson, Todd A. Sherman, and Peter J. Garon of CSUN and Jenny Schaffer of U.C. Berkeley. Valerie Matsumoto of Stanford helped research the Frederick L. Anderson papers.

The California State University Foundation and the American Philosophical Society assisted this project with summer travel grants. I am especially indebted to the National Endowment for the Humanities, first for the advice of its consultants and then for a fellowship that freed me to write for an entire year. I would like to express my gratitude to Professors Edward Coffman, Robert Dallek, Robin Higham, Peter Karsten, Leonard Pitt, and Russell Weigley who were kind enough to provide evaluations for my grant requests.

My thanks to the people at Oxford University Press who devoted so much time and care to this book: Sheldon Meyer, Leona Capeless, Melissa Spielman, and Tessa DeCarlo. Finally, and most of all I want to thank my wife Robbie Schaffer for her counsel, encouragement and love.

Northridge, California   R. S.
May 1985

Contents

Introduction

Several years ago I came across a remarkable passage in the official history of the United States Army Air Forces in World War II. The commander of U.S. Strategic Air Forces in Europe, it said, opposed recommendations frankly aimed at breaking the morale of the German people by bombing them. According to the air force historians, this officer repeatedly raised the moral issue involved, and Army Air Forces headquarters in Washington strongly supported him on the grounds that such operations were contrary to air force policy and national ideals. What seemed so extraordinary was the notion that in the midst of a savage, atrocity-filled war, American generals based military decisions at least partly on moral concerns.

Several questions immediately suggested themselves. What did American air force leaders understand by the moral issue? Did they share the ideals their headquarters ascribed to the American people? How did their views of moral questions affect the way they conducted the air war?

Reflection and an examination of air force records suggested further lines of inquiry. To understand how the leaders of the AAF thought about and reacted to the moral issue it was essential to investigate their doctrine and to examine its influence on bombing policies and practices. Personal histories of the air force leaders, including the training they underwent, had to be taken into account. Since the president, the secretary of war, and the heads of the other armed forces held much responsibility for Army Air Forces operations, it was also necessary to determine how those officials viewed the moral issue and how their attitudes affected American bombing. Similar questions presented themselves about lower-level figures—air force officers and civilians, such as the atomic scientists—who contributed to morally significant actions in the air war.

Apparent discrepancies in the official history suggested further questions. If American air leaders preferred not to bomb or terrorize civilians, as the history suggests, why did they do so in Germany, Japan, and the Balkans? Why did the very officer who is said to have raised the moral issue deny, after the war, that moral or religious concerns had led him to oppose the bombing of cities? How does one distinguish between the image the U.S. Army Air Forces wished to project at home and to the world and the personal feelings of the men who ran that organization?

Efforts to answer such questions led eventually to a number of generalizations. One is that virtually every major figure concerned with American bombing expressed some views about the moral issue—a phrase that usually meant to them the bombing of cities and civilians, though it also referred to air attacks on artifacts of civilization, such as libraries, cathedrals, monasteries, and famous works of art. A second is that while members of certain wartime organizations tended to share a common way of viewing the moral issue, it is impossible to place all air force leaders, all politicians, or all members of any of the groups that determined how America used its air arm into simple categories. The people who conducted the air war and those who advised them were divided among themselves and sometimes divided within themselves about moral questions that bombing raised. A third generalization is that while moral constraints almost invariably bowed to what people described as military necessity, there was substantial dispute over what military necessity meant.

Explaining the role of the moral issue required that I tell part of the story of the American air war. Yet this is not a comprehensive history. It omits navy and Marine Corps air actions and says little about fighter and tactical bomber units. It considers only instances of strategic bombing which at the time, or in retrospect, raised significant moral questions. People who served in the Army Air Forces may find part of this account oddly unfamiliar, since some of the issues it focuses on may never have been stressed to them during World War II. What many of them will recall most clearly is hardly visible in these pages—things like determination to complete one's job, the power of hundreds of bombers waiting to take off with their engines roaring and huge bodies shaking, the sensation of flying through puffs of smoke lit by muffled red flashes, things like comradeship, and the death of friends. Civilians who lived through that war may also find in these pages many things they do not remember at all. This is partly because their government, like any belligerent government, withheld information from the public about certain sensitive and controversial events.

People of Allied nations who recall World War II generally think of it as a "good" war, a struggle for survival and liberation. The elements that now make it good in their memory formed a context within which American leaders conducted the air war against the Axis. One of the most important of those elements was enemy behavior. In April 1945 an air force historian visited a recently liberated Nazi death camp at Buchenwald. He smelled the stench, saw typhus-ridden inmates, and observed human bone remnants piled near the crematorium. Then he noted, "Here is the antidote for qualms about strategic bombing."[1] Long before that time, people who directed the American air war had learned of the torture and mass murder that the Nazis had perpetrated, of German fire raids on British cities, of atrocities Japanese troops had committed against Allied civilians and prisoners of war, and of some of the crimes of Axis satellite officials. Enemy atrocities were sometimes taken as moral justification for U.S. air actions that killed and terrorized enemy civilians.

I have tried to present an account of events that will enable readers to form their own evaluations of what American leaders did in the air war. This is not a work of philosophy or theology. It offers no arguments about how people ought to have dealt with moral problems other than arguments the participants themselves presented. Yet many of the questions raised by what was done are of such universal and enduring significance that it will be impossible not to wonder about the answers.

For instance, it might be asked how it was that different groups of American air war leaders reacted in different ways to enemy atrocities or to the location of military targets within areas heavily populated by civilians. Why did some feel those acts and circumstances justified U.S. bombing that was bound to kill large numbers of enemy civilians, while other Americans refused to allow what the enemy did or the location of his resources to justify harsh actions against his people? Are there circumstances in which an enemy's behavior does warrant such actions? How certain should military leaders be, before attacking civilians and destroying cultural artifacts, that significant military advantages will result? How often was something done in the name of military necessity that could have been avoided through more careful reflection? In the midst of a great war, does thinking about the morality of attacking civilians dampen fighting spirit and weaken the ability to fight? Can leaders consider the humanity of the enemy's people without conveying an appearance of weakness to their own troops and to the enemy? If war leaders steel themselves to the moral consequences of their acts, do they risk destroying what their country is fighting for?

A few of the people in this book questioned whether there could be innocent civilians in a modern warring nation. Some felt that in centrally controlled societies virtually all civilians, whether they wish to or not, support the nation's military effort. Should belligerents therefore feel free to attack the entire enemy populace, or are there degrees of civilian involvement that impose restraints on the killing of civilians? Certain officers thought that members of armed forces were at least as valuable to humanity as civilians, that they were the "flower" of a nation's youth. If this is so, to what degree should troops be exposed to death to spare the lives of women and children, the enemy's or one's own? How much suffering should troops endure to save civilian lives, and how many civilians is it right to kill to spare men and women in uniform? Perhaps the questions most likely to occur to the reader (as they occurred to me throughout the creation of this work) are, What would I have done and what would have happened had I done it?

While no one who writes a book such as this could possibly be indifferent to the issues it raises, I have tried to keep my own views in the background. Nevertheless, the facts and interpretations presented here are bound to stir controversy and will, I hope, engender a searching debate.

Wings of Judgment

— 1

Leaders of the American Air War

The men who directed the United States armed forces in World War II were born near the beginning of a century when fundamental values of Western societies came under devastating attack. Faith in the progress of humanity clashed with the realities of twentieth-century war and mass extermination. A new psychology suggested that humans were dominated by feelings they did not understand and had an instinctive drive toward self-destruction. Beliefs once regarded as universal certainties began to appear to be nothing more than the transient views of particular social groups at a particular phase in their history.

One of these beliefs was that war itself could be subject to humane, rational limitations. For nearly two hundred years a model of war had developed in the West which held that, if at all possible, inhabitants of "civilized" nations should be spared from attack, great cities preserved, and the artifacts of high culture left unharmed. Over the years this paradigm had stretched and cracked. Civilians had suffered gravely in Sherman's march to the sea and in the siege of Paris in 1871. They had been severely hurt by blockades and caught in the crossfire of guerrilla war. But the model itself survived, even through World War I. Then, in the next two decades, technological change and the developing theory of air power subjected the model to insupportable strains, producing by the end of World War II a revolution in the morality of warfare. As American civil and military leaders found themselves caught up in that revolution, their responses depended partly on their character as individuals, partly on the collective experience acquired by the time their country became a belligerent.

The Top Command

The connections between President Franklin D. Roosevelt and the actions that involved the U.S. air forces* in the moral revolution were generally indirect, mostly vague, and very important. Roosevelt had a passion for secrecy. Careful to avoid precise commitments that might limit his freedom of action, he left an ambiguous record, or no record at all, of his views on sensitive issues. Yet his general outlook, which the leaders of the military arms noted and absorbed, suggested boundaries for permissible behavior by the American military services.[1]

Roosevelt was determined to secure two great objectives: the destruction of Axis military power, which he regarded as the gravest possible threat to his country and to democratic societies everywhere, and a postwar security system in which the United States would play a major part. Achieving these objectives promised to be an arduous task. It entailed not only raising and equipping armed forces and employing them against powerful, determined enemies, but also undertaking certain inherently conflicting actions. The United States would have to cooperate with allies whose interests at times diverged radically from its own. The American public, traditionally isolationist and suspicious of other powers, would have to support the alliance. While the American armed services would have to act ruthlessly against the country's enemies, whatever was done—at least to the Germans and Italians—should not conflict too painfully with the humane image Americans held of themselves.

Without public and congressional support, Roosevelt knew it would be difficult, if not impossible, to achieve his larger goals. He had to attend not only to the anxieties of the American people but also to their ideals. This placed a limitation, if not on the means the armed forces employed, then on what the public could be allowed to understand about the methods used.[2]

Roosevelt long before had come to see himself as a realist. As assistant secretary of the navy in the Wilson administration he had ridiculed Navy Secretary Josephus Daniels when the outbreak of World War I shocked Daniels's "faith in human nature and civiliza-

---

*The air arm of the U.S. Army changed its name several times. It began in 1907 as the Aeronautical Division of the Signal Corps, became the Signal Corps Aviation Section in 1914, and from 1918 to 1926 was called the Air Service. Its official title was the Air Corps from 1926 until 1941, then the Army Air Forces. An independent U.S. Air Force replaced it on September 18, 1947. Here the term "air force" is used generically and the official names are employed when discussing the air arm at a particular time.

tion and similar idealistic nonsense." Nevertheless, when it was his own turn to lead the country into war he followed a procedure employed by his predecessors and explained his objectives with moralistic rhetoric, presenting the struggle against the Axis powers as a conflict between darkness and light which required the enemy's absolute capitulation. In his annual message to Congress a month after the Japanese surprise attack on Pearl Harbor he declared, "There never has been—there never can be—successful compromise between good and evil. Only total victory can reward the champions of tolerance, and decency, and faith."[3] The implication was that the president sanctioned the sternest actions against enemy nations, provided those actions did not clash in an obvious way with the ideals of the people of the United States.

As far as his secretary of war, Henry L. Stimson, was concerned, this was a perfectly satisfactory approach, for Stimson regarded the conflict between the Allies and the Axis as a moral contest. Born two years after the Civil War to a family of the New York City upper class, Stimson had grown up and gone through Yale and Harvard Law School at a time when people of his kind believed strongly in moral certainties and in fusing the ideal with the practical in one's lifework. Like others of his circle, he wished to do good for society, to serve the public interest through government work or in his private vocation. For such people at that time, capitalism and country were sacred in themselves and were elements of the evolutionary process leading humanity to higher material and moral goals.[4]

Such beliefs might have produced banal optimism, but not in Stimson, for part of his heritage was a Puritan seriousness, a sense of human frailty and of the necessity for discipline and order. The practice of law on Wall Street reinforced these conceptions and impressed him with the way historical precedent limited what people could change. Consequently, when the chaos of the twentieth century descended, Stimson was not disillusioned but actually hopeful that he and people like him could impose some order on a disordered world.[5]

Stimson was deeply attached to what was then called civilization, meaning chiefly the culture of Western Europe and its offshoots in the United States. To him, civilization included not only capitalism, Western Christianity, and certain political forms, like representative and constitutional government, but also literature and the arts, to which he had been exposed at his mother's home, where prominent artists and writers gathered, and on numerous trips to Europe. Yet the secretary was not wholly Europe-centered. As governor general of the Philippines and as a tourist in the Far East, he had developed an appreciation for the civilizations of that part of the world and the belief that he understood "the oriental mind."[6]

When Roosevelt called on him in 1940 to direct the War Department, Stimson was admirably suited for the post. Having headed the department under President William Howard Taft and served as Herbert Hoover's secretary of state, he had more than the requisite administrative experience. His persistent, methodical, lawyerly approach to complex problems, his knack for choosing exceptionally talented and hard-working younger men to assist him, his absolute dedication to the struggle against the fascist powers, which he considered barbaric and debased, more than compensated for his advanced age. (He was seventy-two at the time.)[7]

Stimson also had an affinity for the military way of life. War was part of his heritage. His family had taken part in most of the important North American conflicts from colonial times through the Civil War (Stimson's father had fought for the Union). Henry L. Stimson had begun military service with the National Guard, enjoying the strike duty to which his unit was called. In World War I he had served at the front as an artillery officer, though he missed the big battles because he was ordered home to help with training. Stimson took pleasure in leading and molding the young men under his command and developed great respect for the dignity of military life and for its ceremonies and orderliness, its sense of professional calling, its directness and activity. At one time he considered himself more a soldier than a lawyer.

Like others of his class and time, Secretary Stimson considered war an antidote to the softness and materialism he observed around him in America's industrial society. Though he lived very comfortably, he liked the spartan quality of a soldier's existence, the excitement of facing danger, the opportunity for stoic endurance of physical harshness. He thought great sacrifice of life was inevitable in modern war, a consequence that had to be accepted. In 1915 he had written that "every man owes to his country not only to die for her, if necessary, but also to spend a little of his life in learning how to die for her effectively."[8]

The secretary's attitude toward war and the military profession eased his relations with the heads of the armed services, in particular with the army chief of staff, General George C. Marshall. There were important similarities between the two men. Both were formal, dignified, and somewhat distant. Even Franklin Roosevelt found it difficult to penetrate Marshall's reserve. When he tried to approach the general with his usual deft informality, calling Marshall by his first name, the chief of staff responded coldly. He even declined to laugh at the president's jokes.[9]

Marshall, like Stimson, held a bleak view of war's inevitable costs. The chief of staff followed the tradition of Ulysses S. Grant, believing that armies must concentrate on vital objectives, which often could be secured only through massive loss of life. At a meeting with the other American military chiefs and the president, Marshall endorsed an early attack on France rather than a more indirect approach to German-occupied Europe, which he thought would prove less fruitful in the long run. He recognized that the assault he favored would cost a great many troops; but, he observed, the fact was that the troops could be replaced. He applied this same cold practicality to his analysis of the war on the eastern front, where, he said in 1941, he hoped the Russians would be "wise enough to withdraw and save their army, abandoning their people, if necessary."[10]

This austere officer, a superb organizer within his own sphere and usually an excellent judge of subordinates, commanded the respect of everyone who dealt with him. He was the preeminent uniformed official of his country during the Second World War. When the United States formed a Joint Chiefs of Staff in 1942 to coordinate the actions of the military services, he dominated it. First among equals on the Anglo-American Combined Chiefs of Staff, he became, with Roosevelt and Churchill, one of the principal Western strategists of a war fought on many fronts with traditional land and sea forces and with the newly emerging weapons of air power.[11] His hand therefore appeared along with those of the president and the secretary of war in most of the morally significant events of an air war whose details were planned and executed by the leaders of the Army Air Forces.

The Air Leaders

About two dozen general officers were chiefly responsible for developing American air strategy and directing air power in World War II.[12] Few of these men wrote memoirs, we have just a handful of full-length biographies, and only a minority left collections of personal papers. But from these sources and from brief biographical accounts and official records we can learn something about the air leaders as a group and a good deal about a number of exemplary officers.[13]

While some of the air leaders had influential family connections, collectively they could hardly be said to have sprung from the social elite to which Roosevelt, Stimson, and several leaders of the other services belonged. Hoyt S. Vandenberg, who headed the Ninth Air Force in Europe and became an assistant chief of air staff at Army Air Forces headquarters, was a nephew of Senator Arthur M. Vandenberg of Michigan. Commander of Mediterranean Allied Strategic Air Force Nathan Farragut Twining came from a family of naval officers. But James H. "Jimmy" Doolittle, commander of several air forces in the European theater and leader of the first United States bombing raid against the Japanese homeland, was the son of an itinerant carpenter. Curtis E. LeMay, who as head of the XXI Bomber Command directed the devastating incendiary attacks on Japanese cities during 1945, recalled a boyhood spent along the small gray houses and shabby brick corner stores of West Columbus, Ohio. The father of Carl "Tooey" Spaatz, commander of American strategic air forces in Europe and then in Asia, published a rural weekly newspaper. Spaatz's deputy chief for operations, Frederick L. Anderson, was the son of a farmer turned auto dealer. The head of the AAF, "Hap" Arnold, spent his childhood in a suburban Pennsylvania town where his father practiced medicine. Haywood S. Hansell, Jr., LeMay's predecessor at the head of the XXI Bomber Command, was the son of an army surgeon. Arnold's chief of air staff, Barney Giles, grew up on a Texas farm. The father of Thomas D. White, an assistant chief of air staff for intelligence and later the commander of the Seventh Air Force in the Pacific, was an Episcopal bishop.[14]

Although almost all these officers were born in the United States, their geographical origins within the country were diverse. Vandenberg and Twining were born in Wisconsin. Spaatz and Arnold came from Pennsylvania, Eaker and Giles from Texas, Power and Frederick Anderson from New York, Norstad and White from Minnesota. There was one each from Illinois, Virginia, West Virginia, New Mexico, Washington, D.C., the state of Washington, Massachusetts, and California. Only six were born in cities, a disproportionately small number considering the way the American population was distributed at the time. In comparison with the leadership of both the navy and the rest of the army, the very small number from the Southeast is striking.

These men were vigorous and relatively young during the Second World War, their average age a little over forty-two when the Japanese attacked Pearl Harbor. Arnold was the oldest at fifty-five, Norstad, at thirty-four, the youngest. While few of them had seen combat in World War I, several matched the image of the intrepid, daredevil aviator who thrived on stunts, speed, and danger. Doolittle and Hansell had served in Air Corps aerobatic teams, and Eaker, Spaatz, and Quesada had once flown over Los Angeles for more than 150 hours in a Ford Trimotor named the *Question Mark*.[15]

If anyone appears to conform to the daredevil stereotype, it is Jimmy Doolittle. This dynamic officer, who spent nine of his first twelve years in Nome, Alaska, became an amateur boxer and a gymnast, worked as a hard rock miner, and in 1918 joined the aviation section of the Army Signal Corps, where he learned to fly pursuit planes so skillfully that he was made an instructor. Doolittle loved stunt flying. He used to walk on wings and perform other tricks that were strictly against regulations. He also liked to break records. In 1925 he won the Schneider Cup race, flying a Curtiss Navy seaplane, and he took the Thompson trophy at the 1932 National Air Races in a land-based aircraft. Doolittle flew a Curtiss P-1 through South America in 1926 on a demonstration tour. While intoxicated, he performed some acrobatic stunts at the officers' club in Santiago, Chile, and fell off a window ledge, breaking both ankles. After a short hospital stay he demonstrated his plane for Chilean officials, then flew over the Andes—with both legs in casts.[16] What Doolittle is best remembered for is the air raid of April 18, 1942, which he personally led against targets in Japan, taking off in a B-25 medium bomber from the deck of USS *Hornet*.

Doolittle was a good deal more than just a man of action. A highly trained engineer, he spent a year at the University of California School of Mines in Berkeley, took aeronautical engineering courses at McCook Field, Ohio, and received master of science and doctor of science degrees in aeronautics from the Massachusetts Institute of Technology. His research tested theory against the personal experience of flyers, including himself. As a professional engineer he headed a laboratory established by the Daniel Guggenheim Fund for the Promotion of Aeronautics, where, in 1928 and 1929, he did pioneering research in blind flying, assisting in the development of horizontal and directional gyroscopes and performing the first all-instrument flight. He was also a liaison between the military and business worlds, representing, on his South American tour, both the Air Corps and the Curtiss company. During the 1930s Doolittle left the regular army to run the aviation department of Shell Oil Company, but he never cut his military ties. As a reserve officer he served in 1934 on a board headed by former secretary of war Newton D. Baker that investigated air defense policy; he was the only member of the Baker board to recommend severing the Air Corps from the army. Returned to active duty in 1940, Doolittle helped automobile manufacturers convert their plants to warplane production. His chief work during the war was as a manager of large military enterprises, commanding, at different times, the Eighth, Twelfth, Fifteenth, and North African Strategic Air Forces.[17]

If Doolittle is the airman as manager link between the air force and industry, then technological expert Haywood S. Hansell exemplifies the airman as planner. A member of two minorities within the air leaders' group, Southerners and men from army families, Hansell was, like Doolittle, a fighter pilot, an engineer (educated at Georgia Tech), and a commander. It was he who first sent very long-range bombers from the Marianas against the Japanese home islands. His most important contribution to the development of the AAF was in strategic planning. In the 1930s, when the Air Corps Tactical School developed the principles on which prewar and wartime plans were built, Hansell served as an instructor. Later he headed the European Air War Plans Division in AAF headquarters and became a member of planning committees for the U.S. Joint Chiefs of Staff. A reflective man with an analytical mind and a feeling for history (he later wrote biographical studies of AAF leaders and histories of AAF plans and operations in World War II), Hansell was one of the chief designers of the American air war against both Germany and Japan.[18]

General Ira C. Eaker played a crucial role in the prewar development of the American air force, as a promoter of public and congressional relations. Eaker's career goes back to World War I, when, following graduation from college, he became an infantry officer, then switched to the Signal Corps Air Service. After holding a variety of staff and command positions in the interwar years, he organized the VIII Bomber Command in England, became commanding general of the Eighth Air Force, commanding general of all U.S. Army air forces in the United Kingdom, and then air commander-in-chief of the Mediterranean Allied Air Forces. At the end of the war in Europe he returned to the United States as deputy commander, Army Air Forces, and chief of the air staff.[19]

Throughout the interwar period Eaker worked to develop a favorable public image for the air force. Public relations, important to all the services, was especially significant for the Army Air Corps, whose leaders were struggling to free themselves from constraints laid down by a land-minded military bureaucracy. Since theirs was a new service which in the early years had only a small constituency among military suppliers, Congress, and the general public, the airmen had to work especially hard for a share of the small military budgets of the 1920s and 1930s. Attempting to focus public and congressional attention on their arm, they staged events that served some plausible military or scientific purpose but were also designed to make headlines.

The interwar years were an era of ingenious publicity stunts, and some of the most exciting were produced by the airmen. In 1921 Air Service fliers under the direction of General William L. "Billy" Mitchell sank the surrendered German battleship *Ostfriesland*, the cruiser *Frankfurt*, and other vessels, demonstrating the vulnerability of warships to air attack and doing it in a way bound to generate publicity. Air force officers took part in international goodwill tours which drew attention to the way warplanes could travel long distances across international boundaries. They ran endurance tests, like the flight of the *Question Mark*, the aeronautical equivalent of a marathon dance. At the request of the Roosevelt administration, the Army Air Corps took over airmail-carrying operations in the winter and spring of 1934, receiving a great deal of publicity—much of it, to the Air Corps' regret, focused on crashes and the death of Air Corps pilots. One of the most spectacular of the interwar publicity events was the 1925 court-martial of General Mitchell, the deputy chief of the Air Service, who figuratively immolated himself in an effort to alert Americans to the neglect of air power by the U.S. military establishment.*[20]

Eaker was admirably suited to public relations work. A graduate of a teachers' college, he spent his spare time acquiring education and, especially, sharpening his command of the English language. After World War I he was stationed in the Philippines, where he signed up for university classes. When the Air Service sent him to Long Island, New York, he traveled to Columbia Uni-

*Mitchell, who wished to establish an independent air arm, was court-martialed when he accused the War and Navy Departments of "incompetency, criminal negligence, and almost treasonable administration of the National Defense." After a long trial, which enabled the general to expound his ideas to the press, he was found guilty of conduct prejudicial to good order and military discipline.

versity for night classes in contract law. He studied at George Washington University during a tour of duty in Washington, D.C. In 1934 he received a degree in journalism from the University of Southern California.

Recognizing his special competence, Eaker's superiors placed him where he could publicize the air force. From 1924 to 1926 he was executive assistant in the Office of Air Service in Washington, writing speeches and reports for Chief of Air Service General Mason Patrick. With Henry H. "Hap" Arnold, he handled publicity for the Billy Mitchell trial. During one six-month period, beginning in December 1926, he piloted an Air Corps plane on a goodwill tour of Central and South America, then returned to Washington where, as executive officer to the assistant secretary of war, he promoted the interests of his service by flying senators and congressmen to Air Corps installations. Eaker was chief pilot of the *Question Mark*. He commanded one of the routes of the government's air mail program. As assistant chief of the Air Corps Information Division in the late 1930s, he prepared answers to civilian and congressional inquiries and carried out special projects designed, as he said, "to further the Army Air Corps image with the press, the public and Congress." With Hap Arnold he coauthored three books about the air force. As he explained years later, he was one of a small group of Army Air Corps leaders who kept the idea of air power alive in the interwar years by persuading newspaper columnists, magazine writers, and radio reporters to promote the views of the airmen, and by developing a constituency among Congressmen and other political leaders throughout the country.[21]

During the Second World War Eaker served under General Carl Spaatz, combat commander, manager of large-scale air operations, and the man whose forces conducted some of the most significant and controversial American air actions of World War II. Spaatz came from a line of Pennsylvania Dutchmen. His grandfather had migrated from Germany and started the *Boyerton Democrat*, a weekly originally printed in German, a language Spaatz's paternal grandmother spoke to the end of her life. A mediocre student but a football player for his seminary, Spaatz decided to go to West Point, probably because of something he had read about it in a book. He graduated in 1914, receiving an infantry commission. After learning to fly at the Signal Corps aviation school in San Diego, Spaatz served on the Mexican border, helping General John J. Pershing's search for bandit-revolutionary Pancho Villa. When the United States entered World War I he went to France, where he was stationed for a time in Billy Mitchell's headquarters and where he organized and ran an American flying school. One of the few top AAF leaders who saw combat in World War I, Spaatz commanded the Second Pursuit Group, downing three enemy aircraft.

Spaatz shuttled between base commands and positions in Washington during the interwar period, becoming assistant chief of the Air Corps in 1940. After service in the Plans Division and as chief of the air staff and head of the AAF combat command in Washington, he was dispatched to England, where as commanding general of the Eighth Air Force he directed the first American bombings of occupied Europe. At the end of the year he was shifted to the Mediterranean theatre, becoming commander of the Twelfth Air Force and then of the Northwest African Air Force. During the Allied invasion of Italy, Spaatz was deputy chief of staff of the Mediterranean Allied Air Forces, and from January 1944 until after Germany capitulated he directed the U.S. Strategic Air Forces in Europe. Then he moved to the Pacific to oversee the final strategic bombing missions against Japan, including the atomic attacks on Hiroshima and Nagasaki. Spaatz was present at the surrenders of both Germany and Japan. In February 1946 be became commanding general of the Army Air Forces.[22]

A dour-looking officer with a lean face, red hair, a closely cropped mustache, and a prominent nose, Spaatz was tactiturn and not at all flamboyant. Eaker remembered him as thrifty with words, a man who said, "I never learned anything while I was talking." During the war Hap Arnold, the air force chief, decided that Spaatz should receive a publicity buildup to make him the symbol of American air power in action. Spaatz demurred, preferring that his own chief commanders receive the attention of the AAF publicity apparatus.[23]

Relentlessly pragmatic in situations that required diplomacy and patient determination, Spaatz was an expert team player. Even when he disagreed strongly with the views of superiors, he dutifully carried out their orders, sometimes working quietly to modify their decisions. He had a powerful concern for the record, wanting it to show that in touchy situations he had done exactly what his superiors had told him to do. One of Spaatz's more observant subordinates remarked, "If Eisenhower had asked him in writing to drop his bombs in the Arctic Ocean on D-Day, he would have complied." Spaatz himself told an air force historian that after

receiving a verbal order to drop the atomic bomb, he had insisted
that the order be in writing. "The military man," he once declared,
"carries out the orders of his political bosses."[24]

Spaatz was an excellent military executive and, in his way, a
shrewd politician, a commander-manager who inspired great respect from his fellow leaders. General Doolittle, who served under
him in North Africa, Italy, and England, told an interviewer that
Tooey Spaatz as "perhaps the only man that I have been associated
with whom I have never known to make a bad decision. His judgments were almost always rapid and almost always right. I don't
know of any major decision that he ever made that wasn't sound."[25]

Spaatz was chief lieutenant for Hap Arnold, the exuberant,
driving, magnetic commander who headed the Army Air Forces
during World War II. Descended, like Spaatz, from German ances-
tors, Arnold grew up in a household so firmly disciplined that when
he entered the U.S. Military Academy shortly after the turn of the
century, he experienced a feeling of freedom he had never known
before. Something of a romantic, Arnold wanted to enter the
glamorous world of the cavalryman, but for reasons beyond his
control he began his service as an infantry officer. He soon trans-
ferred to the Aeronautical Division of the Signal Corps, learning to
fly from Orville Wright, and became an instructor at the army's
first aviation school. In 1911 Arnold flew the first United States
airmail and the following year took an airplane to 6,540 feet, setting
a world record for altitude. During World War I Arnold supervised
the army's aviation training schools and afterward rose steadily to
the top of his service. In the 1920s and early 1930s he commanded
army air bases, served as chief of the Air Service information
division, became in 1935 assistant chief of a combat organization—
the GHQ Air Force—and in 1938 head of the Air Corps. When the
War Department was reorganized in March 1942 and the air arm
raised to coordinate status with the army and navy, Arnold became
commanding general of the Army Air Forces. A member of the
United States Joint Chiefs of Staff and of the Combined Chiefs of
Staff, he played a central role in directing air operations around the
world.[26]

Despite his position within a vast military hierarchy, Arnold
was not what is usually thought of as an organization man. He was
too intensely curious, especially about technology, too vibrant, too
impatient and mercurial, with a brain that fired off showers of ideas
he wanted put into action immediately. Robert A. Lovett, assistant
secretary of war for air, whose office adjoined the general's, said

Arnold "responded to emotional stimuli in a very youthful fashion; he would be on top one minute and down in the depths the next." At times, with so many things that he had to have done at once, he simply exploded, or as he put it, got things off his chest.[27]

Arnold, who once described himself as "personally never satisfied," drove his subordinates. At a Sunday morning meeting during the early wartime buildup of the AAF, he was impatiently criticizing the information that a soft-spoken matériel officer had just presented when the officer pitched forward in front of Arnold's desk, dead of a heart attack. Not surprisingly, Arnold, who suffered from ulcers early in his career, developed heart disease himself and several times during the war was felled by coronary failure. The archetypical "can-do" military leader, he abhorred pessimism and pessimists, hating to be told a job was impossible. In his memoirs he wrote of his family's early wish that he become a minister, then reflected that he really had become a preacher, selling the idea of air power with as much evangelism as it would have taken him to "sell the 'Wages of Sin.'"[28]

It took more than salesmanship and drive to run the air force, and Arnold had men underneath him who could do those things the chief of the AAF was unsuited to. In Assistant Secretary Lovett, an investment banker with a cool sense of humor who had flown navy combat planes in World War I, he found "a man who possessed the qualities in which I was weakest, a partner and teammate of tremendous sympathy, and of calm and hidden force. When I became impatient, intolerant, and would rant around, fully intending to tear the War and Navy Departments to pieces, Bob Lovett would know exactly how to handle me. He would say, with a quiet smile: 'Hap, you're wonderful! How I wish I had your pep and vitality! Now . . . let's get down and be practical.' And I would come back to earth with a bang."[29]

Arnold came to accept administrative arrangements that reconciled his own desires for immediate action with a bureaucracy's need for deliberateness. One of Arnold's staff officers, General Laurence S. Kuter, recalled that when the AAF started its vast expansion after Pearl Harbor, Congress gave the commanding general a vast organization that surrounded him with officers who Arnold believed had no spare time to speculate or to play with imaginative ideas and suggestions. Kuter thought Arnold felt "actually lonesome in his high office." Every now and then the commanding general would develop a hot idea and give it to a "project officer" to put into effect at once. Kuter or another member of the air staff would intercept this officer, look over the idea, and find some way of working it into the structure of AAF programs or, if that was impossible, show Arnold tactfully why it could not be enacted forthwith. Whether he liked this treatment or not, General Arnold allowed it to go on, and the AAF ran with a semblance of smoothness. Meanwhile he set up his own informal advisory council of young colonels, such as Lauris Norstad, Charles P. Cabell, and Jacob Smart, bounced ideas off them, and engaged in long-range thinking.[30]

Arnold had an inclination, one he shared with Roosevelt, to pick the minds of experts. In November 1943 he secured a team of some of the country's best-known historians to evaluate prospects for the collapse of Nazi Germany in the light of historical events, such as Germany's internal breakdown at the end of World War I. To work on specific projects designed to hasten the fall of the Axis, he established committees of businessmen and academicians, sometimes intermingling them with air force and other military officers. Aircraft manufacturers, like Donald Douglas, with whom Arnold became a close friend and hunting companion and a relative by marriage, supplied him with information about technological developments. He developed personal relationships with scientists like Robert A. Millikan of the California Institute of Technology, cooperated with the government's scientific war agencies, and established the AAF's own civilian Scientific Advisory Group chaired by Theodore von Karman. Toward the end of the war he remarked, "We must have the long-haired professors in von Karman's board see all the gadgets and data and drawings so as to give us a Buck Rogers program to cover the next 20 years."[31]

Hap Arnold and his subordinates formed strong emotional bonds. Ira Eaker remembered his chief, whom he had first met at Rockwell Field in 1918, as "one of the handsomest military figures I've ever seen." Arnold was then thirty-two years old, "six feet tall, erect, and wore his uniform with pride and grace." His personality was "tremendous." He "always had a glint in his eye, sort of a half-smile [the reason people called him Hap]. He won your complete admiration and support just by being there." Strong ties also connected other AAF leaders with one another. Thus General Doolittle said of General Spaatz, "I suppose if it were possible for one man to love another man, I love General Spaatz. I guess it's a better word . . . that I idolize General Spaatz."[32]

These links, forged even before the Second World War, arose from a shared military education and from similar experiences as flyers, officers, and members of a service hierarchy. Perhaps the most important tie was their common relationship with death.

Death—faced, survived, inflicted on others—is one of the chief unifying forces among members of martial professions, and in the formative years of their military lives the men who were to run the U.S. Army Air Forces had an extraordinary closeness to death. Fatalities were common among military flyers, even in peacetime. During Hap Arnold's early years in the Air Service, the death rate for American aviators reached one for every 12,800 miles and the casualty rate for Air Service flyers went as high as 50 percent. Arnold himself barely survived. One day in 1912, when Arnold had already made more than a thousand flights in flimsy military aircraft, his plane went into a terrifying stall and dive. By tremendous effort he managed to get control and brought the plane down. Then he announced to a fellow officer, "That's it. A man doesn't face death twice." It was four years before he overcame his fear sufficiently to fly in an airplane.[33]

It was not only his own death that an air officer had to think about (or not think about) but the deaths of close friends and colleagues. At one point General Eaker could not recall a week or a month when someone from the airdrome where he was stationed had not died or lost a close friend in a crash. Arnold had seen Lewis C. Rockwell, a West Point classmate whom he had encouraged to take up flying, plunge to his death during an exhibition. Mortality was woven into the airman's occupation. Most army air bases, Rockwell Field for example, were named for dead flyers, many of them killed in accidents.

The constant evidence of death had its effects on rising air officers. Besides intensifying fraternal bonds, it engendered a sense of fatalism. When Arnold resumed flying he decided, "When I'm going to die, I'm going to die." It also shaped the way air officers felt about the deaths of those who served under them. Eaker believed it made army flyers more "realistic" about losses than other military men before combat actually began. "I won't say you get callous," he remarked, "but you get realistic." He thought air force commanders were more inured to loss than most civilians or even most military commanders; General Arnold, he recalled, had lived with tragedy throughout his career and was therefore more hardened to it than some civilian leaders.[34]

An incident in General Doolittle's career illustrates the hardening process. While Doolittle was a flying instructor, two of his students were killed in accidents. After one of them had taken off, crashed, and burned, Doolittle, without looking at the wreckage, turned to another student and said, "Next!" One of the other instructors asked, "Doesn't that kid's death mean anything to you?" Doolittle replied that he would think of the dead boy that night, but his immediate job was to make flyers of his men.[35]

The constant presence of death was bound to affect the way air officers felt about killing people of enemy nations. Like all soldiers in battle they became used to death around them, but in their case, during World War II, the deaths were not just of enemy troops but of civilians, and many of them came to accept civilian casualties as an inevitable consequence of their work. General Eaker told an interviewer after the war that a military man had to be "trained and inured" to do his work. "Otherwise you'd never do the job." General Curtis LeMay remarked that a person in LeMay's profession could not "meditate on the process of death," nor "mope around about the deaths he has caused personally, by deed; or impersonally, in the act of command," for if he began to think of what he was doing to people on the ground it could drive him crazy.[36]

Yet training and combat and all the evidence of mortality did not eradicate all traces of a tender core. General LeMay, one of the toughest of the air commanders, told in his autobiography how he reacted to one horrible incident. In the spring of 1938, when LeMay was about to leave on a South American tour, he heard that a military plane at an air show in Colombia had crashed into a crowd of spectators at full speed, killing sixty people and crippling or mutilating scores of others. He imagined propellers twisting into the soft bodies of women and children and gasoline spurting out. Then, he said, "you didn't like to think of it any further." But that night he dreamed about a time in his childhood when he and his brother and other children had climbed up and over a barn roof. His brother fell, dropping onto a pile of broken bottles. Blood spurted from him. Everyone began yelling. When LeMay woke from the dream he felt himself grieving for the Colombian dead. A few days later he was in Colombia, attending their funeral. Seeing the weeping faces of their relatives, he thought, "How very much alike we are after all." Then he reflected on the airmen he had known who now were dead.[37]

The special training of officers like Eaker, Arnold, and LeMay, their professional experience, and their common humanity all conditioned the way they reacted to moral issues that arose in their work. What made those reactions so important in the revolution of military morality was the way the attitudes of air leaders were linked to the changes in military technology and theory, which placed civilians, cities, and the treasures of humanity in the battle-field. These changes became a subject of intense inquiry by the officers in the American and other air forces who created and applied the doctrines of strategic air warfare.

2

American Air War Doctrine and the Bombing of Civilians

The foundations of the doctrine with which the U.S. Army Air Forces entered the Second World War lay chiefly in the battlefields of World War I. Its formulators had observed how young men from all parts of the world had died by the hundreds of thousands in battles on the western front to secure very small amounts of territory, rarely achieving any important military purpose. Officers like Hugh Trenchard of the Royal Flying Corps, Billy Mitchell of the Air Service, and the Italian general Giulio Douhet believed that in the next war the airplane could prevent this kind of stalemate, making war again an effective instrument of national power. They envisioned fleets of warplanes heading toward the vital centers of an enemy nation to paralyze and destroy them with poison gas, incendiary bombs, and explosives, terrorizing civilians until they begged their government to surrender. In the future war, bombers would spare the lives of soldiers by moving the battlefield from the trenches to the cities.

The most original and influential of these theorists was Douhet, who before World War I had begun to formulate a fairly coherent doctrine of air strategy. Novel as it is in major respects, Douhet's theory had roots in earlier military thought. Like the nineteenth-century Prussian strategist Karl von Clausewitz, author of *On War*, Douhet considered war an act of force used by one nation to compel other nations to do its will. He tried, as Clausewitz had done, to view war without illusions, to examine the most extreme form it might take.

That form, as Douhet conceived it, was a conflict of whole

peoples, employing the entire human and material resources of society, a struggle in which the distinctions between combatant and noncombatant vanished. In modern war everyone took part, "the soldier carrying his gun, the woman loading shells in a factory, the farmer growing wheat, the scientist experimenting in his laboratory." In this total war the primary object of military action would no longer be the enemy's armed forces, as in Clausewitz's time, but the vitals of the nation itself, the source of enemy military power, now exposed by technology to attack from the air.[1]

In some respects General Douhet's vision of war resembled the view of the American naval theorist Admiral Alfred T. Mahan. Admiral Mahan had recommended far-ranging offensive action as the best way for a naval power to defend its trade, protect its homeland, and secure its other objectives. Douhet likewise considered strategic attack by far the best form of defense. Mahan wrote of the necessity to secure command of the sea, an idea paralleling Douhet's belief that a nation must dominate the third dimension by seizing command of the air. This would be done not through the inefficient method of individual air combat, but by striking, at the beginning of hostilities, at whatever enabled the enemy to fly—airports, supply bases, and production centers. For Mahan the chief means of war was a long-range battle fleet. For Douhet it was an air force independent of other military arms.[2]

Once it had secured command of the air, this independent air force could disrupt the mobilization of the enemy army and hamper the enemy's navy by bombing oil supplies, naval bases, arsenals, and ships at anchor. Or it could head directly for the chief objective, the population centers: Rome, Paris, or London. Bombers would terrorize the nation, breaking its physical and moral resistance. Douhet felt civilian workers were more susceptible than troops to a collapse of morale and that, unlike an army, they would be unable to resume their operations after an attack. "How could a country go on living and working," he asked, "oppressed by the nightmare of imminent destruction and death?"[3]

The future war, as Douhet imagined it, would begin with warplanes bombing a city, dropping high explosives, poison gas, and incendiaries. The attack would erupt suddenly and last just a few minutes. "First would come explosions, then fires, then deadly gases floating on the surface and preventing any approach to the stricken area. As the hours passed and night advanced, the fires would spread while the poison gas paralyzed all life." Soon civilians in other cities, learning of this catastrophe, would be terrorized, making it all but impossible to keep order or maintain public services and production. Even if a semblance of order could be maintained and some work carried on, the sight of a single enemy plane would stampede the inhabitants into a panic. Normal life would be impossible. And on the next day, if ten or twenty or fifty cities were bombed, no one would be able to prevent the desperate, panic-stricken citizens from fleeing to the countryside. The nation's social structure would break down completely. Even before the armed forces could mobilize, the people, drive by suffering and horror and by the instinct of self-preservation, would rise up and demand an end to the war.[4]

While Douhet wished to regard war "unemotionally as a science," he was very much aware of the moral questions people might raise about the type of warfare he prophesied. "Tragic" was the term he used in his 1921 treatise, *The Command of the Air*, to describe the situation of people caught in this cataclysm. Still, as one who had witnessed the First World War Douhet believed that some good would derive from turning areas where civilians lived into battlefields. Because "the decisive blows will be directed at civilians, that element of the countries at war least able to sustain them," the end would come with merciful speed. Future wars might prove more "humane" than those of the past because they might, in the long run, shed less blood.[5]

In *The Probable Aspects of the War of the Future*, published in 1928, Douhet probed further into the moral characteristics of the conflict he envisioned. Writing shortly after the signing of international agreements to limit naval armaments and ban poison gas, and in the very year the Kellogg-Briand Pact sought to outlaw war itself, Douhet declared that "all the restrictions, all the international agreements made during peacetime are fated to be swept away like dried leaves on the winds of war." Methods of warfare could not be described as human or inhuman because "war will always be inhuman, and the means which are used in it cannot be classified as acceptable or not acceptable according to their efficacy, potentiality, or harmfulness to the enemy." The waging of the war of 1914–18 "by means recognized as humane and civilized" had left millions dead and millions mutilated. Whatever could be done to hurt the enemy would be done, for that was the purpose of warfare. Moral limitations on the means of war were "nothing but international demogogic hypocrisies." The conflict of the future would be "an inhuman, an atrocious performance. And no one will shrink from using such terrifying offensives . . . no matter how inhuman and atrocious they might be considered."[6]

General Douhet expressed no regret at the disappearance of moral distinctions between making war against civilians and attacking enemy armies. Nations must resign themselves, he felt, to air attacks on their populated places in the same way an army commander resigns himself to the loss of troops when he knows that is the way to secure victory. Douhet may really have preferred to sacrifice some civilian lives for those of soldiers, since he criticized "that peculiar traditional notion which makes people weep to hear of a few women and children killed in an air raid and leaves them unmoved to hear of thousands of soldiers killed in action." All human lives were "equally valuable," he remarked. But he immediately contradicted himself, saying that although "because tradition holds that the soldier is fated to die in battle" his death did not upset people much, the fact was that "a soldier, a robust young man, should be considered to have the maximum individual value in the general economy of humanity."[7]

Giulio Douhet was more than a revolutionist of strategy. He was one of the small group of theorists in the early twentieth century who rationalized the collapse of the moral barrier between killing troops and destroying the populace of "civilized" countries. He presented himself not as one who consciously willed that change, but as one who had come to understand that military and technological evolution, particularly the evolution of strategic air warfare, had made the barrier obsolete. Douhet urged his readers to confront the brutal facts of the future war, to view them "without false delicacy and sentimentalism."[8] Whatever his intent, his words encouraged nations to get ready for the kind of war he had made seem inevitable.

How much influence did Douhet exercise on the American air force? Opinions vary. Some leaders of the AAF stated that they had not encountered Douhet's writing until their own views of air warfare were largely formed. A few attributed more influence to other theorists, such as William Mitchell.[9] Yet there is ample reason to believe not only that Douhet's ideas were available to the commanders and planners of the U.S. Army Air Forces early in their military education, but that the Italian theorist influenced their thinking directly and indirectly, whether they realized it or not.

Virtually all the World War II U.S. air force leaders attended the Air Corps Tactical School (ACTS), where Douhet's writings had been available in English translation almost from the time he produced them. Part I of *The Command of the Air*, the most important section, was translated into English within months of its publication in Italian. Four copies of it were available in 1923 at the Air Service Field Officers' School (the name by which ACTS was then known). In 1931 five copies of Douhet's piece, "The War of 19——," which had been published in *Rivista Aeronautica* the year before, appeared in the ACTS library. In 1933 Dorothy Benedict, assisted by an ACTS instructor, George C. Kenney, retranslated excerpts of three of Douhet's works that had previously appeared in French. The school library also held a summary of the article "Air Warfare Doctrine of General Douhet" by Charles De F. Chandler, excerpted from the March 1933 issue of *Air Service*. The chief of the Air Corps sent several copies of Chandler's article to the chairman of the U.S. House Committee on Military Affairs with the notation that it "presents an excellent exposition of certain principles of air warfare."[10]

A few American air leaders acknowledged Douhet's influence. Carl Spaatz, who had attended the school in 1925, recalled that most of his contemporaries there had read *The Command of the Air*. Haywood Hansell recalled how the instructional staff at ACTS had "infected" him with their enthusiasm for the doctrines of Trenchard, Billy Mitchell, and Douhet. One instructor, possibly Hansell himself, attributed to Douhet "the real conception of the strategic air offensive," and called his doctrine the foundation on which the great European air forces were built, its ideas "accepted as fundamental axioms today."[11] General Douhet's ideas recur through the manuals used at ACTS from 1926 through the 1930s. Some passages appear to paraphrase the words of the Italian theorist.[12]

Other European military writers influenced American air doctrine, including Hugh Trenchard, B. H. Liddell Hart, and especially Clausewitz, whose work, if not fully understood, was widely respected in the U.S. Army between the world wars.[13] General Hansell recalled that the Air Corps Tactical School had taken as axioms for its own analysis of air warfare Clausewitz's view of war as an instrument for advancing national policy, and his definition of war as an act of violence intended to compel the opponent to do one's will. Hansell also regarded this passage from *On War* as having been important at ACTS:

> Now philanthropists may easily imagine that there is a skillful method of disarming and overcoming an enemy without causing great bloodshed, and that this is the proper tendency of the art of War. However plausible this

may appear, still it is an error which must be extirpated, for in such dangerous things as War, the errors which proceed from a spirit of benevolence are the worst. . . .[14]

A far less seminal thinker than Clausewitz or Douhet, but one whose influence on the development of American air power cannot be underestimated, is General Billy Mitchell. Mitchell's articles, books, and speeches, his appearances before investigating boards, and his court-martial all drew public attention to the idea of an independent air force and helped acquaint the American people and Congress with the importance of air weapons. Foreseeing the Japanese attack on Pearl Harbor years before it occurred, he analyzed the strategic problems a Japanese-American conflict would pose. One of his solutions, the firebombing of Japanese cities, became the core of U.S. air strategy in the last six months of World War II. His experimental sinkings of captured warships gave a semblance of combat reality to his principles and exemplified what would become an important element of American air strategy—daylight attacks against small targets. While Mitchell never developed an original, carefully structured theory of air war, he publicized ideas about doctrine that sometimes paralleled and occasionally derived from the thinking of more systematic theorists, particularly Douhet.[15]

In the years immediately after the First World War, Mitchell's ideas about air strategy seemed to shift back and forth. In a 1919 report he insisted that the entire nation, not just the armed forces, must be regarded as combatants. Proper strategy entailed killing and destruction far from the front lines. The targets of attack might include women, children, or anyone who did not bear arms, since these civilians were "vastly more important as manufacturers of munitions than if they were carrying rifles in trenches." In *Our Air Force*, published in 1921, the same year as Douhet's *Command of the Air*, he predicted that future wars would include the destruction of whole cities using airborne gas. Yet in other works written the same year, he described air power as essentially an adjunct to the land army. By 1923 he had begun to change his position again, and in official internal documents suggested that gases could be developed to poison water supplies and destroy crops, that manufacturing centers should be considered target areas (though he recommended that civilians be notified when factories were about to be destroyed), and that national morale was a worthy target, though he believed that direct attacks on population centers would occur infrequently—as reprisals. Like Douhet, he discussed what appeared to him to be the positive moral value of strategic air warfare:

by ending conflicts more rapidly and decisively, the bombing of vital centers would take millions fewer lives and consume less treasure than the traditional struggle of army against army. Strategic bombing would be "a benefit to civilization."[16]

These shifts reflected more than just a natural evolution of thought. So long as he remained a career officer, Mitchell was subject to restraint by superiors in the U.S. Army who regarded the Air Service as an auxiliary to ground forces.[17] Perhaps even more important, the publicly expressed official policy of the United States government appeared to rule out the kind of warfare Mitchell foretold.

During World War I President Woodrow Wilson had said, "I desire no sort of participation by the Air Service of the United States in a plan . . . which has as its object promiscuous bombing upon industry, commerce, or populations in enemy countries disassociated from obvious military needs to be served by such action." Wilson's secretary of war, Newton D. Baker, had insisted in 1918 that the United States must not take part in "promiscuous bombing" of industry, commerce, or the civilian population. The secretary later described indiscriminate bombing as the type of inhumane departure from civilized practice that had recently characterized America's ruthless enemies in the Great War.[18] These ideas, which remained official War Department policy through World War II, at least on paper, were supported in the United States by an influential body of anti-military, anti-interventionist, and anti-war opinion. Consequently, while Douhet, writing in a fascist country that glorified violence, could openly discuss unlimited terror bombing of civilians, it was altogether another matter for Mitchell to do so in the United States—the country Douhet once called "the father of the most humanitarian and pacifist proposal"[19]—particularly while Mitchell and the Air Service were trying to cultivate American public opinion.

After his court-martial Mitchell resigned from the service, breaking the ties that had limited what he was able to say about air war. From 1926 to his death ten years later, his strategic doctrine could scarcely be distinguished from Douhet's. In his posthumously published memoirs of World War I, Mitchell explained that the only way to secure the object of war—imposing one's will upon the enemy—was to seize, control, or paralyze his vital centers: his "great cities" and factories, his food and finished products, the sources of his raw materials, and his means of transportation. Countries that had followed the traditional, centuries-old theory of war protected these centers by "covering them with the flesh and blood of the people, putting out in front of them what we call armies." Under that theory, it was necessary to smash the hostile army to open the way to the enemy's vitals. By 1914 the traditional methods had made such victories terribly costly, requiring that the enemy army be slowly killed off, and that in the process all the hostile nation's personal and material resources be destroyed. The participants in the Great War (except the United States, which entered very late), emerged from the conflict exhausted. Any future ground war that followed the old principles could only end in "absolute ruin."

"Fortunately," Mitchell said, the new element of air power could overcome these problems. By attacking the vital centers with fire, chemical weapons, and airborne bombs, it could completely paralyze them and reduce them to ruins at a modest cost in men and dollars.[20]

There were several important parallels between Mitchell's ideas and those presented at the Air Corps Tactical School. Subject to the same pressures that had impinged on General Mitchell, the school fluctuated on the employment of air power just as Mitchell did. Like the general, it produced at one point a strategic doctrine which resembled the vision of Douhet. Its early manuals offered the accepted army view that aircraft were aids to ground forces and that armies, not cities, were the objective in war. Then in 1926, the same year that Mitchell broke loose from official inhibitions, the school made a drastic change. Its 1926 manual *Employment of Combined Air Forces* not only accepted the idea of an independent air arm, whose first task was to secure command of the air; it also declared that the true objectives in war were the enemy population and the enemy's vital points, not his armies in the field. Like Douhet and Mitchell, it argued that air attack, as "a method of imposing will by terrorizing the whole population," was vastly preferable to a war of slow attrition. But it assumed that terror would not necessarily require large-scale killing, and spoke of "conserving life and property to the greatest possible extent."[21]

Four years later a school manual discussed in passing certain moral implications of air war against civilians. *The Air Force,* published in 1930, quoted General Hans von Seeckt, former chief of the German Army Command, as saying, "It is important to attack civilian populations in the back areas of the hostile country." The manual explained how the air force of a great power might strike at those populations. Bombers could hit city dwellers directly with high explosives, chemical spray, or chemical bombs, or they might attack them indirectly by destroying water supply and power systems or by disrupting the distribution of food. Successful assaults on these objectives, the manual said, would lead to "terrible suffering of non-combatants."[22]

The authors of the 1930 manual classified as "political objectives" targets attacked in order to strike directly at the heart of the enemy civilian population. They maintained that a decision to direct an air force against a political objective would "never be adopted except as the result of a careful estimate of the results to be accomplished when weighed against the suffering of women and children, and the effect upon public opinion in neutral countries." But if national policy demands that an air force be used in that way, the "highest authority" would decide both the specific task to be accomplished and the general method to be used.[23]

Since the men who wrote that manual had no sure way of predicting how the highest authority would react to the circumstances they described, they could not have been certain that the top leaders of the United States would carefully weigh civilian suffering against projected military results. Rather, they expressed what they expected or perhaps hoped the highest authority would do. Assuming the traditional deference which American officers accorded civil authority, they removed crucial moral decisions from the sphere of the air force officer, making him the morally neutral or amoral instrument of civilian policymakers.

During the 1930s Army Air Corps doctrine began to diverge in important respects from the approach of Douhet and Mitchell. Air Corps Tactical School instructors continued to believe, as the two air-power prophets did, that civilian morale would be decisive in the next war, and agreed with Douhet that it was more vulnerable to destruction than the morale of soldiers and far more difficult to restore. But they differed with both men about the best way of breaking civilian morale and forcing an enemy to surrender. The thrust of Douhet's strategy was toward total destruction of urban centers, resulting in a complete breakdown of civilian morale and enemy will to fight. Mitchell thought a few gas bombs could paralyze a city.[24] The school questioned these ideas, refined the notion of what constituted a vital target, and attempted to devise a more systematic method of breaking enemy resistance—by shattering the society's economic structure.

The officers at ATCS, who lived in an era of economic collapse, thought the economies of advanced nations, with their high living standards and large urban centers, were extremely vulnerable to air bombardment. A complex web of functions supported both civil populations and military arms, and in wartime, when the enemy was straining to supply both sectors, selective bombing of the web's most vital points—transportation, factories, sources of energy, and raw materials—would produce devastating effects. The effects would be circular and cumulative. Destroying the civilian economy would depress civilian morale. Demoralized workers and wrecked factories would be unable to produce the tools of war. Denied materials they needed to fight, the armed forces would collapse, further undermining national will to resist.[25]

By the middle of the decade Air Corps Tactical School instructors ceased to favor direct attacks on population centers. They knew that selective bombing was much less likely to provoke hostility to the Air Corps within the United States than was Douhet's approach. Selective bombing also fit very well the kind of equipment and bombing techniques the Air Corps was developing, and it seemed the most efficient way of using the nation's scarce military resources.

In 1935 the Boeing Company tested a prototype model of the B-17, a heavy bomber which, when equipped with a precision bombsight and under ideal daylight test conditions, could drop bombs inside a small target area. Carrying several defensive guns, capable of flying at high altitudes and at a speed then thought to give it an advantage over pursuit planes, the B-17 appeared able to destroy precise objectives at long range—not just enemy factories, but parts of factories.[26]

B-17s were very expensive by pre–World War II standards, and in the mid-1930s, when the Roosevelt administration was trying to keep a growing budget under control and peace organizations were constantly pressuring the U.S. government to limit military spending, they were hard to come by. It seemed more efficient to use them against a limited number of small but crucial economic targets than to have them saturate large population centers in the hope of crushing the enemy's will to resist. As Generals Eaker and Arnold wrote in their 1941 volume *Winged Warfare*, "Human beings are not priority targets except in special situations. Bombers in far larger numbers than are available today will be required for wiping out people in sufficient numbers by aerial bombardment to break the will of a whole nation."[27]

When these words appeared in print, General Arnold was already looking toward a time when bombers *would* be available in far larger numbers, in fleets large enough to level entire cities. In April 1941 he had witnessed the German blitz of London, noting after a raid that had killed hundreds of civilians and injured thousands of others that fewer than five hundred German planes had caused so much wreckage. In the United States, he reflected, "we are thinking in terms of not less than 500 and perhaps more than a thousand bombers." If eight hundred or a thousand planes had hit London in one night, he wrote, they might have wiped out the city. "Air power means employment of airplanes in numbers large enough to secure complete destruction."[28]

Before Pearl Harbor it would have been extremely imprudent for the chief of the Army Air Corps to have made these reflections public. Besides, they represented only one school of thought in the air force. Other officers, testing their theories with the experience of nations already at war, believed the evidence confirmed the principle of selective bombing. The Air Corps Tactical School studied raids launched against civilians in China, Ethiopia, and Spain and found them wanting in efficiency. In a June 1940 lecture at the school, Muir S. Fairchild, the director of air tactics and strategy, remarked that Japanese bombing of Chinese cities had actually increased the morale of the Chinese nation, and was more responsible for unifying the populace than any other factor. For that reason, and because direct attacks on population centers produced only temporary results which did not build on one another and had minimal effects on a nation's ability to make war, the school preferred a strategy of delivering selective precision attacks against the enemy's national economic structure.[29]

If the greater efficiency of selective bombing influenced ACTS to reject Douhet's mass bombing approach, was the school also rejecting Douhetian ethics? The evidence is not entirely clear. While ACTS textbooks for 1935 and 1936 stated that world opinion opposed "employment of air power in direct attacks against civilian personnel," they did not express agreement or disagreement with that view on moral grounds and observed that, regardless of world opinion, the major powers anticipated air war against civilians. The text of a lecture, "The Aim in War," apparently first delivered by Haywood S. Hansell, Jr., states that "we may find the air force charged with breaking the will to resist of the enemy nation. Let us make it emphatically clear that that does *not* mean the 'indiscriminate bombing of women and children.'" However, when this lecture was given in 1939, this passage was crossed out; so was the next section, which explained that efficiency is a sufficient reason to avoid that type of bombing. The transcript of a school conference in 1939 on bombing objectives in Japan notes that direct attack against the civilian populace, though probably highly effective in breaking the morale of the people, is rejected "due to humanitarian considerations." But the the transcript added; "This objective should be borne in mind, however, as a possible means of retaliation. Nothing in recent or remote Japanese history indicates that were she physically able, Japan herself would not adopt this mode of attack."[30] The implication was that a form of air war otherwise too inhumane to employ might become permissible if the enemy employed it first.

While individual officers at ACTS may have thought it morally repugnant to attack enemy civilians directly, school doctrine envisioned a kind of war that would do great indirect damage to the civilian populace. The approach the school favored—breaking down the national economy through attacks on vital installations—was bound to injure large numbers of civilians. Despite precision bombsights and the accurate results achieved in practice runs, airmen, particularly veterans of air combat, must have realized that they could not avoid killing or wounding civilians when they tried to bomb those installations. The key targets were in cities, usually near workers' housing, and the more heavily the enemy defended the targets, the more difficult it would be to drop bombs only on designated places.[31]

Besides, the Air Corps' vital-centers approach was intended to injure civilians—psychologically. Major Fairchild put it this way:

> Obviously we cannot and do not intend to actually kill or injure *all* the people. Therefore our intention in deciding upon this method of attack [against the national economic structure] must be to so reduce the morale of the enemy civilian population through fear—fear of death or injury for themselves and their loved ones—that they would prefer our terms of peace to continuing the struggle, and would force their government to capitulate.

Fairchild was not talking about generating fear with radio broadcasts and propaganda leaflets. To break national morale and the national will to resist, he said, it would be necessary to inflict "intense suffering" upon the civilian populace.[32]

When Major Fairchild wrote these words, other nations had already begun to inflict death and injury on civilians. The United States government denounced their actions. President Roosevelt protested vehemently against continuing Japanese air raids on Chungking, where the Nationalist government of China had located itself after the Japanese invasion. When the Soviet Union bombed Helsinki and other cities during its 1939 attack on Finland, the president, echoing the position that President Wilson had taken in World War I, stated, "The American Government and the American people have for some time pursued a policy of wholeheartedly condemning the unprovoked bombing and machine-gunning of civilian populations from the air."[33] But when World War II began, and American air force planners were called on to produce an actual program for fighting prospective enemies—Germany, Japan, and Italy—the plan they came up with not only included ways of disintegrating national economic structures but, in a reversion to the approach of Mitchell and Douhet, proposed to attack civilians directly when certain specified conditions occurred.

In the summer of 1941 the U.S. Army was trying to estimate military needs for a global war, and delegated to the Army Air Forces the task of determining air war requirements. The AAF assigned a group of officers in its Air War Plans Division to draw up a strategic war plan to guide its calculations. The project's director was Colonel Harold L. George, a dynamic, enthusiastic veteran bomber pilot who had flown in World War I, participated in Billy Mitchell's experimental attacks on warships, and in the mid-1930s headed the Department of Air Tactics and Strategy at the Air Corps Tactical School. His assistants included Haywood Hansell; Kenneth Walker, an intense, methodical apostle of strategic bombing who had been an instructor at ACTS when George was a student; and Laurence S. Kuter, who taught bombardment at the school and was known for his keen mind and sardonic sense of humor.[34]

In a few days, under tremendous pressure, these officers distilled ACTS doctrine into essentially what became the American strategic bombing program for World War II. Their plan, AWPD-1, included neutralization of the German Air Force, air defense of the Western Hemisphere, defensive air operations in the Pacific, and direct air support of Allied surface forces in an invasion of the European continent, followed by bombing attacks on Japan. Its basic objective for Germany, against which most American resources would first be directed, was to destroy that nation's ability to make war by breaking down its national economic and social structure. At least at first, strategic bombing would be concentrated "tenaciously" against specific target systems vital to a continued German war effort and to the means of livelihood of the German people: electric power, transportation, and oil supplies.

Up to this point the plan followed the most recent ACTS doctrine, including attacks that would affect German civilians severely but indirectly. Then it added the suggestion that direct attacks on civilians might be effective "as German morale begins to crack." Timing was all-important. If the bombing of urban areas began prematurely, it might stiffen popular resistance, especially if the attacks were weak and sporadic. But if the German people were already demoralized by continued deprivation and suffering and were losing faith in the ultimate triumph of their armed forces, sustained bombing of cities might destroy their morale entirely. Once the psychologically correct point had been reached, the entire bombing effort might be aimed at civilian morale. This would not necessarily be at the very end of the war, for the planners suggested that immediately after the effects of bombing material targets had become quite evident, or right after the German armies had suffered a major defeat, it might be "highly profitable to deliver a large-scale, all-out attack on the civil population of Berlin."[35]

Taken as a whole, American air power doctrines, like the theories and practice of other modern nations, offered unpleasant prospects to the inhabitants of enemy countries. While the doctrine taught to its officers modified the Douhetian principle of all-out attacks on cities, it did so on the pragmatic ground of efficiency, not a promising basis for insulating civilians against air attacks. American doctrine continued to accept the principle which underlay the mass-bombing strategies of Mitchell and Douhet—that in modern total war, civilians and armed forces were inseparably linked in national war machines. It also accepted their argument that one way to break those machines was to smash civilian will, though the relatively small-scale attacks that the fascist countries and the Soviet Union delivered against civilians before the United States entered the war had failed to secure that objective. The ACTS doctrine, presented by Major Fairchild, was to break national will indirectly, through measures that would cause great suffering for the enemy populace. The Air War Plans Division went still further. Although it gave direct attacks on civilians the lowest priority, it specified circumstances under which American bombers might make German civilians their objective. The chief of the Army Air Forces, meanwhile, looked forward to a time when waves of bombers would demolish entire cities.

There was, of course, the official policy of the United States government, expressed most recently by President Franklin Roosevelt. Examined carefully, however, that policy offered no absolute prohibition against bombing enemy cities or endangering enemy civilians, no promise that the United States would not join the moral and military revolution already under way among the world's great powers. For the policy ruled out only "unprovoked," "promiscuous," or "indiscriminate" attacks on civil populations, and these terms were sometimes difficult to define in real war situations, even when decision makers wanted to.

Still, the absence of impediments to joining the moral and military revolution did not guarantee that American flyers would take part in it or, if they did, determine the extent of their participation. Other factors had to be considered, including the idealism of the American people, the impact of that idealism on military decisions, the values of American political and military leaders, and the way the war developed after the United States became a belligerent. The effects of these factors can be observed by examining the way the Army Air Forces applied their doctrine under war conditions, beginning with the first American air offensive launched from the British Isles.

— 3

American Air Operations in Europe: Occupied Countries and Axis Satellites

While air-power theorists in the 1920s and 1930s had discussed certain general moral consequences of the kind of war they envisioned, actual use of air weapons during the Second World War raised specific ethical questions that prewar thinkers had not considered. Under what circumstances is it right to take the lives and destroy the homes of friendly civilians in countries occupied by the enemy? When does war make it justifiable to damage or destroy the physical heritage of one's own civilization? Should civilians in countries allied with and dominated by the principal enemy be dealt with as harshly as those living in the territory of the chief opponent? These difficult questions arose for American leaders as the United States Army Air Forces sought to apply its airpower doctrine to Nazi-dominated Europe.

American Doctrine and European Practice

Before the late summer of 1940, the German and British air forces attempted to maintain a distinction between combatants and bystanders. A 1936 Luftwaffe training manual announced that "attacks on cities for the purpose of terrorizing the civilian population are absolutely forbidden." Though the German Condor Legion had bombed helpless civilians during the Spanish Civil War, Hitler's air arm refrained for several months after the outbreak of World War II from attacking English population centers. The Nazis' first objective was to secure command of the air as preparation for a landing on the British Isles. Their airmen attempted to eliminate the Royal Air Force by destroying its bases, supplies, planes, and aircraft factories. But when these efforts failed they began to attack London, seeking to draw the last RAF reserves into combat while hitting military targets. German bombardiers aimed at docks and large factories. They might as well have directed their bombs at residential districts, for their accuracy, especially in night raids, was extremely poor. From the beginning of September 1940 through mid-May 1941 they killed nearly 40,000 people in London, Coventry, and other urban centers, and wounded and destroyed the homes of many thousands more.[1]

At the beginning of the war the British tried to strike specific military and economic targets, but they too turned to bombing heavily populated urban areas. By the end of 1939 they realized that day raids were terribly costly and not very effective. Yet their attempts to bomb particular objectives at night did not work either. A War Cabinet study of raids conducted during June and July 1941 concluded that only one in four of the crews that claimed to have attacked their objectives had actually flown within five miles of the target. Early the next year the British government decided to abandon "precision" bombing. It ordered RAF Bomber Command officially to do what it had already been doing on and off for a year—bomb German urban areas with the aim of disrupting the German economy by killing, wounding, "dehousing," and terrorizing workers, and keeping them out of factories even if the factories could not be hit. "A primary object" of Bomber Command raids, an RAF directive of February 14, 1942, stated, was "the morale of the enemy civil population and in particular of the industrial workers." If raids that destroyed German cities also demolished important military objectives or factories, so much the better. There was also the psychological benefit of paying the Germans back in kind. Some British officials even believed that urban area bombing, if properly done, would destroy German will to fight and force the Nazis to surrender.[2]

When the United States Army Air Forces arrived in England in the spring of 1942, the British wanted them to join in this type of bombing. The Americans refused. Like the leaders of the American Expeditionary Forces in World War I, U.S. air commanders did not want their forces thrown piecemeal into battle. They had come to England to build up the Eighth Air Force and use it in selective attacks against German targets, which at this stage of the war did not appear to include residential districts. AAF leaders believed they could succeed where the RAF had failed—in precision daylight bombing. They expected to defeat the enemy's air force and go on to destroy vital centers, eliminating Germany's ability to fight and crushing its will to resist.[3]

High-level Army Air Force leaders challenged British urban area bombing, but not on moral grounds. General Spaatz, the first Eighth Air Force commander, told an interviewer after the war that "it wasn't for religious or moral reasons that I didn't go along with urban area bombing." It was because he believed attacks on "strategic targets" would be more effective. General Eaker, Spaatz's successor as head of the Eighth Air Force, agreed. He explained that he had "never felt there was any moral sentiment among leaders of the AAF." On the question of bombing to break civilian morale, Eaker differed with the British for the same reason Spaatz did—he thought it would not work. Although many people after the war condemned the head of RAF Bomber Command, Air Chief Marshal Arthur Harris, for bombing German civilians, Eaker declined to join them, because he recognized that Harris's chief purpose was "to destroy Hitler's tyranny and prevent it from killing British civilians."[4]

This does not mean, however, that Army Air Force leaders considered the morality of bombing unimportant. Spaatz and even Eaker, despite his claim that there was no moral sentiment among people like himself, felt that RAF methods, however misguided technically, were justified by what the Germans had done. When Spaatz had first come to England in 1940 as an observer, he had not cared whether the British won or lost, but what he called "intimate contact with the ruthless methods" of German warfare, including the "indiscriminate" blitz of London, had convinced him to take the British side.[5]

Apart from their personal views, American air force leaders had a very persuasive reason for concern about the moral issue. Over the years the AAF had arrived at its position partly by cultivating public support, and its leaders expected public opinion to help it attain supremacy in the postwar national defense system. As Hap Arnold told General Eaker in June 1943, "We want the people to understand and have faith in *our way of making war*."[6] It was essential to convince the public that AAF bombing methods did not violate ethical principles widely held at home. If there was going to be any bombing that appeared to conflict with those principles, it was better if the British did it, not the AAF.

This was the kind of arrangement the Americans wanted when they argued at the January 1943 Casablanca conference for an agreement to continue daylight precision bombing. General Eaker made the case for the American position to Prime Minister Churchill and, not surprisingly, all his arguments were pragmatic, not moral ones. Eaker explained how American attacks would complement and assist RAF night area raids. Daylight bombing could destroy targets the RAF missed. It was more economical than area attacks because it concentrated bombs on the target. American crews were trained for day bombing, whereas if the AAF accepted the British request to use them at night they would have to be retrained. American bombers would also need extensive refitting to bomb in darkness. Dividing missions between American day bombers and the night bombers of the RAF would prevent congestion in the air space over England. B-17s would destroy enemy fighters and would ignite German targets, creating beacons for RAF night raids. By attacking "the devils" around the clock, the AAF and the RAF would give the Germans no rest.[7]

Though Churchill remained deeply skeptical about the American approach, he accepted it. The British agreed to a Combined Bomber Offensive whose primary aim was "the progressive destruction and dislocation of the German military, industrial and economic system, and the undermining of the morale of the German people to a point where their capacity for armed resistance is fatally weakened." General Arnold called the Casablanca agreement "a major victory, for we would bomb in accordance with American principles using methods for which our planes were designed."[8]

Bombing the Low Countries and France

Allocation of the AAF to daylight raids meant that the Eighth Air Force tended to fly at first to France and the Low Countries, where its precision bombing techniques were supposed to enable it to knock out German objectives while harming friendly civilians as little as possible. But the Americans did not always hit their targets accurately; they had problems with faulty navigation devices, German air and anti-aircraft defenses, harsh weather, and their own inexperience. The United States Strategic Bombing Survey, which analyzed the effects of American bombing in the Second World War, estimated that from January through September 1943 daylight bombers of the Eighth Air Force landed about one bomb in five within a thousand feet of the target. Through accident or careless attacks on what the air force termed "targets of opportunity," United States B-17s did extensive damage to civilians. Raids intended to destroy military and industrial objectives in Paris, Nantes, Lille, Rouen, Lorient, Amsterdam, and elsewhere killed thousands of inhabitants, seriously undermined the morale of friendly civilians, provoked vehement complaints from governments in exile, and provided material for Nazi propagandists.[9]

To counter these effects, the Allies broadcast assurances in French that the United States felt the deepest sympathy for the French people. The AAF aimed its bombs only at the Nazis, they said, and at enterprises that helped the Nazi war effort. At the same time, they cautioned civilians to vacate areas within two kilometers of war factories.[10]

In an effort to limit damage to friendly civilians, General Spaatz told Eighth Air Force combat commanders to follow the RAF's official rules for bombing occupied countries. These rules forbade intentional bombing of civilian populations and required airmen to take reasonable care to avoid undue loss of civilian life. Nevertheless, the problem of incidental casualties persisted, evoking sharp reactions, especially from the French. Alarmed by the political havoc American bombers were creating, the British sent General Eaker (who succeeded Spaatz as the Eighth Air Force chief) a series of warnings against alienating the inhabitants of occupied Europe.[11]

General Eaker, meanwhile, received a very different kind of message from Washington. Civilian War Department officials felt he should ignore the official RAF policy, since the RAF was breaking its own rules. They urged him to do everything he could to cripple German U-boats berthed in French ports where, hidden in concrete shelters, they seemed impervious to direct air attack. Undersecretary of War Robert P. Patterson thought it absurd to confine the American bombers to fruitless raids on the submarine pens while the British disrupted U-boat maintenance by blowing up homes of French maintenance workers. Assistant Secretary of War for Air Robert A. Lovett told General Eaker in March 1943 that the RAF had nullified any restrictions against bombing towns in occupied territories by "cutting loose" on places like Lorient. Since the

AAF could not penetrate the Lorient U-boat shelters, Lovett recommended that U.S. flyers try to "wipe out the town as the RAF does."[12]

Eaker declined to follow this advice. Instead, bowing to RAF entreaties, he ordered his target selectors to weigh, along with the military importance of objectives, the possibility that bombing would kill or injure large numbers of civilians. Then he sent the target lists to the British Air Ministry for approval. General Eaker was not very happy about these new procedures, for he feared the Allies were letting German propaganda decide which objectives they were to attack, permitting the Nazis to shield military installations behind friendly civilians. He wondered if the British realized that for the B-17s to do their work they would have to hit civilians. "It is not clear in my own mind," he wrote Charles Portal, the British chief of air staff, ". . . whether you believe the destruction of the Renault plant in Paris was of sufficient military importance to justify the killing of French civilians who may have lost their lives in that attack."[13]

As the time approached for the Allied invasion of Normandy, Operation OVERLORD, the problem of friendly civilian casualties intensified, becoming entangled with a controversy over how best to use airpower to support the landing. Arthur Harris, the head of RAF Bomber Command, wanted to continue battering German cities. Air Marshal Arthur Tedder, deputy to the Supreme Allied Commander, General Dwight D. Eisenhower, favored a plan to impede German reinforcements to the invasion zone by systematically destroying marshaling yards and other rail facilities weeks before the landing.[14] General Carl Spaatz, who had assumed command of U.S. Strategic Air Forces in Europe, had other ideas about using air power to assure the success of OVERLORD.

The transportation plan was essentially the brainchild of a British scientist, Solly Zuckerman. Earlier in the war, Spaatz had worked with Zuckerman on the bombing of the island of Pantelleria preliminary to the Allied landings on Sicily, an attack that forced the enemy garrison to surrender. The scientist had impressed the general at that time with what Spaatz described as his "very coldly analytical and precisely applied" method of planning bombardment. Zuckerman's approach had almost persuaded the American that in modern war the best general was a "mathematical genius." But Spaatz and his staff strongly objected to Zuckerman's plan for bombing transportation.[15]

The Americans wanted to concentrate their attack on oil. They argued that systematic precision bombing of Nazi oil resources would do more to assure the success of Operation OVERLORD than raids on marshaling yards, which were difficult to shut down completely and fairly easy to repair. Attacks on vital synthetic petroleum plants and refineries would cause the Germans to conserve fuel, restricting their movements in the west. The heavy bombers would draw the Luftwaffe into air battles in which it would suffer such heavy losses to American gunners that by D day the Allies would command the air over the landing zone. Then, shortly before the invasion, Allied planes would sever rail and road bridges, effectively isolating the battlefield from German reinforcements.[16]

Behind these arguments lay another, unspoken in Allied war councils. General Spaatz and some of the other Americans believed that air power alone would defeat the Germans if the airmen were permitted to use it against strategic targets instead of having it diverted to other theaters and to projects like the Zuckerman plan. At one point Spaatz believed the invasion would fail, after which the air forces would have the chance to win the war on their own. At another time he complained to Zuckerman that while Air Marshal Harris would be allowed to go on bombing Germany and would be "given a chance of defeating her before the invasion," his heavy bombers would be confined to tactical attacks.[17]

As the struggle over the Zuckerman plan went on for weeks, Spaatz found himself with many allies. British intelligence and economic warfare experts, the British War Office, and part of the RAF high command shared his doubts about transportation bombing. Prime Minister Churchill and the British War Cabinet anticipated grave political consequences from the Zuckerman plan, for they feared that bombs intended for railroad cars and marshaling yards would kill as many as 40,000 French and Belgian civilians and injure 120,000 more. However, General Eisenhower, who assumed control of Allied strategic air forces before the invasion, approved the plan as more likely than the alternatives to affect German resistance seriously before D day.[18]

Churchill urged President Roosevelt to intervene to mitigate the predicted "French slaughters," but Roosevelt refused. He agreed with General Arnold and the War Department that Eisenhower be allowed to make his own decision. He explained to the prime minister that he shared his distress at loss of life among the French populace and felt no possibility should be overlooked for "alleviating adverse French opinion," provided it did not interfere with military success. Yet he would not limit military action by the responsible commanders which, in their opinion, might aid the invasion or prevent additional Allied losses.[19]

Churchill acquiesced, but Spaatz continued to press for an oil-bombing program, threatening to resign if Eisenhower refused his request. The result was a compromise in which Spaatz's bombers, while adhering to the letter of the Zuckerman plan, were allowed to hit petroleum targets surreptitiously. AAF planners arranged for U.S. planes to attack marshaling yards adjacent to the oil facilities in Ploesti, Rumania. But they designed the bombing runs so that "stray" bombs would land in the oil works.[20] This kind of procedure, in which the AAF aimed at one target with the intent of securing a "bonus" by destroying a second objective, became an important element of its tactics throughout the war.

Like Prime Minister Churchill, General Spaatz argued that the Zuckerman plan needlessly endangered friendly civilians. He wrote General Eisenhower that "many thousands of French people will be killed and many towns laid waste in these operations. I feel a joint responsibility with you and I view with alarm a military operation which involved [sic] such widespread destruction and death in countries not our enemies, particularly since the results to be achieved from these bombing operations have not been conclusively shown to be a decisive factor."[21]

These moral and political objections were never Spaatz's principal reason for opposing the Zuckerman plan. Still, it is worth noting that he felt they should be considered and that they might carry some weight with General Eisenhower. W. W. Rostow, an economist who worked with Spaatz's targeting staff, felt practical considerations predominated in Spaatz's headquarters, though some people, including the general, did consider the welfare of Allied civilians. "Although it was not an overriding criterion," Rostow recalled, "we took some comfort that our proposals would be much less costly in terms of the lives of civilians than would the marshalling-yard attacks." Spaatz's aides also worried that since American heavy bombers would have to do most of the bombing, blame for French and Belgian casualties would fall on the AAF.[22]

The raids on marshaling yards, together with attacks on bridges, severely damaged German transportation before D day. They did not silence the proponents of the oil plan, who continued to speculate that if they had gotten their way in the first place, the war might have ended sooner. Pre-invasion bombing killed some

12,000 civilians in the occupied countries, far fewer than the prime minister and his aides had estimated but more than enough to demonstrate that the issue raised by Churchill and seconded by General Spaatz had been far from trivial.[23]

In the transportation bombing controversy, as in the entire air war over occupied Western Europe, American leaders subordinated the likelihood of civilian casualties to the promise of military gains. For General Eaker, the deaths of French civilians had to be weighed against the damage air raids could do to German production; while he acted, under British pressure, to limit French casualties, the restrictions disturbed him. General Eisenhower, warned about the likelihood of heavy civilian losses, nevertheless approved the Zuckerman plan because it offered the best hope of decreasing German resistance to OVERLORD. To Secretary Lovett, the criteria for obliterating a French city were, first, the existence of enemy targets within its boundaries, and second, whether the RAF had taken similar action in France. While General Spaatz called attention to civilian losses that might result from the Zuckerman plan, this by itself did not mean that he felt the moral issue transcended military necessity. He considered the Zuckerman plan militarily harmful, a waste of men and planes that were needed to bomb really important targets like oil refineries.

Franklin Roosevelt conceivably might have sided with Churchill in the marshaling yard dispute and urged General Eisenhower to reconsider Zuckerman's plan. This would have been politically risky, however. If things had gone wrong on D day, the president could have been blamed for interfering with the Supreme Commander. It would also have been an unusual step, since Roosevelt ordinarily allowed his generals considerable leeway in achieving what was, after all, the best hope for most civilians in Nazi-held territory—an early Allied victory.[24] But it would have been neither unprecedented nor impossible. Roosevelt did intervene with the military chiefs, directly or indirectly, to shape crucial decisions, for example the decision to invade North Africa. In the case of the Zuckerman plan he disagreed with Churchill that the chance of "French slaughters" justified his interposition.

To the president and to most of the other Americans responsible for the air war, death and injury among friendly civilians were inescapable consequences of modern warfare. They were analogous to casualties among the Allies' own troops. They did not like to see them. They avoided them when they could. But they were inevitable if the Allies were to prevail over the Nazi empire.

The Bombing of Italy—Axis Partner, Occupied Cobelligerent

Human casualties were only a part of the losses suffered in the air war, for in addition to bringing death and injury, destruction of homes, and disruption of lives, warplanes severely damaged places and objects of great cultural significance. It was a problem in every battle area. The Germans devastated historic sections of British cities. RAF bomber crews demolished beautiful old structures in Germany. Even before the Allies landed on the continent, their air forces ruined cultural artifacts in the Low Countries and France, despite efforts to avoid hitting them. Nowhere was the threat of war to the physical treasures of Western civilization more ominous than in Italy, where Allied armies struggled against the Germans and against the Fascist legions of Benito Mussolini. For nearly two years air and land battles menaced Italy's universities, libraries, archives, and museums, its ancient ruins and venerated religious buildings, and the splendor of its art and architecture. While one group of Americans threatened Italian cultural treasures with devastation from the air, others, including members of the AAF, sought to limit the damage inflicted by U.S. warplanes. The war in Italy became, on one level, a conflict between destruction and preservation.

From the earliest phase of the Italian campaign—the air raids preceding the landing on Sicily, July 10, 1943—until the first operations of the U.S. Fifteenth Air Force four months later, American air units stationed in the Mediterranean theater rarely took part in long-range strategic bombing, but instead blasted enemy supply lines or acted as airborne artillery, bombarding hostile battle positions. Since these positions often lay in or near inhabited places, American flyers and their colleagues in the RAF wrecked towns and villages in Sicily and lower Italy and devastated much of Naples, a transshipment center for Axis forces in the Mediterranean.[25]

These raids terrified the inhabitants, a fact that Allied leaders tried to turn to political advantage. They hoped air attacks, by panicking the Italian people, would weaken their will to fight and cause their government to surrender—making the prophecies of Douhet come true in his own country. General Spaatz, who then commanded the Northwest African Air Forces, was struck by the way bombing attacks appeared to affect enemy morale. When the Italian garrison on Pantelleria capitulated, following days of incessant bombing, Spaatz declared that "the human mind cannot adjust itself to bombardment on an ascending scale." He proposed to apply this principle to the mainland of Italy by offering the Italian government a chance to surrender while his planes destroyed Naples. If it declined his offer, the next target would be Rome.[26]

General Spaatz's superiors also proposed to bomb Rome or, more precisely, certain targets within its boundaries. Roosevelt and Churchill agreed to have the U.S. Army Air Forces attack Rome's San Lorenzo and Littorio marshaling yards and the San Lorenzo railroad station. Destroying these facilities would impede the movement of German reinforcements to Sicily and Southern Italy, but to Allied leaders the psychological and political effects of the raid, including the possible collapse of Mussolini's government, were as important as their military consequences.[27]

Yet they recognized that an attack on any part of the Eternal City could gravely damage the Allied cause. Even a precision daylight raid designed to spare Rome's historic and religious centers might shock Catholics in Europe and the United States. Nazi propaganda would surely depict it as an assault on a shrine of Christendom. Still, Allied leaders accepted those risks. While General Arnold felt it would be impossible to guarantee the safety of all churches near the target area, he felt that General Eisenhower, who then commanded the Allied forces in the Mediterranean, should make the decision to bomb the yards without regard for politics or religion. Army Chief of Staff George C. Marshall agreed, for he was implacably determined that no "outside considerations" be allowed to interfere with the firm prosecution of the war. General Marshall told the Combined Chiefs of Staff that while it would be a "tragedy" if Saint Peter's were destroyed, it would be a "calamity if we failed to knock out the marshalling yards."[28]

Eisenhower, who regarded the targets in Rome chiefly as psychological objectives, maintained that the Allies could secure their military goal of blocking enemy rail traffic by striking facilities further south; but after it appeared that he could spare several planes from the battle for Sicily, he decided to proceed with the Rome operation. The attack was scheduled for July 19, 1943.[29]

At the president's request, the Combined Chiefs of Staff told General Eisenhower that all pilots must be thoroughly instructed in the geography of Rome, particularly the location of Vatican City, where no bombs should be allowed to fall. They sent Eisenhower names and locations of major churches that must not be hit: Saint John Lateran, Santo Paolo, and Santa Maria Maggiore. The president conveyed these precautions to the pope, assuring him that in the struggle for Italy, the Allies would respect the neutrality of

Vatican City and other papal domains and would spare churches and religious institutions if they possibly could. Meanwhile, the Combined Chiefs arranged to control public information, by rushing reports out before the Nazi broadcasts began, by distinguishing the marshaling yards from the city of Rome itself, and by stressing the military importance of the places bombed.[30]

Shortly after 11:00 A.M. on the 19th, under clear skies, the first of several waves of B-17s wheeled over Rome and began dropping high explosives on the marshaling yards from about 23,000 feet. Medium bombers flew in at lower altitudes to hit the Littorio and Ciampino airdromes. Damage was so concentrated and severe that the yards and airfield were crippled for days.[31]

Yet even this textbook example of precision bombing caused unwanted damage, killing civilians near the railroad facilities and wrecking one of Rome's most magnificent churches. A bomb landed about a thousand feet from the marshaling yards in the nave of the Basilica of San Lorenzo, which for some reason had not been circled on the briefing maps. The explosion caved in the roof and front façade, destroying thirteenth-century frescos and fourteenth-century mosaics and severely damaging other parts of the Basilica.[32]

As Allied leaders anticipated, the raid's psychological impact was extremely powerful. American warplanes had appeared over the Italian capital at the very time that Hitler was trying to bolster a worn, discouraged Mussolini at a conference in Feltre and while King Victor Emmanuel was considering whether to oust the Fascist premier (which he did six days later). Together with the heavy bombing of Naples and other towns and with Allied success in Sicily, the air attack on Rome deepened Italian war weariness.[33]

After the July 19 raid the Italian government tried to make Rome an open city. General Eisenhower postponed a scheduled second air raid on the Rome marshaling yards and called a halt to all morale bombing in Italy, but his superiors, fearing that an agreement to safeguard the Italian capital against attack would give military advantages to the Germans who occupied it, declined to commit themselves to a formal arrangement. President Roosevelt advised that the Allies stall on open city proposals. "General Eisenhower knows that we do not want to burn Rome," he told the Joint Chiefs of Staff, and left it to Eisenhower to decide whether to bomb the marshaling yards again.[34]

Since the Germans chose not to make a stand inside the city, it was spared the kind of damage suffered by London or Berlin, but the AAF did a first-class job of wrecking its rail facilities. When General Arnold visited the Italian capital in June 1944, he went to see what was left of the marshaling yards and noted in his diary, "Over 800 railroad cars thrown around—turned upside down—burned—tossed on top of one another—over a stretch of the entire yard. . . . The station and warehouses completely destroyed. It was a delightful mess from my viewpoint," but "none of the apartments bordering the yards were injured in any way."[35]

Partly in reaction to the American bombing of Rome, the Italian government capitulated on September 8, 1943. This was just the prelude to the most serious fighting in Italy, for German troops disarmed the Italian army and, establishing strong positions in difficult terrain, prepared to make the Allied advance slow and painful. The prospect of continuing ground battles and air attacks threatened cultural treasures throughout the peninsula.[36]

Several people in the United States and other countries had foreseen this problem and started preparations to limit the damage. Months before the landing in Sicily, American university and museum officials discussed ways to preserve the artworks and cultural monuments of Europe. In the fall of 1942, William Bell Dinsmoor, president of the Archeological Institute of America, arranged for the chief justice of the United States Supreme Court, Harlan Fiske Stone, to write the president about the problem. Stone recommended the establishment of a national agency to preserve and restore European artistic and historical monuments and records and to return looted objects to their owners. Roosevelt referred Justice Stone's proposal to the State Department and the Joint Chiefs of Staff while Dinsmoor took up the preservation issue with the secretary of war.[37]

The responses were all positive. High-level American officials recognized the political importance of preservation. Some of them shared the values of the preservationists. Stimson and John J. McCloy, the assistant secretary of war, were deeply interested in safeguarding cultural monuments, and not just to shield the United States against Nazi charges of barbarism. They considered European culture part of the heritage their country was fighting for. Later in the war McCloy intervened personally, flying to the headquarters of an American army in Germany to prevent the destruction of Rothenburg ob der Tauber, a medieval walled city his mother had once visited. Secretary of State Cordell Hull sympathized with Justice Stone's objectives and thought the proposed organization would serve America's practical interests by proclaiming its desire to protect "symbols of civilization" from injury and plunder. While the Joint Chiefs of Staff did not expect any military advantage from the proposed agency, they agreed to have American commanders cooperate with it in ways that did not interfere with military operations.[38]

The president then gave his approval and on August 20, 1943, Secretary Hull announced the founding of the American Commission for the Protection and Salvage of Artistic and Historic Monuments in Europe. Headed by Supreme Court Justice Owen J. Roberts, with leading museum officials, the Librarian of Congress, Francis Cardinal Spellman of New York, and archeologist Dinsmoor on its board of directors, the commission advised and assisted the Army Military Government School and the Army Air Forces, and coordinated the work of two agencies that had begun to prepare lists and maps of cultural artifacts, the American Defense Harvard Group and the Committee of the American Council of Learned Societies on Protection of Cultural Treasures in War Areas.[39]

These civilian agencies played a crucial role in protecting cultural monuments and artwork. In mid-July 1943, shortly after the landing on Sicily, the ACLS group took over the Frick Art Reference Library in New York. Using lists of cultural monuments prepared by the Harvard Committee, along with Italian tour books and some maps supplied by the War Department, it prepared map copies for the armed services. By the end of August the Roberts Commission was sending negatives of each map, with cultural monuments designated, to Army Air Force Intelligence in Washington. By April 1944 ACLS workers produced 160 city maps and seven regional maps for Italy alone.[40]

The Army Air Forces were very cooperative. AAF reconnaissance planes photographed sensitive areas, and prints of these photographs, with rectangles marking places of special importance, were given to briefing officers. Special orders warned flyers to avoid cultural monuments in Rome and Florence and limited their attacks on other towns and on papal properties. In 1944 the Mediterranean Allied Air Force distributed copies of a photographic atlas of Italian cultural, historical, and religious monuments prepared by the ACLS group.[41] Yet there were distinct limits to air force cooperation. These arose from actual or imagined military necessity, from the practices of American flyers, and from the influence of authorities outside the AAF.

The effects of military necessity can be seen in the atlas of Italian monuments. A preface by the MAAF commander, General

Lauris Norstad, to the February 1944 edition divided Italian towns into three categories. The first group—Florence, Rome, Venice, and Torcello—were never to be bombed without express authority from MAAF headquarters. The second category included places the Army Air Forces considered to have no current military importance, for instance Assisi, Urbino, Ravenna, the old walled city of San Gimignano, and Montepulciano, a spectacular hilltop village of medieval houses and Renaissance palaces. If possible, flyers were to avoid bombing these towns, but if they considered it essential for operational reasons to hit objectives in any of them, they were not to hesitate and MAAF headquarters would accept full responsibility. Centers such as Orvieto, Pisa, Siena, Verona, and Frascati, which currently contained or were located near important military targets, comprised category three. These targets were to be bombed and "any consequential damage" accepted. Airmen were forbidden to hit towns in the second and third groups when clouds totally obscured objectives, but if they were attacking at night and could identify targets with markers, or if overcast was less than complete, they could decide on their own whether to bomb and their judgment would not be questioned. If the German army was using places in categories two or three for ground operations, all restrictions were lifted.*

While instructions accompanying the atlas urged flyers to minimize the chance of damage, MAAF told them that if damage occurred to towns in the second and third groups it would assume all responsibility. It also explained that they were not to do anything that might increase the risk to themselves. Vatican City was off limits. During attacks on Rome flyers were expected to spare other churches and religious institutions belonging to the Holy See, if possible. However, none of the safeguards for papal properties were to interfere with attacks against military objectives.[42]

In addition to these specific instructions, air force officers and other Americans serving in the Italian theater received from General Eisenhower a warning not to damage cultural monuments needlessly:

> [I]f we have to choose between destroying a famous building and sacrificing our own men, then our men's lives count infinitely more and the buildings must go. But the choice is not always so clear-cut as that. In many cases the

---

*Allied airmen did not hit every place in category three. Orvieto, a beautiful city in Tuscany, escaped unscathed. However, Frascati, with its famous sixteenth-century villas, contained the headquarters of General Field Marshal Albert Kesselring; B-17s demolished the town in one hour.

monuments can be spared without any detriment to operational needs. Nothing can stand against the argument of military necessity. . . . But the phrase "military necessity" is sometimes used where it would be more truthful to speak of military convenience or even of personal convenience. I do not want it to cloak slackness or indifference.[43]

Eisenhower referred here to the behavior of certain Allied officers and enlisted men in Sicily and Italy. Assistant Secretary of War McCloy had recently written to him, after a trip through the Italian theater, that "crimes are being committed in the name of military necessity." While McCloy particularly meant vandalism by ground troops, American airmen were also sometimes responsible for serious damage to cultural artifacts. Attacks intended to interfere with harbors, road, and rail transportation destroyed nearby areas. AAF fighter bombers, aiming at bridges in Pisa, devastated the center of the city. In an attempt to blow up the dock and transportation facilities of Livorno, B-24s of the Fifteenth Air Force damaged residential buildings, wrecked the ducal palace, the civic museum, and several churches, and almost completely demolished the cathedral. AAF planes gutted Impruneta, near Florence, after the Germans had evacuated. For no apparent military reason, American flyers bombed the ruins of Pompeii.[44]

The most controversial air operation of the entire Italian campaign took place February 15, 1944, when U.S. bombers together with artillery destroyed the Abbey of Monte Cassino. Its demolition exemplified the third type of limit on efforts by the American air force to help save cultural treasures—the influence of outside authorities.

Monte Cassino Abbey, founded in the sixth century by Saint Benedict, whose remains lay within its walls, had great artistic as well as religious significance. Four stories high, covering more than seven acres on the top of a mountain, the yellow and gray stone building's scores of windows looked across the Liri Valley. There, in an especially bloody series of battles during the winter of 1944, Allied forces were trying to crack the Nazi Gustav line and break through to Rome. The Germans had men and supplies close to the abbey, but U.S. Army commander General Mark Clark and most Allied leaders in the area did not believe German troops occupied the monastery itself. The evidence was conflicting. Generals Eaker and Jacob L. Devers, who flew over the abbey in a small plane, said they had spotted a radio antenna jutting from the building and enemy soldiers moving in and out, which suggested that the Germans were using the abbey to aim their artillery. However, records kept by monks who were in the building at the time support Clark's view. Besides, even if the monastery was being used for artillery observation, destroying it would have made little difference to the Germans, who had better observation posts on nearby mountains and on Monte Cassino itself.[45]

These were rational considerations. To the men down below, trying to protect themselves from exploding German shells, emotional factors were far more potent. They believed Nazi troops were using the building to direct artillery fire, and it disturbed them just to see the huge structure, with all its windows, peering down at them.[46]

The order to destroy Monte Cassino Abbey originated in Allied headquarters. General Bernard C. Freyberg, commander of the New Zealand Expeditionary Force, was preparing to send his troops against German defenses along the mountain. He asked for the bombardment as a military necessity. With some reluctance, his superiors complied.[47]

Once the decision was made, the Army Air Forces turned the operation into a massive show of air power. Freyberg originally requested thirty-six bombers; then he decided he wanted the building flattened, and the AAF sent him more than two hundred. Destroying the abbey did not help the Allies militarily. An American division commander, General Fred L. Walker, wrote in his diary the next day, "This was a valuable historical monument which should have been preserved. The Germans were not using it and I can see no advantage in destroying it. No tactical advantage will result since the Germans can make as much use of the rubble for observation posts and gun positions as of the building itself." Still, the air bombardment cheered the soldiers struggling up the mountainside. An American officer who survived the climb recalled how "the tired infantrymen, fighting for their lives near its slopes," cried for joy as "bomb after bomb crumbled [the abbey] into dust."[48]

The bombing of Monte Cassino Abbey also made a strong impression on people in higher headquarters. General Barney M. Giles, chief of AAF Air Staff, called it, together with a subsequent series of raids that pulverized the nearby town of Cassino, "the finest example of bombing that I have ever seen." As proof Giles cited General Freyberg's report that Cassino was so completely devastated that he found it hard to maneuver his forces in the wreckage. Three months after the battle, General Arnold flew over the ruins of the abbey and the town and called them "two more wrecked targets—monuments to the destructive force of Air Power."[49]

The outcry from the Vatican and other church sources was bitter, and the Nazis made much of it. American officials responded by claiming that the abbey had housed German soldiers (though it actually contained only refugees and a few monks) and released statements by Roman Catholic leaders in the United States approving what had been done. President Roosevelt called the abbey a German "strongpoint," claimed there had been German artillery in the building, and told the press that the bombing, though unfortunate, had been a military necessity.[50]

The weekend before the raid on Monte Cassino Abbey, air force flyers produced another piece of bad publicity by bombing Florence. While the AAF had declared the great art center off limits to attack, American B-26s blasted the Campo di Marte marshaling yard during the Liri Valley battle. The art historian Bernard Berenson, about two miles away, wrote that "the bursting of shells was deafening and made everything tremble. It sounded as if vertically overhead and directed at one's person." Three planes dropped their bombs on the city itself, leading General Eaker, commander of the Mediterranean Allied Air Forces, to warn Fifteenth Air Force chief Nathan Twining against promiscuous attacks. The reasons Eaker offered for not bombing Florence were the "unfortunate political consequences which flow from such instances" and the advantage indiscriminate bombing gave to enemy propaganda.[51]

Eaker recognized how the bombing of places like Monte Cassino Abbey and Florence might affect the image of his service. To help General Arnold "combat" press and public discussion of bombing damage to church landmarks and antiquities, Eaker sent him a copy of the atlas of Italian monuments. "Please be assured," he explained, "that we do everything possible to prevent wanton or careless destruction of these relics and that we shall, at the same time, acquaint press representatives here of our efforts in that direction."[52]

These comments and other remarks and actions of air force leaders during the Italian campaign suggest a complex and somewhat contradictory set of attitudes toward cultural artifacts and monuments. Sensitive to charges of barbarism, always concerned about the reputation of the AAF at home, reluctant to give the German propaganda machine any unnecessary assistance, they tried to avoid indiscriminate destruction of famous buildings, religious shrines, and works of art. Their official reasons for doing this were entirely practical. They were willing to destroy objects of great beauty and religious importance if that was what it took to win battles and save the lives of Allied servicemen. Yet some of them felt personal sympathy for the endangered places and artworks. Although General Arnold insisted that only military considerations ought to govern Eisenhower's decision whether to bomb Rome, Arnold himself took as much pleasure as any American tourist in the art and architecture his bombers spared. During a visit to Pisa, which U.S. warplanes had damaged heavily, he wrote in his journal, "Took photographs of Leaning Tower and visited cathedral—a magnificent building with wonderful paintings."[53] But Arnold was excited and awed by the destructive power of American bombers, by the way they transformed Monte Cassino Abbey from a cultural and religious monument into what he called "a monument to the destructive force of Air Power." He was pleased by the way his air force, in destroying Monte Cassino, had shown what it could do.

These conflicting attitudes resembled crosscurrents among the highest American military and civilian leaders. Roosevelt wanted to avoid burning Rome. McCloy and Stimson wished to preserve old and beautiful places. Eisenhower tried to keep pretended military necessity from permitting needless damage to the treasures of Italy. Army and civilian government officials helped the Roberts Commission and other agencies preserve and repair artistic and cultural works. Yet civilian and military leaders alike believed that when the needs of war clashed with the wish to preserve the physical heritage of Western civilization, preservation must give way.

At times war leaders seemed to show more solicitude for buildings and art works than for human beings. While armies and air forces did grave damage during battle, or by vandalism or accident, no government deliberately set out to destroy the treasures of Italy.[54] That would have marked the people who adopted such a policy as barbarians. Yet combatants frequently viewed civilians as legitimate targets. Civilians contributed to war economies and their morale was thought to sustain the governments that ruled them. Consequently, leaders of the warring powers chose to direct violence against them. This happened during the early part of the Italian campaign. It also occurred in Germany's Balkan satellites, where American planes took part in a campaign of terror bombing.

The Bombing of Axis Balkan Satellites

After the Italian government surrendered, American and British officers, who believed that morale bombing had hastened Italy's capitulation, proposed to use the same technique against Hitler's allies in the Balkans. They considered Bulgaria especially vulnerable. The Bulgarian populace had already shown how sensitive it was to air attacks when two British raids on railroad targets in 1941 panicked the inhabitants of Sofia, causing a mass departure from the capital.[55] Two years later Allied officers proposed to deliver much heavier raids against Bulgarian civilians, who, they believed, had heard about the American air attacks that demolished whole towns in Sicily, Italy, and Sardinia and were terrified at the prospect of similar treatment.

In October 1943 Major D. Dalziel of the Northwest African Air Force planning section proposed a massive surprise attack on Sofia to coincide with a Russian offensive. Late in the afternoon a hundred heavy bombers would appear over the capital, saturating business, government, and residential districts with incendiaries and high explosives. Night bombers would follow at intervals and early the next morning the daylight planes would return, this time carrying leaflets as well as bombs, warning the inhabitants that if Bulgaria did not surrender in twenty-four hours their city would be leveled. Dalziel had recently learned that Balkan specialists at NAAF and in Middle Eastern RAF and U.S. Army headquarters thought the same tactic would work against the Rumanians. He recommended that area raids should also be launched against Bucharest, the Rumanian capital, five days after the Bulgarian operation ended.[56]

The British Chiefs of Staff devised a plan similar to Major Dalziel's, and though the American Joint Chiefs doubted an attack against Sofia would have much military effect, they went along with the British proposal. Joint Chiefs planners thought the political and psychological consequences of bombing the Bulgarian capital might yield important political and psychological results, embarrassing an unstable government, bolstering anti-fascist Greek and Yugoslav guerrillas, "all of whom hate the Bulgars," and perhaps persuading the government of Bulgaria to pull its forces out of Greece and Yugoslavia, which would shift more of the burden of occupying those areas to Germany. At the recommendation of the U.S. Chiefs, the Combined Chiefs of Staff directed General Eisenhower to mount an attack on Sofia when he determined that planes could be spared from Italian operations and from the strategic bombardment of Germany.[57]

The raids began November 14, 1943. Ninety-one B-25 medium bombers blasted the city's marshaling yards and airfields, wrecking a large number of buildings and terrifying the inhabitants. Some 300,000 Sofians lived and worked in a fairly small area, protected by feeble anti-aircraft batteries and a rudimentary civil defense system. Unlike Berliners and Londoners they had not become hardened to continuous air attacks, and when the planes appeared they fled, just as in 1941; those who could not go sent their families to the countryside. Disorderly evacuation made chaos of the city's economy. In outlying areas, mobs of confused refugees crowded into scarce living quarters and drove up prices in village markets.[58]

Despite the impact of this and two smaller raids in the following weeks, Allied planners at NAAF felt the operation had failed. Bulgaria did not surrender. They concluded that the raids had not been powerful enough and called for even larger attacks aimed directly at civilians. The planners argued that if aerial bombardment of Rumanian and Hungarian nerve centers were to cause those countries to capitulate as well, Germany itself might collapse. It was time, they believed, to redirect Allied bombers from strategic military targets to morale-wrecking operations in the Balkans that could bring the war to an early end.[59]

Although the Combined Chiefs of Staff did not share these expectations fully, they permitted the Balkan raids to continue on a growing scale. On January 10, 1944, 143 B-17s struck Sofia in a daylight attack, followed by a night bombardment by 44 RAF Wellingtons. The combined assault smashed electrical and water connections, destroyed residential and other buildings, and killed thousands of people. Fires broke out all over the city. Desperate inhabitants thronged the roads and jammed the railroad terminal, carrying whatever possessions they could, but those who reached the countryside, in bitter cold weather, found that their predecessors had occupied almost all shelter. It took a week before public employees could be persuaded to return to work and restore basic services.[60]

The Bulgarians had hardly recuperated from the January attack when Allied bombers returned. British planes dropped incendiaries on Sofia on March 16. On the 24th they burned the royal palace in Vranya to the ground. Forty American B-17s bombed Vrattsa, a town of some 16,000 inhabitants. On the 29th and 30th hundreds of U.S. heavy bombers and British aircraft set a fire storm in Sofia, destroying the National Theatre, the city arsenal, and the Holy Synod. Inside unburned buildings books exposed to superheated air ignited. The inhabitants again tried to evacuate the city. Food supplies began to run out. This time weeks went by before public facilities reopened.[61]

Then came the vast American raid of April 4, 1944, when three hundred U.S. heavy bombers attacked the Sofia marshaling yards, destroying no less than 1,400 railroad cars and many buildings and leaving the area around the yards burning for two days. The highest concentration of bombs landed not on the rail facilities but on Sofia itself.[62]

In Rumania, hundreds of U.S. heavy bombers pounded urban railroad yards with disastrous results for civilians. "Our attack on the marshalling yards at Bucharest was a bloody affair," Eaker wrote Secretary Lovett. There had been a practice alarm at 10:30 in the morning and when the American warplanes appeared an hour and a half later, people thought it was a continuation of the practice and did not go to their shelters. "We killed about twelve thousand people." Eaker explained. "Six thousand of them were refugees on trains in the yards; six thousand of them were Rumanians living about the yards."[63]

In the campaign against Balkan targets, the Americans pursued a contradictory policy. General Eaker directed his field commanders to take "the greatest care that non-military objectives suffer as little as possible" and warned them that the value of the attacks would be "largely nullified if material is given to the Axis for 'Terror propaganda.'" Yet the target priorities he issued were (1) towns in Bulgaria, (2) Budapest, and (3) Bucharest, and he explained to the commanders that the purpose of the raids was political as well as military.[64] American flyers were expected to terrorize Balkan civilians without appearing to use terror tactics.

General Eaker thought the raids on these cities and the Allied air attacks on Belgrade, Yugoslavia, and the Ploesti oil fields in Rumania paid "big dividends." They restricted the flow of oil from Rumania to the Reich. They helped the Russians by dislocating rail traffic to the German divisions opposing Soviet forces. They encouraged anti-German guerrillas in the Balkans. And among the inhabitants of Balkan countries they instilled a "keen civil desire" to get out of the war.

This bombing program originated, of course, at a higher level. It had the approval of American military and political leaders who, however committed they might have been to precision bombing as a principle, accepted morale bombing raids against East European satellites designed to drive them out of the war. In March 1944, after the Nazis occupied Hungary, General Marshall told the Joint Chiefs of Staff that a relatively minor bombing operation against the right objectives might yield extremely favorable results, and suggested that the Mediterranean theater commander, General Henry Maitland Wilson, be allowed some latitude in selecting Balkan targets. Wilson, a British army officer, wanted to hit cities and towns.[65]

Nevertheless, several persons concerned with U.S. air strategy began to express serious reservations about the American raids in Southeastern Europe. Their doubts were of two kinds. Critics of the Balkan air operations considered them diversions, with limited military value, from the really important tasks of the Army Air Forces, particularly the strategic bombing offensive against German military and economic power. This was the view of operations analysts working in the American embassy in London and of General Spaatz, commander of the U.S. Strategic Air Forces in Europe, including the Fifteenth Air Force, which was frequently dispatched to bomb urban targets in the Balkans. When the British Chiefs of Staff suggested allowing the Mediterranean theater commander to send Fifteenth Air Force planes against political targets in the Balkans, Spaatz wrote General Arnold that he did not want to divert strategic bombers to "the intangible attempt to break enemy morale by area bombing." He could not subscribe, he said, to changing AAF strategy from precision attacks on military and industrial objectives to area attacks against populations. His deputy for operations, General Frederick L. Anderson, also challenged the efficacy of Balkan terror raids, contending that morale attacks would work only if joined to effective bombing of industrial installations.[66]

By March 1944 the Joint Staff Planners of the American Joint Chiefs of Staff had come to share that position. They argued that additional raids on Bulgarian cities with forces the Allies could reasonably afford to send could not possibly force Bulgaria to capitulate. Only Soviet military success, Allied victories in Italy, and successful air actions in Germany could hasten its surrender.[67]

The second objection concerned the political effects of terror raids in Eastern Europe. Informants working with the Office of Strategic Services reported in the spring of 1944 that while these raids encouraged defeatism in Axis satellites and incited hatred against the German and Balkan governments for failing to protect civilians, they produced equally intense hostility toward the Western Allies. Bombing of civilians in Bucharest and especially in Sofia had led citizens to denounce the Americans and British as hypocrites whose acts belied their humanitarian propaganda. People were more angry than intimidated. Pro-American sentiment observed before the air attacks had dissipated. Meanwhile, in Hungary the Germans were channeling public anger at terror raids against the Allies and the Jews.

If the Balkan air raids hurt the Americans and British in the propaganda war, they helped the Russians. In Sofia the Soviet legation quietly exploited the terror raids, while the Communist underground declared that Russians did not attack women and children. Even upper- and middle-class townspeople, who had favored the Americans before the raids, seemed to be turning toward the USSR.[68]

When news of these developments reached the U.S. ambassador to Great Britain, John G. Winant, he described the problem to President Roosevelt. Winant observed that while the Russians had confined their bombing largely to military targets, 85 percent of the planes that struck Sofia, Budapest, and Bucharest were American. The ambassador believed that periodic long-range bomber raids on marshaling yards, which could be repaired quickly, had little military importance, a fact so obvious that other people were bound to conclude that the raids were really political attacks. By continuing them the Americans would make enemies and strengthen the position of the Russians.

Winant then mentioned an especially troubling fact: Americans did not select the targets for these political raids—the British did. Earlier in the year the Combined Chiefs of Staff had given Charles Portal, RAF chief of air staff, the authority to send American planes against Balkan cities.[69]

Roosevelt referred the Balkan problem to his advisors. Secretary of State Hull recommended changing the policy. Arguing that the bombing had already achieved its main psychological effect by showing the people of the Balkan satellites how vulnerable they were to Allied air attack, Hull proposed to limit air attacks more strictly to military objectives so that "civilian losses would then be attributed to accidents of war, rather than to deliberate and indiscriminate destruction." The Joint Chiefs of Staff concurred. They agreed to recommend that bombing in satellite countries be restricted to targets of military importance, with due consideration of the probable number of incidental casualties. The Combined Chiefs of Staff adopted that proposal in late July 1944. Nevertheless, attacks on Balkan urban areas continued. As late as November 27, 1944, while the Soviet army was approaching the gates of Budapest, the Fifteenth Air Force dropped sixty tons of bombs on the center of the city.[70]

It was no secret to anyone in Eastern Europe or in the Anglo-American military and political commands that the raids on Balkan towns were intended to terrorize civilians. Yet at least as far as the records show, Americans concerned with bombing in that area, even those who objected to it, did not discuss its moral aspects. It is true that the British selected the targets. Yet the U.S. Joint Chiefs of Staff accepted their Balkan bombing program despite doubts about its military value. So long as it worked, the State Department regarded it as an acceptable means of bringing the war home to the people of the area. General Eaker, the Mediterranean Air Force commander, considered it useful, partly because of the "keen" desire it fostered among the Balkan peoples to leave the war. Those who opposed it argued on practical military and political, not moral grounds: it diverted resources from more crucial military objectives; it had already achieved its objectives; it helped the Russians at American expense.

Perhaps some of the critics thought the Balkan raids were morally objectionable but considered it wiser, in the midst of a war, to confine themselves to pragmatic arguments. Whatever the case, the United States, despite reservations, took part for many months in a program of bombing aimed at altering people's minds, trying to force governments to surrender by attacking the will of their citizens. Once that objective became acceptable it would be extremely difficult to limit the bombing of civilians, for despite the German and British raids on cities since 1940, no one knew how much violence it took to break the will of an enemy people, or even if breaking the will of civilians could bring about capitulation. The only way to find out was to try. In other theaters the United States ended up trying—attempting over the practical and even the moral objections of certain civilian and military officials to defeat the enemy by making not just his economy and armed forces but the minds and wills of his civil population the objects of air attack.

— 4

The Bombing of Germany:
Early Operations

The landscape of Germany at the end of the war in Europe was strewn with wrecked towns, charred skeletons of cities, and the stone and twisted steel remains of industrial plants. Allied ground armies had created many of these ruins, but most stood, as General Arnold might have said, as monuments to air power, including the power of the U.S. Army Air Forces. They also symbolized a controversy, arising during the war and continuing long afterward, over the morality of what was done. For in the hope of breaking Germany's will to fight, the Army Air Forces had engaged at times in actions—terrorizing enemy civilians, blowing up towns and villages of the slightest military or economic importance, and destroying urban centers—that in the minds of some observers raised significant moral questions.

These actions arose in part from military doctrine and the carefully thought-out designs of strategic and tactical planners, from evolving military circumstances, and from the desires of America's allies, especially Great Britain, to influence the way the United States fought the war. Perceptions by American civil and military officials of what the American people expected and would tolerate affected what was done, and so did the diverse, sometimes conflicting, occasionally self-contradictory attitudes of those officials about what was ethical in war.

No one better exhibited conflicting views of the ethics of air warfare than the chief of the AAF. General Arnold wanted his service to use the selective bombing technique against Germany because he considered it the most efficient method for winning the war. Yet he also described it as a morally superior way of conducting war. In the spring of 1943 he sent his combat commanders a memorandum offering both ethical and practical reasons for precision bombing. As a "spur to . . . conscience," he urged them to make sure that Army Forces planes bombed as accurately as possible, so that American flyers would not have to risk their lives repeatedly to destroy targets that could be eliminated in one blow. And he also warned his generals to avoid needless harm to enemy civilians. Careless, inaccurate bombing, he explained, would spread and intensify feelings of hatred in the "victim populations," poisoning relationships between countries after the fighting ended. He invited his lieutenants to note the "humanitarian but nonetheless practical" aspects of the problem: "War, no matter how it may be glorified, is unspeakably horrible in every form. The bomber simply adds to the extent of the horror, especially if not used with discretion; but when used with the proper degree of understanding, it becomes, in effect, the most humane of all weapons."[1]

Yet other things that Arnold said suggested a far from humanitarian attitude toward enemy civilians. He accepted as a "fundamental principle of American democracy" that personnel casualties were "distasteful" and that the United States would continue to fight "mechanical rather than manpower wars."[2] This statement had an ominous meaning for the people of hostile nations. "Mechanical" war was the kind of conflict Douhet envisioned. It promised to expose civilians to whatever instruments of war American technology could devise and to substitute their lives for the lives of American troops. This was not just theory. The AAF chief demonstrated in several ways that he was entirely willing, under appropriate circumstances, to use violence against German civilians.

One of those circumstances arose when Allied troops landed in North Africa and discovered that the Germans had left them booby-trapped souvenirs. Arnold reacted to the news with one of his "hot ideas." The AAF would retaliate by dropping explosive devices in fountain pens, watches, and pocketbooks onto German territory. The project was to be completely secret, even from the army, though the AAF was part of the army chain of command.

Arnold's staff tried to find someone to procure the devices. They took his proposal to Vannevar Bush, head of the Office of Scientific Research and Development, the U.S. government's center for technological war research, but Bush refused to touch it. He suggested that they speak to the Office of Strategic Services, which designed and procured similar gadgets. OSS also declined to cooperate. Its research director, Stanley Lovell, argued that an order to build Arnold's booby traps could not be kept secret from the other services. The Joint Chiefs of Staff would have to originate it. Beyond that, OSS studies showed that such weapons were "fantastically expensive" if their cost was measured against possible results. The only companies that could build the intricate mechanisms were swamped with similar work, and OSS had learned that when the Germans used booby traps in North Africa, killing several women and children, they had shifted local sympathies from the Axis to the Allies.

Arnold's own intelligence chief opposed the booby trap plan. So did General Benjamin W. Chidlaw, his assistant chief of staff for matériel, not because of "any 'squeamishness' as to the use of such weapons or gadgets," Chidlaw explained, but because the probable results did not justify the costs of engineering, manufacture, training, and operation, or the diversion of materials from other projects.[3] Arnold's "hot idea" came to nothing.

On other occasions Arnold made it clear that he did not intend to exempt German civilians from U.S. air attacks. In April 1943 he told his matériel chief that the Eighth Air Force was going to use incendiary bombs for three purposes: to destroy precise industrial objectives; to create beacons for RAF night attacks on cities by starting fires in day raids on densely built-up areas (including residential districts, such as workers' housing clustered near factories); and for "burning down the densely built-up portions of cities and towns by day attack alone when the occasion warrants." A few days later he instructed an aide to tell members of his Air Staff that "this is a brutal war and . . . the way to stop the killing of civilians is to cause so much damage and destruction and death that the civilians will demand their government cease fighting. This does not mean that we are making civilians or civilian institutions a war objective, but we cannot 'pull our punches' because some of them may get killed."[4]

Among Arnold's lieutenants there were similar crosscurrents of thought. General Eaker felt that all Allied war leaders (presumably including himself) deeply regretted the necessity of endangering "defenseless women and children," as Eaker put it, but he also felt that every one of those leaders realized it was necessary to do so to prevent a greater loss of human life. They were strengthened he believed, by "certain knowledge that this war against evil was to save the lives of the just." The Allies were killing bad people to save good ones, killing outlaws to spare the righteous. "When I watched bombs falling and hitting houses and churches," he recalled, "I had a distaste for the whole business, but they were shooting at us. You don't have any moral question about it at all."[5]

Curtis LeMay shared Eaker's view that one did not ask about the morality of wartime actions. After the war he remembered how the losses of his airmen in battle used to torment him. "But to worry about the *morality* of what we were doing—Nuts. A soldier has to fight. We fought. If we accomplished the job in any given battle without exterminating too many of our own folks, we considered that we'd had a pretty good day." LeMay also suggested that while killing civilians disturbed him at some level of his consciousness, he suppressed his feelings about it:

> You drop a load of bombs and, if you're cursed with any imagination at all, you have at least one quick horrid glimpse of a child lying in bed with a whole ton of masonry tumbling down on top of him; or a three-year-old girl wailing for *Mutter* . . . *Mutter* . . . because she has been burned. Then you have to turn away from the picture if you intend to retain your sanity. And also if you intend to keep on doing the work your Nation expects of you.[6]

General Spaatz experienced a similar division of feelings about the morality of attacking ordinary Germans. It was impossible for him, as a German-American whose own family spoke the language of the people he was bombing, to entirely dehumanize the inhabitants of the *Reich*, however much he despised their government. Nevertheless, his reasons for not wishing to bomb the urban areas in which millions of them lived were practical, not moral ones. Though he announced that his policy was not to make the German people a target, he also stated, as noted earlier, that it was not for moral or religious reasons that he objected to urban area bombing. Some of his contemporaries thought he actually favored raids to terrorize the German populace. General Laurence Kuter observed that Spaatz, perhaps under British influence, was "pretty well persuaded for awhile" that terror would win the war. Kuter remembered feeling "pretty much alone" at the time in his opposition to terror bombing. Solly Zuckerman claimed that while Spaatz "had no faith, as such, in the destruction of cities . . . he was not averse to spreading terror."[7]

Most of these observations by Kuter and Eaker, Zuckerman, LeMay, and Spaatz are from the postwar period, some of them from many years after the event. They may be colored by personal bias, by a desire to appear humane or to protect the reputation of the Air Force, or perhaps by a wish not to appear soft. To understand the attitudes of American air leaders and the effects of their attitudes on the way they fought the war, it is necessary to go beyond recollections—to analyze what the men who wielded American air power actually did in the air war against Germany.

From the first flight of American B-17s over the Nazi homeland in January 1943 until the following autumn, the AAF pursued a precision bombing strategy.[8] While the RAF continued night area attacks, the Americans hit small but significant military and industrial targets. Eventually, though, enemy resistance, problems with weather, and other difficulties, along with the greater success of certain RAF raids, led them to alter their approach.

A classic instance of the early division of labor between the AAF and the RAF was a series of raids on Hamburg in late July and early August 1943. Arthur Harris, the head of RAF Bomber Command, sent his night bombers to destroy the city with incendiary attacks. The result was a fire storm that swept through a large part of the city with hurricane-force winds and temperatures high enough to melt metal utensils and destroy bricks. In the daytime, between RAF raids, the Americans struck at shipyards and factories, but found their targets so obscured by smoke that they were able to do only modest damage. Less than 1 percent of the estimated 44,600 civilians who died in these raids appear to have been victims of American bombs. The B-17s had proven more "humane," to use General Arnold's term, than the RAF night bombers, but they had not been nearly as effective.[9]

Hamburg turned out to be one of the few even moderately successful Eighth Air Force operations that summer, a period of great difficulty and intense frustration for U.S. commanders and their men. Poor weather kept B-17s grounded day after day, undermining morale (as inactivity usually does to combat forces) and dulling skills, for the flyers had to learn from experience how to bomb effectively and survive in the sky. Commanders of American forces in other theaters, desperately short of airpower, noted that B-17s were sitting on the ground in England and pressed AAF headquarters to send them the heavy bombers for their own campaigns.[10] Perhaps most frustrating of all for U.S. air force leaders was that every day they could not bomb was a day the Germans could produce more fighter aircraft and recover from previous bombings, and a delay in the series of attacks that would eventually cripple the Nazi war machine.

When the Eighth Air Force did get off the ground it sometimes endured grievous damage. A hundred planes and a thousand men

were lost in July alone. That same month seventy-five flyers suffered mental breakdowns. While this was a very small proportion of
Eighth Air Force crews, men who survived air battles often suffered in other ways, becoming drained of emotions, empty of all
values and feelings except those connected with combat.[11]

One reason for American losses, even in a period of little
activity, was a flaw in doctrine. While before the war most American bombing experts had assumed that the "flying fortresses" could
defend themselves effectively with the concentrated firepower of
their machine guns, combat experience showed that the bombers
really needed long-range fighter escorts. But only short-range escort planes were available at that point in the war. The Luftwaffe
simply waited until the escorts, approaching the point of no return,
headed back to England. Then they roared in to attack the bomber
formations. On missions deep into Germany the Americans had to
fight their attackers most of the way across Europe and back again.

This is what happened August 17, 1943, up to that point the
most critical day of the war for the American bombing offensive.
That morning a large force of B-17s took off to attack the Messerschmitt aircraft works in Regensburg. A few hours later another
armada left England for Schweinfurt, an even more vital objective,
since factories on its outskirts made ball bearings which were used
in all kinds of machinery and war equipment. American planners
believed that if AAF warplanes destroyed those factories, they
could paralyze the Luftwaffe and possibly the entire German war
economy.

Both forces reached their targets. They inflicted heavy damage. But American losses were disastrous.[12]

Colonel Bierne Lay, who flew on the Regensburg mission, sent
his commander a report of the ferocious German resistance,
though he said it gave him a dry mouth and an unpleasant feeling in
his stomach just to recall what happened. At one point a twelve-
ship squadron of yellow-nosed Messerschmitt 109 fighters swept
around in a wide U-turn and began to attack in pairs and fours.

> A shining silver object sailed past over our right wing. I recognized it as a
> main exit door. Seconds later, a dark object came hurtling through the
> formation, barely missing several props. It was a man, clasping his knees to
> his head, revolving like a diver in a triple somersault. I didn't see his chute
> open.
>   A B-17 turned gradually out of the formation to the right, maintaining
> altitude. In a split second, the B-17 completely disappeared in a brilliant
> explosion from which the only remains were four balls of fire, the fuel
> tanks, which were quickly consumed as they fell earthward.

Our airplane was endangered by various debris. Emergency hatches, exit doors, prematurely opened parachutes, bodies, and assorted fragments of B-17's and Hun fighters breezed past us in the slip-stream.

I watched two fighters explode not far beneath, disappearing in sheets of orange flame, B-17's dropping out in every state of distress, from engines on fire to control surfaces shot away, friendly and enemy parachutes floating down, and, on the green carpet far behind us, numerous funeral pyres of smoke from fallen fighters marking our trail. . . .[13]

Of 146 B-17s that left for Regensburg, 24 never returned. German defenders shot down 36 of 230 bombers in the Schweinfurt operation and damaged 27 others so badly that they could not fly again. The double mission cost the Eighth Air Force over 550 crewmen killed or captured, leaving it crippled for weeks, emotionally and physically. The worst part was the fact that the fortresses had not damaged the ball-bearing factories enough. The B-17s would have to return to Schweinfurt.[14]

The Regensburg-Schweinfurt operation and the Hamburg raids deeply impressed American air commanders. Their combined lesson appeared to be that sometimes urban area raids could be more fruitful and a lot less costly than precision attacks. After Hamburg, AAF generals began to talk about launching heavy air assaults against the German capital. General Eaker, the Eighth Air Force commander, and Frederick L. Anderson, who headed Eaker's VIII Bomber Command, both wanted to attack it. Anderson felt that a big American daylight raid on the Nazi capital would produce a "terrific impact" on the German people, intensifying the panic set loose by the Hamburg fire storm. The people of the United States, he thought, would welcome an attack against Berlin as "an indication of the power of Air" in the European theater.[15]

After Regensburg-Schweinfurt, American officers considered using the British method of aiming at residential districts to make their bombing more effective and less costly to the AAF. Four days before the Eighth Air Force returned to the Schweinfurt ball-bearing works, a group of its combat leaders discussed the problem of blowing up urban objectives. One of them was Curtis LeMay, who had led the Regensburg raid. Participants explained that houses as well as factories made good aiming points since they enabled airmen to "put down enough bombs to destroy the town." This made additional missions to the target unnecessary.[16]

At about this time the Eighth Air Force staged its first daylight area raid following these principles. On October 10 it sent 138 planes to attack Münster. The sky was clear. The aiming point was the center of the city.[17]

Though the bombing of Münster was unique at this stage of the war, as an attack specifically directed at the core of a German town, it was actually the prelude to a long series of de facto area raids in which American bombers used radar to locate targets in bad weather. Airborne radar was extremely imprecise. Crews that managed to locate the city they were supposed to hit (for they sometimes missed it altogether) were fortunate to land their bombs within two thousand feet of the target. Nevertheless, Assistant Secretary of War Robert Lovett encouraged Eaker to conduct this kind of raid, describing it as area bombing.[18]

Eaker needed no encouragement. While he still preferred selective daylight bombing, he thought it was clearly better to bomb inaccurately than to keep his planes grounded during the foul winter weather of 1943–44. Radar attacks had some impact on German production, and Eaker thought the enemy considered American bombing through solid clouds dangerously demoralizing. "We learn from enemy reaction from secret sources," he told AAF headquarters, "and from his squealing and press and propaganda, that he abhors these attacks on his cities. They cause great gloom in Germany."[19]

Some officers in AAF headquarters felt the same way. Henry A. Berliner, an aircraft engineering executive who served as a colonel in AAF intelligence, wanted to launch radar-guided area raids on all kinds of German cities every time weather prevented visual bombing. These attacks would disperse fighter defenses, weaken enemy morale, and by "dehousing" civilians in wintertime, force the Nazi government to divert scarce resources to the care of bombing victims. Without impeding the regular strategic air offensive, which would continue in fair weather, the AAF could stage "at least one Hamburg a month."[20]

General Arnold, who intended to destroy the German air force before the Allies landed in France, liked the idea of using radar bombing to help clear it from the air. Radar raids together with visual attacks would force the Germans to either defend their cities at intolerable cost to the Luftwaffe or permit the cities to be devastated. On November 1, 1943, he directed that whenever day-time precision bombing attacks could not be staged, heavy bombers using radar should attack area targets selected with regard to their effects on the German air force.[21]

As part of this attrition strategy, U.S. heavy bombers, accompanied by new long-range fighters, delivered a series of mostly blind bombing raids on Berlin in March 1944. The strategy worked. After one raid General Frederick Anderson reported, "Already the German radio is squealing like a stuck pig, and the force they have put up against us is a good [indication] of the fear that they hold for our daily . . . bombing of their country." Anderson wanted to blast both the German air force and German cities, for in a discussion about drawing the Luftwaffe into battle he remarked, "Well if it comes up here where we get one of those damn cities that we can see and have our force on . . . there won't be a damn house left. . . ."[22]

The British, meanwhile, were encouraging the AAF to bomb populated areas. Their encouragement sometimes took the form of publicity suggesting that the Americans were unwilling to attack the center of Berlin while the RAF paid nightly visits to the German capital and other cities. At least that was how Generals Doolittle and Frederick Anderson interpreted what they read in the English press. Some American commanders believed that the Royal Air Force wished Europeans, who resented it for its area raids, to detest the AAF as well. General Charles P. Cabell, director of plans for the U.S. Strategic Air Forces, felt that the British, "up to their ears in area-bombing, which is practically indiscriminate attack," hoped to draw the Americans into the same kind of warfare in order to nullify any political advantage the AAF might secure through selective bombing.[23]

If that was the British intention, the American response must have pleased them, at times at least. During April and May the Eighth Air Force delivered five heavy attacks on the center of Berlin, intended, in the view of Eighth Air Force Intelligence, to bring about capitulation before the landing in Normandy or, if that did not occur, at least to produce major disorganization as the Allied onslaught began. At the same time General Spaatz allowed the AAF to attack transportation targets in the Reich without regard for the consequences to civilians, although he himself had pointed out, in arguing against the Zuckerman plan, that those consequences might be severe. On May 15 he sent the Fifteenth Air Force commander, General Norstad, a list of transportation targets located in France. Explaining that these targets had been chosen to minimize civilian casualties, he noted, "This consideration does not apply in Germany."[24]

While the attacks on German cities and transportation facilities appeared to achieve the military results AAF leaders desired, they precipitated a public relations crisis centering on moral issues. In the March 1944 issue of *Fellowship*, an anti-war religious journal, the English pacifist Vera Brittain attacked Allied area bombing. What made Brittain's article especially important in the United States and threatening to AAF public relations was an introduction signed by twenty-eight noted clergymen and anti-war activists who stated that "Christian people should be moved to examine themselves concerning their participation in this carnival of death." The *New York Times* printed a front-page story about the incident, and a flurry of controversy followed in secular and religious media.[25]

This unusual show of dissent alarmed the AAF, the War Department, and the Roosevelt administration. Undersecretary of War Patterson denounced the protesters and charged that they encouraged the enemy. Stephen Early, President Roosevelt's secretary, sent a letter to *Fellowship* stating that the president was disturbed and horrified by the killing that was going on, but that the easiest way to prevent many more civilians from being killed was to use every effort to compel the Germans and Japanese to change their philosophy, since as long as that philosophy lasted there would be more death, more destruction, and more wars. Shortly after D day Secretary Lovett, during a visit with air force leaders in England, warned General Spaatz of feelings in Congress and the country about the inhumanity of indiscriminate bombing, and predicted serious trouble if indiscriminate attacks became announced AAF policy. He urged Spaatz to use utmost caution in carrying out his bombing program.[26]

Lovett did not object personally to bombing civilians, particularly German civilians, whom he wanted to punish so severely that they would never support another war. After viewing reports of an RAF obliteration raid on Essen, he wrote RAF Marshal W. L. Welsh, "I have read 'The Battle of Essen' and have studied the pictures with great interest and, I confess, some of that sadistic barbarism that I was joking about the other night."[27] It was the image of the American air force that concerned him.

That image, so essential to the AAF in its wartime struggle for resources, so crucial to its leaders' vision of a postwar independent air arm, continued to preoccupy AAF officials. Around the world they worked closely with filmmakers, publishers, and journalists, arranging to have the story of air power told so that after the war, as General Arnold explained, the United States would not tear down what "cost us so much blood and sweat to build up."[28] The picture the AAF presented to the men and women who served in its ranks and to the American public was of precision bombing— destroying railroad installations, oil tanks, ammunition dumps, and factories—not indiscriminate burning or blowing up of German homes.

Criticism by pacifists and clergymen compounded another problem. However much they may have disliked Nazi leaders, most Americans simply did not hate the German people. Millions of U.S. citizens, Generals Arnold, Spaatz, Eisenhower, and Kuter among them, had roots in Germany. Many Americans distrusted or even detested the British. A substantial part of the American people felt their country should not even be fighting the Germans, who after all had not attacked United States territory.[29] And as Secretary Lovett believed, a good number of Americans were idealistic and humane and did not wish to kill or injure German women and children.

The problem confronting AAF leaders was how to maintain the air force's favorable image among people at home if American bombs kept falling on German civilians, whether as an incident to precision attacks, through the scattering of bombs in radar-guided raids, or as part of a strategy the American leaders were beginning to consider, that of forcing a rapid end to the war by terrorizing the people of Germany. For as the war continued not only the British but some of the AAF's own staff officers and even members of the American civil and military high command began to urge the bombing of population centers in order to break enemy morale.

Morale Bombing: The Controversy within the Army Air Forces

A few months before the landings in France, a group of American officers in Spaatz's headquarters considered whether AAF bombers should attempt to break German morale through raids aimed directly at civilians. In February 1944 Spaatz appointed a Special Planning Committee to determine which targets to destroy after German air force production facilities had been wiped out. He was still committed to defeating Germany through selective bombing of military and industrial targets. But by this time Allied planes had crippled the Luftwaffe so badly that he thought small groups of bombers, on days when weather made precision bombing difficult, could safely sweep through Germany at lower altitudes, attacking undamaged towns, hitting neglected strategic targets, and demoralizing the inhabitants by showing them that their government was powerless to protect them.[30]

The Special Planning Committee, however, rejected morale as a target system. It concluded that if the kinds of places Spaatz proposed to bomb were struck at all, the AAF should hit only towns with industries, and then only the industries themselves. The committee made no mention of any moral arguments against terror bombing. Their reasoning was entirely pragmatic, based on an analysis of German history, politics, sociology, and psychology. It centered on two questions: How does one break the will to resist of a totalitarian society? Whose will does one break?[31]

The committee believed that German civilians were already demoralized—and considered that fact irrelevant. For as long as Nazi controls persisted, the German people could not stop the war if they wanted to, and controls were as strong as ever. Air attacks actually increased Nazi party influence by forcing the people to depend on their leaders to restore normal conditions.

If it was impossible to win by breaking the morale of the German people as a whole, were there particular elements that might be induced to bring resistance to an end? It seemed doubtful to the committee that the Allies could cause Germany to surrender by cracking the will of Nazi leaders, for the chief Nazis had a simple, persuasive reason to stave off defeat at all costs: personal survival. Outside the party there remained no centers of civilian power, because Hitler had destroyed or co-opted almost all potential opponents. Industry never played an openly political role but exerted its influence through other social groups, and for several years Nazi officials had assumed key management positions. Banking and finance had no national leaders. The church, subordinated to the Nazi government, could not express independent views if it had them. The civil service and judiciary were pervaded by Nazism. The middle class had long ago lost any influence in national politics. The working class, though profoundly tired of the war, had never held real power, even in the days of the Weimar Republic, and now was impotent against Nazi domination.

That left the army, the one group strong enough to seize power. For months, party members had been tightening Nazi control of the high command and entering the ranks of junior officers, yet the German army had an interest in preserving its honor, and it would want to dissociate itself from Nazi leadership when the war ended. However, only when it judged that defeat in the field was inevitable was the army likely to oppose the party. Civilian war weariness made no difference whatever to the military high command, except that if civilians refused to work or if soldiers refused to fight, it might be necessary to start shooting them. For the German army what really counted were the means of war, weapons and factories that turned out war matériel. Therefore, the committee concluded, the AAF should continue to destroy military and industrial targets instead of trying to break civilian morale.

Analysts working in the U.S. Embassy in London felt much the same way as Spaatz's planning committee did, and so did the Office of Strategic Services, which concluded from its own analysis that terror raids were unlikely to produce desirable political action as long as the Nazi control apparatus remained, and that until the apparatus crumbled, terror raids would strengthen Hitler's regime. Nevertheless, AAF headquarters in Washington continued to gather data that could be used to plan morale attacks. It prepared lists of German towns and cities arranged by population size and, for each one, calculated a "yardstick" or ratio between the population figure and a number representing the installations that sustained community life, such as power and communication facilities. Using this data, air force analysts estimated the bomb density needed to damage each metropolitan area substantially.[32]

After the Allies landed on French soil, pressure to attack German civilians became even stronger. Much of it continued to come from the British, whose citizens had again become targets for German air raids, this time by unmanned V-1 "buzz bombs." The British government, shaken by this new form of terror warfare, weighed proposals to retaliate by pouring poison gas on the Germans, smashing Berlin in one enormous raid, and terrorizing German townspeople by first warning them that air attacks were coming, then devastating their communities.[33] While American officers in United States Strategic Air Force (USSTAF) headquarters may not have felt the same desire for revenge, some thought the AAF should follow up the Allied landing in France with a psychological warfare campaign, built around air attacks, to break civilian morale and (they hoped) precipitate German surrender. The chief exponent of this view was a citizen soldier, Colonel Lowell P. Weicker, deputy to the U.S. Strategic Air Force director of intelligence and, in peacetime, president of the E. R. Squibb Pharmaceutical Company.

On June 9, 1944, three days after the landing in France and the same day that Generals Marshall and Arnold and Assistant Secretary Lovett conferred with him at USSTAF headquarters, General Spaatz ordered plans drawn up for a program of psychological warfare. This program had three general objectives: to dislocate transportation, to strike enemy morale at a decisive moment, and to gather information that could be used to formulate a doctrine for subsequent morale raids.* The Eighth Air Force would be sent to hit as many undefended German towns as possible in a single day. In order that various types and combinations of incendiary and high explosive bombs could be tested on undamaged areas, the towns were to be "virgin." Planners were to provide for "maximum use of strafing fighters . . . to spread the impact on the population."[34]

The crucial terms here are "undefended" and "virgin." The first implied that towns were to be chosen whose military or industrial facilities, if any, were not considered worth defending. The second suggested that these would be towns the AAF thought too insignificant to have included in its program of hitting military and industrial objectives. The point about dislocating transportation is also significant. The AAF had genuine military reasons for disrupting German transportation. But beyond that, as Spaatz had noted in his arguments against the Zuckerman plan, there was a link between transportation attacks and morale raids, since bombs aimed at rail facilities in small towns would probably kill or injure and would certainly terrorize civilians in the area. The general was asking for dual-purpose raids, similar to the Ploesti marshaling yard bombings that had been arranged to destroy nearby oil fields. It was a way of resolving the dilemma of how to win by breaking civilian morale while preserving the image of the air force.

During the next weeks a series of plans emerged from Colonel Weicker's office. One of these, Operation SHATTER, proposed to send the Eighth and Fifteenth Air Forces against a hundred or more small to medium cities all over Germany. The towns would be chosen on the basis of size, freedom from previous air attack, location of Nazi party, police, or government headquarters, significant industrial targets, and the absence of "conspicuous cultural monuments or educational centers." Together with leaflets and radio broadcasts, the raids were supposed to break the morale of

*It was probably no coincidence that Spaatz requested the plan June 9. Each of his visitors that day had endorsed morale attacks at one time or another.

German civilians by showing them how defenseless they were against Allied air power. To avoid "the stigma of being merely retaliatory terror bombing," the planes would have to attack such targets in each town as government buildings, minor industries, or transportation.[35]

Some of the psychological warfare plans included "black" and "white" propaganda to intensity hopelessness and discredit the German government. "White" propaganda would take the form of threats to bomb particular targets on specified dates, together with warnings to evacuate women, children, and the old and sick to temporary "safe" areas. "Black" propaganda broadcasts, purporting to come from German authorities, would ridicule the threats with statements that real German authorities could hardly disavow, and warmly reassure civilians that they were safe. Then the Americans would blast the towns.[36]

These proposals led to intense discussion in USSTAF headquarters and to considerable opposition, led by the chief target selection officer, Colonel Richard D. Hughes.[37]

In 1944 few Americans knew anything about Colonel Hughes, who today remains an obscure figure, yet he was one of the most respected staff officers in the AAF. The son of an English surgeon whom the colonel remembered as having "a feeling of enormous responsibility toward his fellow humans," Hughes graduated Sandhurst, fought as a British infantry officer in World War I, and for several years commanded the Fifth Gurkha Rifles on India's northwest frontier. Traveling by ship to the United States during a leave in 1926, he met a young American woman and married her soon afterwards. In 1929 he retired from the British army and became a resident of the United States, where he managed a dairy farm near St. Louis. Then, six months before the Japanese attacked Pearl Harbor, he resumed his military career, this time as an officer in the U.S. Army Air Corps. Malcolm Moss, a friend in the Air Corps reserve, and Haywood Hansell persuaded him to join Air Corps Headquarters Intelligence in Washington. By now Hughes had a special reason to fight the Germans. The year before they had killed his brother, commander of the British aircraft carrier *Glorious*, sunk in the Battle of Norway.

Hughes occupied several important positions in the American air force, some of them simultaneously. As a member of the Air War Plans Division, he helped choose the target systems that formed the basis for the AWPD-1 estimates. After Pearl Harbor he continued to work on air war plans, including the plans for the

Combined Bomber Offensive. When the Eighth Air Force moved to England, Hughes returned to his homeland to select the systems of objectives that appeared most vital to the Nazi war effort. The RAF and the British Ministry of Economic Warfare furnished him masses of data, but he felt he needed his own experts to evaluate it and arranged, through the American ambassador, to install a staff of talented American analysts in London. This was the beginning of the Enemy Objectives Unit, which, with Hughes as its guiding force, served the AAF throughout the war in Europe.

Developing close ties with General Spaatz and other American air commanders, this former British officer represented the U.S. Army Air Forces on key inter-Allied committees. The economist W. W. Rostow, who worked with EOU, described him his way:

> Hughes was a memorable figure in London: generally dealing with British and American commanders of much higher rank, his Air Force uniform bedecked with British Army decorations of considerable distinction; his pockets bulging with highly classified papers; articulating his views with a gift for terse prose, selective profanity, and a stutter which often enhanced the effectiveness of his exposition.[38]

Colonel Hughes, who did so much to determine where bombs would fall, took the ethical consequences of bombing very seriously. He felt, as Assistant Secretary Lovett and others did, that ordinary German families must be made to suffer, for like many of his American colleagues he wanted to "bring home" the consequences of war to a people who had allowed their leaders to start two world conflicts. But he did not feel that suffering had to mean widespread killing and the obliteration of communities. In 1943 Hughes told an AAF historian that when the RAF bombed its opponents in his days as an Indian army officer, British authorities invariably warned the tribes, twenty-four hours before attacking, which villages would be bombed and when they would be hit, so that tribesmen could evacuate their families. In his memoir he remarked that in 1920 "there still remained some vestiges of decency in the conduct of bombing operations." When he selected targets for the AAF, he tried to minimize the danger to civilians. Like his physician father, he felt responsible for his fellow human beings.

Regarding himself as part of European civilization, Colonel Hughes identified with the victims of its latest catastrophe, even with the people of Germany, and wished to preserve what he could of European culture. Since the United States would have to rebuild German society after the war and live with the Germans, he felt

America could not afford to wreak limitless destruction. Years later he told his sons that the terror raids of World War II (in which he included Hamburg as well as Coventry, Berlin as well as London, and Dresden, Tokyo, and Hiroshima) had been both impractical and morally idiotic.

Hughes had served on General Spaatz's Special Planning Committee, which had rejected German morale as a target system purely on practical grounds. In a July 5, 1944, memorandum he began his attack on the Weicker group's proposals with a series of equally pragmatic arguments.[39] He insisted that it was pointless to use terror raids to show the Germans how vulnerable they were to American air attacks, since the Germans already knew it. Proposals to warn them, then hit them at designated places, could backfire. Weather, military crises elsewhere in Europe, or failure to bomb the towns solidly through cloud cover might prevent the AAF from fulfilling its promises; then to save face it might have to divert planes from really significant targets, perhaps at a critical point in the war, to hit militarily unimportant cities and towns.

Hughes charged that the Weicker group, despite its claim that it planned something more than just another morale attack, was really pursuing the same "will of the wisp of 'morale'" that the Allies had chased for so long in Germany and the Balkans. Yet while Nazi Party controls remained unbroken it was futile to hope that the terrorized inhabitants could take some action to end the war, and it would remain futile until the Nazi state started to disintegrate from other causes. Why, then, give German propagandists the opportunity to complain about American terror bombing? Why, in pursuit of a small, uncertain, temporary advantage, should the AAF depart from the proven doctrine of selective bombing for which it had trained its men, a doctrine which could actually win the war and which, in the postwar years, would form a solid foundation for American security?

Colonel Hughes then turned to what he called "the moral aspect." He admitted that the United States had been hypocritical at times or Pollyanna-ish about moral issues. Nevertheless, he declared, it "rightly . . . represented in world thought an urge toward decency and better treatment of man by man." While the Japanese might order American prisoners to be shot, the United States did not shoot captured Japanese. "Hot blood is one thing," he remarked. "Reason and the long view is another."

Ignoring the moral issue would lead to practical problems. Hughes reminded his colleagues of what Secretary Lovett had recently said about the reaction at home to "the inhumanity of indiscriminate area bombing," and recalled Lovett's warning of "real trouble" if that kind of bombing became the announced policy of the air force. However "silly" it might appear to "some of us realists" in USSTAF headquarters, Hughes warned, Congress and the country were genuinely concerned about those matters. If the AAF departed from its selective bombing policy, it might cause a rift of unpredictable dimensions between itself and its supporters.

Colonel Weicker issued a vigorous rebuttal.[40] Hughes's comments, he declared, though honestly written and entirely sincere, illustrated a closed mind and a prejudiced point of view that was neither constructive nor helpful when one considered "a subject of such delicacy." Weicker offered examples of psychological warfare that had worked, including the reaction that V-weapons produced in London. Contrary to Hughes's opinion, the black and white propaganda plan contained "fresh elements of power and originality." Attacks on towns throughout Germany would neither use military resources unwisely nor deviate from accepted AAF doctrine, which was broader and less rigid than Hughes appeared to believe.

To Hughes's remarks about the moral issue Weicker responded heatedly. Those statements, he declared, were "characteristic of Colonel Hughes" and a "most laudable expression of the character and ideals" that prompted the colonel's logic. (He added that he said this without "one speck of sarcasm.") He himself considered it "repugnant" to harass civilians and cause them misery, and in that respect the whole war was "deplorable." But "you cannot always use the Marquis of Queensberry's rules against a nation brought up on doctrines of unprecedented cruelty, brutality, and disregard of basic human decencies."

The psychological bombing plan, Weicker insisted, was neither reprisal nor "a new way" to kill women and children. It was a method of pressing home "fundamentals" to the German people, a method that would end the war. If it shortened the war by just one day, and in so doing saved a few British and American lives, the price paid by the enemy should not and could not be a factor for sober, practical consideration. "These Air Forces are not over here just to play cricket. Our Number One responsibility is to get on with winning the war, to shorten it as much as we can, and by so doing, save Allied lives."

As the debate continued, other people who worked for US-STAF took Colonel Hughes's side. Irwin Nate Pincus, an Enemy

Objectives Unit analyst, ridiculed the "8th AF philosopher psycho-analysts of air power" who had "taken down their crystal balls, donned their ceremonial robes, fired a few badly fused incendiaries, and breathed the magic word, 'Morale.'" Pincus found Hughes's remarks "very sweet" and Weicker's rejoinder "ill-tempered." The Enemy Objectives Unit itself attacked the Weicker plan, contending that morale attacks would help the Nazis convince their civilians that the Allies would deal with them harshly if Germany surrendered. Colonel Charles M. Taylor, USSTAF deputy director of plans, called the psychological warfare proposal just one more scheme for drawing the AAF into area and civilian bombing, the greatest diversion from the Combined Bomber Offensive thus far submitted. Taylor thought the Nazis could thwart it easily by announcing, in a broadcast purportedly from the Americans, that the AAF was *not* going to bomb a particular city, so the inhabitants could go about their business. This would either prevent the Americans from bombing it or, if they attacked it anyway, would discredit them with the city's inhabitants. On a memo drafted to inform Eisenhower's headquarters that USSTAF approved the Weicker plan Taylor wrote, "Never sent Thank God!"[41]

Taylor's chief, General Cabell, the USSTAF director of plans, carefully appraised a psychological bombing proposal and concluded that it should not be carried out. Cabell agreed that the time for cracking German morale had arrived. He saw certain advantages in the plan: it would deliver a stinging attack against all of Germany in a very short time and the attacks it delivered, while "a horrible experience for previously undamaged towns," would not devastate them so badly that they would have to be entirely rebuilt. Yet these possibilities, Cabell reasoned, could not compensate for the predictable diversion of AAF resources from really important targets, for the chance that terror raids would strengthen rather than break German resistance, for the certainty that they would be used for propaganda, and for the harm they would do—through their effects on opinion in America and other nations—to the interests of the Army Air Forces and the government of the United States.[42]

Since General Spaatz had asked for a plan like Weicker's in the first place, it is not surprising that his deputy for operations, General Anderson, requested that it be incorporated in further USSTAF planning. But a few days later Spaatz decided not to proceed with it. Colonel Hughes told Cabell that "Tooey, thank God, has come out against Lowell's morale ideas strongly, and spent 15 minutes the other evening telling *me* what Lovett's remarks had been! I laid low and hugged myself."[43]

Spaatz's immediate superior, General Eisenhower, ratified the decision not to go ahead with terror raids. Eisenhower disliked using terror weapons, especially at an inappropriate time. When the British contemplated gas attacks and other reprisals for the German rocket-bombing of London, he told Chief of Staff Marshall that "for the time being, at least, I will *not* be a party to so-called retaliation or use of gas. Let's for God's sake keep our eyes on the ball and use some sense." On July 21, in a conversation with General Spaatz, Eisenhower stated that the AAF would continue precision bombing and not be deflected to morale attacks. Spaatz informed his operations planners that the strategic air forces would continue to direct their efforts toward precision targets and not toward area bombing, though if weather obscured precision objectives, the AAF (using blind bombing techniques) would attack targets such as marshaling yards by bombing through overcast.[44] Given the inaccuracy of those techniques, this was a sizable loophole. Still, it was not the same as ordering flyers to terrorize the inhabitants of those cities.

Nevertheless, it soon appeared that Colonel Hughes had hugged himself prematurely. At the end of the summer of 1944 the policy of the AAF toward bombing cities and civilians began a drastic shift whose instigators included Generals Spaatz and Eisenhower, Secretary Lovett, and others all the way to the top of the chain of command.

— 5

The Bombing of Germany: Transition to Douhetian Warfare

With the successful Allied landing in Western Europe and the advance of Soviet armies in the East, it was clear that Germany had lost the war. But this was quite different from bringing the German government to the point of surrender. Those who controlled the American and British air forces continued to search for ways of using air power to make Germany capitulate. Their proposals continued to include attacks on civilians—to disrupt their morale and break their ties with their Nazi leaders, to teach them lessons about the fate of those who begin wars, to turn them into massive panic-stricken obstacles to the orderly retreat of the Wehrmacht. Before the war American planners had imagined that bombing civilians at the right moment might precipitate Germany's collapse. One of the obstacles to direct attacks on the German populace—a shortage of planes—had ceased to be a problem. Nevertheless, among AAF officers and their advisors controversy persisted about proposals to destroy Germany's will to fight by attacking and terrorizing the German people.

In July 1944, responding to a decision by the British Chiefs of Staff, the Air Ministry produced an analysis of proposals for ending the war through aerial terror raids. It examined suggestions for bombing small towns; for raids on several large cities; for widespread strafing of civilian objectives, such as road and railroad traffic; and for a single devastating attack on Berlin. A copy of this paper went to Washington, where General Laurence Kuter, the assistant chief of air staff for plans, analyzed the proposals and found all of them deficient.[1]

Kuter was sure that none of these proposals would impede German production as seriously as their authors believed, yet they would force the AAF to digress from a fruitful campaign against military and economic objectives, and to share in the hatred that RAF night area bombing produced. Attacks on the German populace could not affect Nazi policy, since the German people had far less influence on their government than did the citizens of a democratic country. Instead of causing a national revolt, the British proposals might actually harden enemy resistance.

These were familiar objections, voiced earlier by Cabell and Hughes and by other opponents of a terror strategy. But Kuter added new ones. The British proposals were bound to kill large numbers of German civilians, and Kuter argued that "we do not want to kill them—we want to make them think and drive them to action." A successful air campaign against civilians could lead to surrender while the German armed forces were still capable of fighting; it would be a serious mistake, however, to end the war by disintegrating the enemy's society before defeating its military forces, if one wanted to prevent future German aggression.* Finally, Kuter contended that it was "contrary to our national ideals to wage war against civilians."[2]

General Arnold did not see the issues the same way. He had what Kuter called "an open mind" on the Air Ministry's proposals and directed that the problem be studied further, with the aim of launching an all-out Anglo-American attack on German civilian morale if that approach seemed promising. His headquarters came up with a number of suggestions, including a plan to announce that particular Nazi shrines, cities, towns, and other objectives would be destroyed, then destroying them one by one until the Nazis surrendered, and a proposal for strafing and bombing the more heavily populated areas of Germany for several days. This would expose a very large number of Germans to the sight of Allied aircraft flying at will over their country and, presumably, deepen feelings of hopelessness.[3]

Kuter disliked these proposals as much as the ones from London. All of them required the AAF to do "the majority of the dirty work." He told General Spaatz's deputy for operations, Frederick L. Anderson, that he wanted the record to show "that our Air Forces

*Kuter was referring here to the way German militarists claimed after World War I that civilian politicians had stabbed an undefeated German army in the back by surrendering needlessly to the Allies. The "stab in the back" legend was used to discredit the Weimar Republic and the peace settlement and contributed to the rise of Hitler.

have been and will continue to be employed exclusively against critical military objectives until the time when it is broadly accepted that morale attacks including the killing of German civilians will tip the scales causing the cessation of hostilities."[4]

Still, as Arnold's chief planner Kuter had to come up with ideas for breaking civilian morale. He determined that if the time ever came to launch that kind of attack, with all the attendant penalties, it should be concentrated, progressive, and joined to a well-defined psychological warfare program that would drive home to the Germans the enormous power of Allied warplanes and their own inability to resist. He suggested that the United States and Great Britain might choose a dozen smaller German cities—"ancient, compact, historic, widespread, and of as much industrial importance as possible"—warn the inhabitants that they were about to destroy one of these towns and urge them to evacuate all of them, then attack a single city with every available American and British bomber. Leaflets with photographs of the damage and new warnings to leave would be dropped on the surviving towns and the process of bombing, warning, then bombing would continue.

"You have available to you some of the finest minds in psychological warfare," he told General Anderson, experts with intimate understanding of Germany, people closer to RAF thinking about morale attacks than his own staff in AAF headquarters. Kuter suggested that they study the problem with a view to early combined planning.[5]

It is not entirely clear how General Kuter regarded the moral issue of terror raids. He said later that he felt isolated from his colleagues in opposing them. But was this because, like Colonel Hughes, he thought them morally wrong? Or did he simply consider them imprudent? When he said that waging war against civilians was against American ideals, was he arguing that the air force should avoid that tactic because the American people might object, or because he shared their objections? It was "imperative," he told Anderson, both to warn German civilians and to show them that the AAF could attack where it wished. Was this primarily because he wanted to spare them from death or injury, or because he thought it more practical to keep them alive in order to control their behavior? Whatever his feelings, the contingency plan General Kuter suggested implied reluctance to shed civilian blood. In a distant echo of the 1926 Air Service manual, it was a proposal for terror without killing.

Some British air leaders felt no such reluctance. At the beginning of August 1944 they urged the Americans to join them in what promised to be an extremely bloody operation, called THUN-DERCLAP, a massive assault against the center of Berlin. RAF Air Staff presented this plan as a way of changing the mental state of the German high command, a method of getting German leaders to surrender before their country disintegrated, confronting the Allies with chaos and the prospect of guerrilla war. But as a Bomber Command paper described the operation, it would affect the minds of Nazi leaders at great expense to ordinary citizens. The idea was to provoke unprecedented terror by saturating the core of the Nazi capital with so many bombs that no one could imagine escaping death. This would not only destroy the country's administrative center, but would make an indelible impression on millions of people nearby who would witness the attack, which was to be made in daylight.

To achieve the concentration of bombs that would produce this terrifying spectacle, American bombers, with their precision bomb-sights, would have to do most of the job. In two hours they would drop 5,000 tons of bombs in a two-and-one-half-square-mile area. Then the RAF would follow with a night raid. Bomber Command believed the operation would kill or seriously injure about 275,000 persons.[6]

General Cabell found this proposal repellent. "I have just read the great opus: 'Operation Thunderclap' prepared in the Air Minis-try . . . ," he wrote Colonel Hughes. "To my mind, which frankly has been greatly influenced by your own thinking, this would be a blot on the history of the Air Forces and of the U.S. We should strongly resist being sucked in to any such venture. It gives full reign to the baser elements of our people, and [to the baser ele-ments] of the characters of our good people." The sacrifices that individual German troops made in France had persuaded Cabell that "no man alive . . . can calculate or recognize a crumbling morale." If there must be morale attacks, they should be raids on objectives that symbolize industrial, economic, or military strength in every section of Germany, not "baby killing schemes."

Cabell knew that proponents of terror raids justified them as a way to end the war quickly and save Allied lives, but he considered this argument a pretense. The real purpose of attacking civilians, he told Hughes, was "retaliation and intimidation for the future." He could not believe the cause of civilization or world peace would be advanced "by killing more women and children."

General Spaatz also disliked THUNDERCLAP, though the reasons he gave for opposing it were entirely pragmatic. He complained to Hap Arnold that the British wanted the U.S. air force "tarred with the morale bombing aftermath which we feel will be terrific." The Air Ministry had been pressuring him to take part in morale raids, he told Arnold. He had resisted, thus far with the support of General Eisenhower.[7]

But Eisenhower's position was changing. Spaatz wrote the Supreme Commander August 24 that he did not want to abandon the policy of striking specific military targets, and would participate in THUNDERCLAP by hitting selected military objectives in Berlin. To this Eisenhower responded, "While I have always insisted that U.S. Strategic Air Forces be directed against precision targets, I am always prepared to take part in anything that gives real promise to ending the war quickly." Eisenhower told Spaatz to continue his present bombing policies unless a situation arose in which, in the Supreme Commander's opinion, a sudden, devastating blow might have an "incalculable" effect. On September 9 he instructed the USSTAF commander to be ready to bomb Berlin at a moment's notice, whereupon Spaatz informed James Doolittle, commanding general of the Eighth Air Force, that "we would no longer plan to hit definite military objectives, but be ready to drop bombs indiscriminately on the town" when Eisenhower gave the order.[8]

As discussions of THUNDERCLAP proceeded at several levels, American officers remained wary of the adverse publicity it might generate in Germany, around the world, and at home. At a September 14 meeting of the Joint Chiefs of Staff, General Arnold mentioned that the British wanted the Combined Chiefs of Staff to endorse morale bombing in Germany. Admiral Leahy, President Roosevelt's military advisor, told the Chiefs it would be a mistake to record such a decision.* The Psychological Warfare Division of SHAEF (Supreme Headquarters Allied Expeditionary Force) considered ways of exploiting the attack by warning residents of Berlin in advance and designating safe areas into which they might flee. To prevent THUNDERCLAP from appearing to be "a simple terror attack," the head of the division proposed to describe it as a gigantic raid on Nazi administrative machinery.† He need not have worried, for problems in assembling enough escort fighters postponed the operation until the winter of 1945.[9]

---

*The AAF official history states that Leahy and Arnold expressed opposition to morale bombing in general. The documents it cites do not support that statement.

†The chief of SHAEF Psychological Warfare Division did not, as the official AAF history states, denounce the THUNDERCLAP raid as "terroristic."

The War-Weary Bomber Project

During the THUNDERCLAP controversy the AAF was developing another program that appeared to conflict with the official policy against indiscriminate air attacks; it provides an insight into the way American civil and military leaders thought about using terror weapons. This was the War-Weary Bomber Project, a plan to take hundreds of worn-out B-17s, fill them with 20,000 pounds of high explosives, and aim them at enemy targets. After setting the bombers on a dead-reckoning course, their crews would bail out and automatic devices would direct the robot planes to their objectives. While the project began as a way of destroying German V-bomb launching sites, air force leaders wanted to direct the robots against fortified German cities and other suitable targets. Hoping eventually to develop the unmanned bombers into precision weapons, they viewed them as forerunners of guided missiles that could destroy industrial centers in Japan. Meanwhile, they intended to use the robot planes for area attacks that would disrupt the German economy, force the enemy to divert large numbers of people to defend against them, and undermine the will to resist.[10]

AAF leaders recognized that War-Weary planes would fall on the Germans indiscriminately. "I can see very little difference," Hap Arnold wrote General Spaatz in November, 1944, "between the British night area bombing and our taking a war weary airplane, launching it, at say, 50 or 60 miles away from Cologne and letting it fall somewhere in the city limits. . . ." Arnold then suggested that the robot planes be turned loose all over Germany so that the Germans, not knowing where they would explode, would fear them as intensely as the English feared German "buzz bombs" and rockets. The "psychological effect on German morale," he said, "would be much greater this way." Spaatz replied that while he doubted the robot bomber attacks would yield important results, he saw no reason not to launch them against undefended towns of "reasonable" size that had military or industrial targets "associated" with them.[11]

The reference to "associated" targets provided an acceptable reason for sending unmanned aircraft on what Arnold regarded as terror raids. It was the kind of proviso Weicker's group had recommended earlier to protect Operation SHATTER from the stigma of being mere retaliatory terror bombing. It represented another instance of the AAF's tactic of striking one type of target in order to hit a second kind. And it was consistent with General Arnold's own approach, for as he told General Spaatz, he would never condone attacks on "purely" civilian objectives.[12]

The robot bombers Arnold wished to unleash over Germany were hard to direct and very inaccurate. Air force scientists worked for months to develop a precision guidance system, but the best they could come up with was a form of radar control which, in test flights, landed the planes within a mile and a half of the target. When the gross inaccuracy of War-Weary aircraft led Assistant Secretary of War John J. McCloy to wonder if they did not violate official War Department policy against indiscriminate bombing, Arnold's staff responded with an argument that rendered the policy virtually meaningless. Robot planes, they said, were more accurate than radar bombing, which the AAF had employed on a large scale with little accuracy since the fall of 1943. And since the War-Weary aircraft were bound to affect German production when launched against large industrial areas, they could not be indiscriminate. Reassured, the War Department approved their use in Germany.[13]

Although General Arnold kept pushing the War-Weary program, only a handful of the robots ever flew. The reason was that the British cabinet feared Germany might retaliate against London with its own robot planes. Arnold and other American military chiefs tried to persuade the British to change their minds, and arranged to have President Roosevelt intercede with the prime minister. Finally, with great reluctance, Churchill acquiesced, but by then Roosevelt was dead, and in any case few suitable targets remained in Germany. The AAF decided to pursue its missile development program at testing grounds in the United States.[14]

The Development of Operation CLARION

While General Arnold never realized his vision of unmanned bombers exploding all over Germany, the air force staged another program at least as threatening to the inhabitants of that country: Operation CLARION. In September 1944, after discussing the proposals from USSTAF and his own headquarters for terrorizing Germany into surrender, General Arnold announced that he wanted a concrete plan for action. He told General Kuter and Colonel Charles G. Williamson of USSTAF to prepare arrangements for sending all British and American air forces in Europe and the Mediterranean on six or seven days of attacks throughout the

Reich. These were not to be obliteration attacks aimed at killing the German people. Their purpose would be chiefly psychological. Arnold wanted roving flights of fighters and bombers to cover all of Germany, striking at military objectives and giving every citizen a chance to witness the strength of Allied air power.[15]

General Spaatz's headquarters responded by resurrecting Operation SHATTER, now described as a plan for attacking transportation, with its targets the system of marshaling yards scattered all across Germany. Transportation links were, of course, highly important to the German war effort. However, it was impossible to strike them in urban areas of any size without endangering large numbers of civilians (as Spaatz had pointed out in his protest against the Zuckerman plan), and many of the places SHATTER listed for attack contained no transportation objectives of any importance.[16]

The USSTAF target section offered familiar objections: Operation SHATTER compromised the strategic bombing program against crucial objectives such as oil. To attack cities with minor transportation targets would expose American commanders to the charge that they were bombing for terror. An Enemy Objectives Unit analyst, Harold Barnett, described the plan as "pure morale bombing" which would kill "many thousands of women and kids." General Frederick Anderson, however, strongly favored SHATTER and was disappointed when bad weather kept USSTAF from launching it.[17]

The British, meanwhile, came up with another set of terror-bombing proposals, HURRICANE I and II . The first envisioned massive RAF raids to destroy what remained of the cities of the Ruhr while the Eighth Air Force hit plants producing Benzol and synthetic oil, the Fifteenth Air Force hammered German objectives in range of its bases in Italy, and the tactical air forces struck enemy transportation as close to the Ruhr as possible. The objects were to demoralize enemy troops and civilians in the Ruhr as Allied ground forces approached, to ruin German transportation in the area, and, with follow-up radar bombing attacks, to precipitate a major evacuation. Then, in HURRICANE II, Allied air forces would strike high-priority strategic targets and launch fighter attacks throughout Germany against airfields and transportation targets.[18]

The debate over HURRICANE was settled by the weather, which prevented the plan from being implemented, but not before it was revealed once again that there was a split in AAF thinking about morale attacks. General Spaatz disliked HURRICANE I because it concentrated too heavily on the Ruhr; Spaatz wanted fighters to roam all over Germany shooting up transportation. Colonel Hughes, seconded by colleagues in USSTAF, preferred to continue hitting oil-related targets and doubted that sporadic raids on transportation or attacks against civilians would contribute substantially to the rapid ending of the war.[19]

Hughes raised questions about the long-range effects of operations like HURRICANE and SHATTER. "Do we want a Germany whose ports are virtually destroyed," he asked General Anderson. Do we want a nation lacking all industry? "Do we want a Germany virtually de-housed, lacking all public utility services, whose population is little better than a drifting horde of nomads ripe for any political philosophy of despair and almost impossible to administer and re-educate?" Colonel Hughes wanted to impress ordinary Germans with the consequences of supporting leaders like Hitler. But he wondered how the air forces were to compel the "individual German family to suffer war as they have never suffered it before" without, at the same time, producing unwanted results. Instead of blindly making day-to-day operational decisions with profound effects on the future, Hughes wondered if the Allied air forces should not ask guidance on these larger issues from the governments of Great Britain and the United States.[20]

The president of the United States was already thinking about the fate of the German people. "We have got to be tough with Germany," Roosevelt told Secretary of the Treasury Henry Morgenthau, Jr., in August, 1944, "and I mean the German people not just the Nazis. We either have to castrate the German people or you have got to treat them in such manner so they can't just go on reproducing people who want to continue the way they have in the past." On August 26 he explained his views to Secretary of War Stimson, who hoped to treat Germany far more gently than Morgenthau or Roosevelt wished:

> It is of the utmost importance that every person in Germany should realize that this time Germany is a defeated nation. I do not want them to starve to death, but, as an example, if they need food to keep body and soul together beyond what they have, they should be fed three times a day with soup from Army soup kitchens. . . . The fact that they are a defeated nation, collectively and individually, must be so impressed upon them that they will hesitate to start any new war. . . .

The president thought too many people in the United States and England erroneously believed that only a few Nazi leaders were responsible for what had happened, not the entire German nation.

"The German people as a whole must have it driven home to them that the whole nation has been engaged in a lawless conspiracy against the decencies of modern civilization."[21]

A few weeks later Roosevelt suggested how the AAF could deal with the inhabitants of the Reich. On September 9 he sent Stimson a letter asking that an agency be established (the future United States Strategic Bombing Survey) to analyze the effects of bombing in Germany and Japan. The president wished it to study the direct and indirect consequences of attacks on specific industries, including problems created by the movement of evacuees from a bombed city; the burden refugees placed on the communities to which they moved; complications these movements caused for transportation, medical care, and food distribution; and the strains imposed on the economic structure through dislocation of industry and commerce. He also hoped to obtain "some indication of the psychological and morale effect on an interior community, which had hitherto been free from attack, of a large influx of evacuees with all the attendant problems." A copy was sent to General Arnold.[22]

This letter originated in the AAF,[23] but when the president signed it and dispatched it to the secretary of war he sent out a signal that anyone conversant with the morale bombing controversy could understand: attacks aimed at terrorizing enemy civilians were acceptable to the commander in chief. The data Roosevelt was looking for would be applied in Japan, but raids that "dehoused" Germans, drove them onto the roads, or weakened the morale of those in previously unbombed areas would also provide the kind of information the president sought and would satisfy his purposes— to bring about surrender and to deter the Germans from starting a third world war. His ideas paralleled the views of General Arnold and other American advocates of airborne terror.

One of Arnold's fighter commanders had come up with an idea that might produce just the results Roosevelt and Arnold desired. In a refinement of SHATTER and of HURRICANE II, General Elwood R. Quesada, head of the XIX Tactical Air Command, proposed sending fighter bombers in pairs to bomb and strafe factories, bridges, railroad stations, residential centers, and other, mostly undefended, targets. He thought 1,500 planes attacking at will across the length and breadth of Germany would precipitate surrender.

Quesada's idea appealed strongly to David T. Griggs, a scientific consultant to the War Department. Griggs, who had worked at the Massachusetts Institute of Technology Radiation Laboratory, was in Europe helping the AAF apply radar to its operations. He supported the principle of postwar air force supremacy as strongly as any general in the AAF, and he perceived in the Quesada plan a way of driving home the significance of air power. After visiting Quesada's headquarters he sent the War Department an enthusiastic endorsement of the proposal, telling E. L. Bowles, Secretary Stimson's science advisor, that the Quesada plan would ruin the Germans' transportation and wreck their morale. The fighter bombers, he thought, would "make an impression on the mind of every German which he would never forget and which would live in the memories of his children and grandchildren as an illustration of the fearfulness of war, so that perhaps we might be spared the job of doing it again."[24]

Griggs's comments reached Chief of Staff Marshall, who found them so persuasive that he sent a copy to General Eisenhower. They also impressed General Kuter in AAF headquarters. Secretary of War Stimson read the radar expert's remarks and found them "intriguing." And so, Stimson recorded, did his assistant secretary, John J. McCloy.[25]

To pursue the question of morale breaking systematically, the War Department decided to consult other scientists, particularly psychologists. It arranged to have Gordon Allport of the Harvard Psychology Department send a questionnaire to leading members of his profession asking about the potential effects of bombing on German and Japanese morale. The responses, which were forwarded to the United States Strategic Bombing Survey, ranged from cursory remarks to a long theoretical discussion of German social psychology, including analyses of Nazi cults and myths and of alleged stages of German psychological development.[26] The psychologists were divided about the effectiveness of bombing as a way to break civilian morale, and those who discussed the ethics of terror warfare were as sharply split as were the people who worked for USSTAF.

Norman C. Meier of the State University of Iowa sent Allport an answer that Colonel Hughes or General Cabell might have written. Meier considered precision bombing more effective and less immoral than area attacks. Indiscriminate destruction of blocks of cities, including hospitals, ancient irreplaceable cathedrals, and other monuments of human culture and progress, was not only "barbaric," placing the perpetrators in the same category as those they criticized for barbarism, but tended to lengthen the war by infuriating the enemy populace and intensifying their will to resist.

Wholesale bombing of civilians in Germany and Japan could be expected to produce hatred and despair, and foster an attitude that would take generations to eradicate, if it could ever be eradicated at all.[27]

Other respondents had no hesitation about attacking civilian morale with warplanes. A psychologist from the University of Wisconsin suggested a plan almost exactly like the one that Weicker's group had proposed: announcing that a town would be obliterated in perhaps two days and informing the inhabitants that an escape route would be left open. This would be a "simple and ferocious method" of getting a community to obey Allied orders against the wishes of their own leaders. Horace B. English of Ohio State University suggested that the best method of shattering morale should be determined experimentally. If the Geneva Convention did not prohibit directing propaganda at interned enemy civilians, he proposed to "make guinea pigs" of civilian Nazi internees to discover what kinds of things would break down their morale and their belief in the Nazi cause. "It's got to be done in Germany," English declared. "Let's find out now, now, if we can."[28]

While psychologists in the United States were attempting to determine if German morale could be broken, planners at USSTAF headquarters continued to develop plans to break it. In December 1944 they came up with a draft of Operation CLARION, a proposal for systematic terror raids subtitled "General Plan for Maximum Effort Attack Against Transportation Objectives." It provided for a vast series of attacks by small groups of planes coming in at low altitudes to bomb and strafe targets all over Germany.[29]

AAF leaders had no difficulty understanding what CLARION was really about, and some of them protested vehemently. General Doolittle warned Spaatz that widespread strafing of civilians behind the battle lines might lead an enraged enemy populace to retaliate against Allied prisoners of war. German propagandists would use CLARION to justify Nazi brutality. And if it led to substantial AAF losses, the American public might question why the air force had changed its tactics for an operation of such uncertain long-term value. Nathan F. Twining, commanding general of the Fifteenth Air Force, added his own cautions, urging Spaatz to consider how the enemy and the American people would react to the inevitable civilian casualties.[30]

These were all very practical arguments, but some air force officers regarded the operation as unethical. In General Cabell's papers there is a copy of CLARION with the handwritten comment:

"This is the same old baby killing plan of the get-rich quick psychological boys, dressed up in a new Kimono."[31]

General Eaker objected strenuously to CLARION. In a letter for Spaatz's eyes only he warned that it would use heavy bombers unwisely, exposing them to very serious, unnecessary risks. It would "take our air effort off the one thing where we really have the Hun by the neck—oil," and would serve as a precedent for those who wanted to turn the bombers into low-level battle-support weapons. Losses would far outweigh prospective results, and the losses would not just be material, for they would involve the reputation of the United States. Operation CLARION, he insisted, would "absolutely convince the Germans that we are the barbarians they say we are, for it would be perfectly obvious to them that this is primarily a large scale attack on civilians as, in fact, it of course will be." Over 95 percent of the people killed would be civilians. He reminded General Spaatz that this operation was "absolutely contrary to the conversations you and Bob Lovett had with respect to the necessity of sticking to military targets." If the time ever came, he added,

> when we want to attack the civilian populace with a view to breaking civil morale, such a plan . . . is probably the way to do it. I personally, however, have become completely convinced that you and Bob Lovett are right and we should never allow the history of this war to convict us of throwing the strategic bomber at the man in the street. I think there is a better way we can do our share toward the defeat of the enemy, but if we are to attack the civil population I am certain we should wait until its morale is much nearer [the] breaking point and until the weather favors the operation more than it will at any time in the winter or early spring.[32]

This letter suggests that General Eaker, like Colonel Hughes and General Cabell, had strong moral objections to attacks that threatened the German people. It appears to contradict his postwar remarks that he never felt there was any moral sentiment among leaders of the AAF. However, Eaker subsequently denied that he had intended in this letter to oppose bombing that endangered civilians. On the contrary, he said, he felt the civilian who supported national leaders in war was just as responsible as the soldier, that "the man who builds the weapon is as responsible as the man who carries it into battle."[33] If his own interpretation is true, then he must have hoped that history would not convict the air force of using heavy bombers against civilians not because he was squeamish about using them, but because he wanted to secure the place of the air force in history. A pragmatist in all things respecting war and an expert on public relations, General Eaker perhaps chiefly feared diverting the strategic bomber from profitable objectives to others that could impair the image of his service.

Assistant Secretary Lovett shared Eaker's anxiety about the AAF's reputation but was willing to attack the German people openly and directly. In a conversation with one of General Quesada's officers the assistant secretary showed great interest in a terror weapon, a new kind of shell that threw white phosphorus pellets in all directions. The pellets ignited on contact with air, causing severe, painful burns. Lovett wished to know if bombs loaded with these pellets or with a combination of pellets and napalm would be effective against troops and even civilian personnel. Lovett stressed the idea, the officer reported, "that if we are going to have a total war we might as well make it as horrible as possible." Later, at the assistant secretary's suggestion, General Quesada began work on a plan for mass napalm raids.[34]

By the beginning of 1945 Lovett and other American officials had begun to worry that Allied armies in Western Europe were losing momentum. The Germans had launched a powerful counterattack through the Ardennes Forest in December, and though the Allies blunted this offensive in the Battle of the Bulge, victory seemed beyond reach. Confronting stalemate, General Spaatz's superiors once more urged him to use the Army Air Forces against the morale of the German people.

Again it was David Griggs who conveyed to the higher authorities a way to attack morale. On January 6 the scientist sent Secretary Lovett a paper urging him to begin the Quesada plan. In ground warfare, he claimed, "man for man and tank for tank the German is our superior." To prevent stagnation on the western front or even defeat in the field, Griggs proposed to exploit Allied air superiority by creating a fighter bomber force that would disrupt the German economy with attacks on small factories, power plants, and communications. Armed with rockets and napalm, the fighter bombers could deny reinforcements to the German army and "strike terror to the heart of the German." Their goal should be "the surrender of Germany to a raiding air force."

Griggs thought the Quesada plan might save the lives of hundreds of thousands of Allied soldiers. It was distinctly possible that it could "cause the surrender of the German nation to air power per se," which would set "a precedent of incalculable value for our future war planning." Air forces, Griggs believed, increasingly did the fighting and destroying while ground troops occupied the territory the airmen devastated. This was the "major lesson of World War II," and American ground commanders and civilian leaders might not learn it unless the AAF commenced the Quesada plan attacks at once.[35]

Griggs's paper, like his earlier remarks, received an immediate favorable reaction in AAF headquarters. Lovett set forth the scientist's ideas in a memo to General Arnold, changing the language somewhat. For instance, Griggs had written that as long as the front was not moving rapidly, the whole effort of the fighter force "should be directed to the disruption of [the] German economy and the terrorization of the German people." Lovett stated the point this way: "if the power of the German people to resist is to be further reduced, it seems likely that we must spread the destruction of industry into the smaller cities and towns now being used for production under the German system of dispersal." Lovett asked Arnold to create a "Jeb Stuart Unit" of fighter bombers, a cavalry of the air named for the Confederate Civil War leader.[36]

The start of the great Soviet offensive the second week of January strengthened hopes that morale bombing could help finish the war. On the 18th General Anderson told his staff to "brush up" on USSTAF's version of the Quesada plan, Operation CLARION, which he linked to the Soviet advance. During a January 31 meeting at the Malta conference, General George C. Marshall told the Joint Chiefs of Staff that he wanted the Quesada plan carried out. Anderson informed him about CLARION and stated that USSTAF would launch it as soon as conditions warranted. The next day, at an Allied air commanders' conference in SHAEF, General Spaatz announced that the opportunity to begin CLARION had arrived.[37]

Three weeks later, on February 22, 1945, and the morning of February 23, thousands of bombers and fighters of the Eighth, Ninth, and Fifteenth Air Forces, joined by the RAF, dispersed across Germany, Austria, and Italy, bombing and strafing transportation objectives and targets of opportunity. General Spaatz wired his commanders the day before the operation that press releases and communiqués must stress the military value of their listed targets (although the lists included small communities of insignificant military or economic importance—for instance, Heidelberg, Göttingen, and Baden-Baden). "Special care should be taken," Spaatz said "against giving any impression that this operation is aimed, repeat aimed, at civilian populations or intended to terrorize them."[38]

CLARION did not prove to be the culminating blow against Nazi power, but according to General Frederick L. Anderson that had not been its purpose. In his instructions to another general who was going back to the United States to talk to the press about the air war, Anderson wrote that

> it should be pointed out that such an operation was not expected in itself to shorten the war—no such optimistic attitude existed here. However, it is expected that the fact that Germany was struck all over will be passed on, from father to son, thence to grandson; that a deterrent for the initiation of future wars will definitely result—a reluctance to participate in any organization that has war as its primary aim certainly will result.[39]

With this idea Anderson's commander in chief heartily agreed.

THUNDERCLAP, *Dresden, and the Public Relations Disaster*

The AAF was continuously caught, at this phase of the war, between conflicting purposes: the aim, sanctioned at the highest level, of terrorizing the German populace; the desire to hit targets that officers like Colonel Hughes considered far more fruitful and more legitimate than enemy civilians; and the hope of protecting itself from the charge of terror bombing. While this conflict usually remained hidden from outsiders, at one point, near the end of the war in Europe, the contradictions became visible, producing a crisis for AAF public relations. This crisis developed out of a series of area raids on eastern German cities beginning with the THUNDERCLAP attack against Berlin and culminating in the bombing of Dresden.

Prodded by Prime Minister Churchill, and with the endorsement of General George C. Marshall, the Allied air commanders prepared to stage these attacks in the winter of 1945. On January 28, RAF Deputy Chief of Air Staff Norman Bottomley and General Spaatz agreed to issue new target priorities: first, oil targets; second, Berlin, Leipzig, Dresden, and "associated cities"; third, "communications" (which really meant transportation facilities), particularly those that could be used for moving German reinforcements to the east; fourth, jet aircraft and communications in southern Germany. The Spaatz-Bottomley directive meant that when bad weather prevented daylight precision attacks on oil targets, Allied air forces would attack cities behind the retreating German army. If possible, they would hit military and industrial targets. But since the weather would prevent the Americans from bombing precisely, they would really be delivering area attacks.[40]

The Allied commanders viewed the eastern German raids as part of a climactic psychological warfare campaign in which massive bombings would panic civilians, who would clog roads and railroads and make it impossible for German troops facing the Soviet army to bring up supplies or reinforcements or to retreat in an orderly way. Thus on February 1, General Kuter, sitting in for General Arnold at the Malta conference, cabled Barney Giles at AAF headquarters that in accordance with a message that Giles had sent earlier, the U.S. Strategic Air Forces had arranged for all available day and night heavy bombers to attack Berlin "with view to increasing existing pandemonium resulting from Soviet advances." The raids were also supposed to wreck what was left of civilian morale, hastening Germany's disintegration. This is what General Marshall had in mind when he announced at Malta that he wanted the AAF to hit Munich. The chief of staff believed an attack on the Bavarian capital, far from Berlin, would persuade refugees driven out by THUNDERCLAP that their situation was hopeless.[41]

Some Allied officers thought the raids in eastern Germany might serve the additional purpose of impressing the Soviet Union. RAF Bomber Command had long believed that by devastating the center of Berlin the Allies would convince the USSR of the effectiveness of Anglo-American air power, and early in 1945, when planning for THUNDERCLAP resumed, the British Joint Intelligence Subcommittee contended that the proposed attack on the German capital might be politically useful in demonstrating to the Russians the desire of the British and Americans to help them in their ground offensive. Shortly before the great powers assembled at Yalta, General David M. Schlatter, Spaatz's deputy chief of air staff, wrote in his diary, "I feel that our air forces are the blue chips with which we will approach the post-war treaty table, and that [THUNDERCLAP] will add immeasurably to their strength, or rather to the Russian knowledge of their strength."[42]

As General Spaatz's headquarters made final preparations, General Doolittle, the commander of the Eighth Air Force, which would have to fly the mission to Berlin, explained to Spaatz why he did not like this operation at all. American planes would have to pass in range of hundreds of heavy anti-aircraft guns to reach an area where there were no really important military targets. The raid would not succeed even as a terror attack because German civilians would have ample warning to take shelter. Besides, terror was induced by fear of the unknown, not by intensifying what the people of Berlin had experienced for years. And THUNDERCLAP, which would be one of the last and therefore presumably best-remembered operations of the war, would "violate the basic American principle of precision bombing of targets of strictly military significance for which our tactics were developed and our crews trained and indoctrinated." Doolittle recommended that the RAF be assigned to area-bomb the capital while the Americans minimized their losses and ensured an effective assault by hitting specific military targets.[43]

Telling Doolittle that he expected it to be a radar-guided, blind bombing operation, Spaatz ordered the attack with specific objectives such as factories, rail facilities, and administrative headquarters listed as aiming points. Then he had his staff prepare for the Munich raid that General Marshall had requested. More than 900 B-17s attacked Berlin on February 3, 1945, accompanied by fighters that strafed transportation targets. Several American bombardiers made visual sightings through holes in the clouds and some hit military objectives, including the Air Ministry buildings and the Friedrichstrasse Station. An estimated 25,000 civilians died.[44]

THUNDERCLAP did not push Germany over the brink, nor did it become the best-remembered operation of the European war. That distinction went to the raid on Dresden, capital of Saxony. On February 13–14 two waves of British planes, dropping hundreds of thousands of high explosive and incendiary bombs, burned out the core of this old city, a center of art and high culture that had remained until then virtually untouched by the air war, despite having a few military and industrial targets within its boundaries. American bombers were to have initiated the attack, but weather delayed them and they followed the British, flying over still-flaming ruins, using radar or visual sighting to bomb the Dresden marshaling yard while American fighters strafed below. The next day they staged a second large attack on the yard, bombing blind. The AAF was unable to determine exactly how much damage was done by the nearly 475 tons of general purpose bombs and over 296 tons of incendiaries its planes unloaded. Nor was an exact death count possible. A conservative figure for this entire series of raids on Dresden is 35,000.[45]

Along with the Nazi extermination camps, the killing of Soviet and American prisoners, and other enemy atrocities, Dresden became one of the moral causes célèbres of World War II. Yet even before the Dresden attack, in the aftermath of the raids on Berlin and other "associated cities," AAF leaders' uneasiness over the effects of American raids on German urban areas was reflected in official air force records.

General Kuter began to write things that conflicted with what he knew about the East European attacks. On the 13th of February he observed in a cable to General Spaatz that the Spaatz-Bottomley directive, which had laid the foundation for the attacks, contained "what can be read as indiscriminate bombing of German cities in priority second only to synthetic oil plants." This, said Kuter, led him to believe that "we are not keeping good faith with the U.S. JCS unless intelligence which I have not seen reasonably shows strong possibility of tipping the scales by this type of bombing." Yet Kuter had known from the beginning of February what the Spaatz-Bottomley agreement said, since he had relayed its contents on to General Giles in AAF headquarters—including a provision for "attack of Berlin, Leipzig, Dresden and associated cities where heavy attack will cause great confusion in civil population from East." Kuter had also attended a Joint Chiefs of Staff meeting at Malta on January 31 at which Chief of Staff Marshall had urged the AAF to bomb Berlin and other cities, including Munich, to show refugees that there was no hope.[46]

General Giles issued similar messages. On February 14 he cabled Kuter from AAF headquarters stating that "the high priority accorded to attacking Berlin and other cities was questioned in our minds." Yet for the previous two weeks he had known about that priority and had not opposed it—rather, he recommended that the city be hit. On February 17 he told General Spaatz that certain instructions Spaatz had given to USSTAF were "acceptable to General Arnold providing that not involved are instructions or implications for the promiscuous bombing of German cities for the purpose of causing civilian confusion." Yet on February 1, confirming Giles's own instructions, Kuter had told him that THUNDERCLAP was about to be staged "with a view to increasing existing pandemonium."[47]

At one point AAF headquarters suggested to Spaatz that when he had attacked Berlin he had not been trying to break civilian morale but had merely attempted to hit transportation targets with precision bombing. It was a plausible hypothesis, because Spaatz had insisted on designating specific objectives as the aiming points. But since he had told Doolittle to anticipate bombing the city blind, and since it was only to be bombed when weather was too poor to aim at oil refineries, Spaatz could not have expected his flyers to hit the listed targets accurately.[48]

A few days after the Dresden raid, an RAF officer at SHAEF made public comments about the eastern German bombing which disturbed American air force leaders even more. Air Commodore C. M. Grierson told a press briefing that one object of the raids was to disrupt the German economy by forcing the Nazi government to move supplies to bombed-out civilians, by attacking towns from which relief was being sent, and by destroying places to which refugees were evacuated. An Associated Press reporter dispatched a story based on Grierson's remarks, and soon people in the United States were reading that "Allied air bosses have made the long-awaited decision to adopt deliberate terror bombing of the great German population centers as a ruthless expedient to hasten Hitler's doom."[49] The story was not entirely true—the British actually had adopted this policy years earlier—but Grierson's remarks and the AP report were substantially correct.

Air Commodore Grierson had finally achieved what U.S. air force officials had suspected the British of intending all along: he had officially and publicly tied the AAF to morale and area bombing. Some American officers thought the RAF officer had done it intentionally, but General Anderson disagreed with that theory. The briefing, he felt, was simply a case of "absolute stupidity by an incompetent officer."[50]

Regardless of the motives behind it, the AAF had to deal with the effects of Grierson's press conference. "What do we say?" the chief of information asked Spaatz from AAF headquarters. "This is certain to have a nation-wide serious effect on the Air Forces as we have steadily preached the gospel of precision bombing against military and industrial targets." General Anderson wanted to issue a statement explaining the AAF position, but Spaatz demurred. He told Anderson, "Reference fuss about terror bombing believe any formal statement about our policy would be inappropriate since it brings into direct contrast before the public a subject which may become a matter of controversy between ourselves & the RAF."[51]

Eisenhower's headquarters agreed with General Spaatz. It decided not to issue an official explanation. All questions raised by Grierson's briefing would be answered by saying:

A. there had been no change in bombing policy;
B. the United States Strategic Air Forces had always directed their attacks against military objectives and would continue to do so, and
C. the censor had passed the story erroneously.[52]

Anderson then sent a message on Spaatz's behalf to AAF headquarters, explaining that while the bombing of Berlin had not been expected to be precise, it was justified by the city's military significance. "It has always been my policy," he declared in Spaatz's name, "that civilian populations are not suitable military objectives."[53]

On February 22 Secretary of War Stimson told a press conference that "our policy never has been to inflict terror bombing on civilian populations." He stated that he had investigated a report that the Allies had decided upon a policy of terror bombing of the German people and determined that it had arisen "from what is considered an excusable but incorrect interpretation of some remark by a briefing officer at Allied headquarters." The basic policy of the U.S. Army Air Forces had not been changed, he said. "Our efforts still are confined to the attack of enemy military objectives. The communication centers we attack become our objective in that they feed the front on which our Allied armies are now engaging the German armies." Yet Stimson did not feel certain that the information he had given out—the AAF's interpretation of the eastern German raids—was entirely true. He pursued the matter further, wondering if the air force really had hit military targets in Dresden. Noting that the results of American bombing there "were practically unobserved," he asked that the city be photographed carefully and the "actual facts made known." Eventually, without making a careful independent inquiry, he let the matter drop.[54]

Still, the controversy could not be quieted. Churchill's government tried to prevent the British people from learning about Grierson's interview, but word of it leaked into the country, stimulating bitter attacks in Parliament. The prime minister tried to color the official record by inserting a statement which implied that the Allied air commanders had violated his wishes when they staged the raids on eastern Germany. Yet Churchill himself had pressed the RAF to bomb Berlin and the other cities in order to harry the German retreat. The Nazis did what they could to tell the world about Dresden. Later, during the Cold War, Communist authorities in East Germany recalled the attack on Dresden in their propaganda against the West. They left unmentioned the fact that the Russians were told about the Dresden raid in advance and had had a chance to veto it.[55]

Within the American air force disputes about the wisdom and propriety of area raids continued. General George C. McDonald, the USSTAF director of intelligence, agreed entirely with Air Commodore Grierson's characterization of the eastern German bombings, and in an emotionally charged memorandum he attacked what he called the policy of "homicide and destruction" into which the AAF had lately been drawn.[56] He reminded General Anderson that until the issuance of the Spaatz-Bottomley directive, which authorized the raids on Berlin, Dresden, and other East European cities, the American air force had generally followed a policy of attacking the enemy's means to resist. The AAF's equipment and training all aimed at that goal. "We had carefully reviewed the results of indiscriminate bombardment in Spain, in England and in Germany and had come to the sober military conclusion that an enemy could be overcome more quickly by systematic denial of military weapons than by attack upon civilian populations," he wrote. The major departure from that doctrine—the bombing of the Balkan capitals in the spring of 1944—had failed. It had not caused or even hastened capitulation, and it had delayed the destruction of enemy oil resources at Ploesti. The raids in Southeastern Europe had offered the people of the Balkans "a contrast between our methods and the Russian ones, which their subsequent welcome of the Russians shows that they well understood." And now the Spaatz-Bottomley directive had put USSTAF and the American Army Air Forces "unequivocally into the business of area bombardment of congested civil populations."

There was no reason to believe, McDonald argued, that this kind of attack would produce military results commensurate with the cost in lives, crew time, and plane damage. The Germans could survive without the manufacturing capacity of Berlin, Leipzig, and Dresden. Destruction of those cities as transport centers might delay but could not critically disrupt the movement of enemy troops and supplies. Nor could "the elusive, if not illusionary target of morale" justify obliterating German cities, for the object of morale attack was revolt, and the German people remained disinclined or powerless to rise against their rulers. Nazi controls were even strong enough to prevent civilian confusion, which the raids were supposed to engender, from seriously hampering military operations.

All these were strategic matters. But beyond the issue of how to win the war there were "secondary, but strong considerations against our adoption of a policy [of] promiscuous bombardment of civilians."

Perhaps, McDonald suggested, reasons existed that he did not know about for repudiating past AAF practices. If so, the air force should face the issue squarely and change its doctrine and procedures drastically enough to reap the full benefits of extermination bombing. It might abandon all its other target priorities, throw away its target folders and bombsights, abandon its study of anything but the weather at air bases, and "settle wholeheartedly to the extermination of populations and the razing of cities." And if this really did turn out to be the best way of waging war, the ground forces should then be directed "to kill all civilians and demolish all buildings in the Reich, instead of restricting their energies to the armed enemy."

For five years indiscriminate aerial bombardment, "latterly conducted on a stupendous scale," had not produced decisive results or broken the German will to fight. If this policy were now to succeed, it could only be done "by effecting a rate of homicide and destruction far beyond anything yet seen, in short, by applying our entire power to a task beyond measurement."

The policy represented by the eastern German bombings, McDonald declared,

> repudiates our past purposes and practices and links us inseparably with a dream and design of aerial warfare limited to indiscriminate homicide and destruction. It places us before our allies, the neutrals, our enemies and history in conspicuous contrast to the Russians whose preoccupation with wholly military objectives has been as notable, and noticeable, as has been our own up to this time.

He therefore recommended that "higher authority" be asked, in the strongest possible terms, to allow the Army Air Forces to continue in their established ways of conquering the enemy.

But by this time American higher authorities had embraced the idea of winning through eradication of cities—as well as other targets—in Japan. And even in Europe they were willing to accept violations of the selective bombing principle, though they did not want outsiders to know about it or the AAF to be blamed for the consequences. On March 15 General Schlatter noted in his diary that the army was asking the air force repeatedly to bomb towns, often so far in the rear that bombing could not possibly offer immediate assistance to the ground offensive. General Spaatz's policy, Schlatter noted, was that "a town as such" would be bombed only when the army specifically required the action and requested each town as an individual target in writing. "He is determined that the American Air Forces will not end this war with a reputation for indiscriminate bombing."[57]

Despite his remarks about making the strategic bomber the most humane of all weapons and his preference for selective attacks, General Arnold regarded terror bombing and the obliteration of urban centers as necessities of war. When the Dresden controversy erupted, and Secretary Stimson asked the AAF to explain its role in that event, Arnold was ill, recuperating from a heart attack in Florida, but still in touch with air force headquarters. His chief of staff, General Barney M. Giles, sent him a message March 7. "The Secretary of War," Giles wrote, "has expressed concern over reports indicating indiscriminate bombing of Dresden and has asked that the City be thoroughly photographed to establish that our objectives were, as usual, military in character." Over this statement and in the margin next to it General Arnold scrawled: "We must not get soft. War must be destructive and to a certain extent inhuman and ruthless."[58]

Reasons for the Change in AAF Bombing Practices

Why had the U.S. Army Air Forces reverted from its selective bombing doctrine to the Douhetian principles of mass attack and terror? There are many answers.

One lies in the resources available to the AAF. The superb bombsights on American B-17s were useless in the kind of weather that hung over Europe several months of the year. American commanders chose to bomb anyway, using inaccurate radar devices, the only kind that Allied technology had come up with, rather than abandon their part of the air offensive. By employing the strategic bomber with less discrimination than their doctrine called for, they created precedents for blind bombing in eastern Germany.

The plenitude of resources that flooded American bases toward the end of the war also contributed to U.S. terror and area attacks. A powerful argument for selective bombing in the prewar years and early in the war arose from shortages of planes, crews, and bombs. When this limitation ceased to exist by the end of 1944 the idea of breaking enemy morale became more plausible, despite the fact that, as McDonald and others observed, there was no evidence that German morale could be broken or, if it could, that shattering civilian morale would make the people in charge surrender. With so much firepower available, it was easier to believe that morale bombing had failed earlier simply because it had not been conducted on a large enough and sufficiently widespread scale. Furthermore, the AAF could hit the remaining strategic targets and still send hundreds of bombers on morale attacks, an impossible feat in the days of the Schweinfurt raids.

Despite the predominance of selective bombing theory, the germ of terror raids and mass bombing lay in the doctrine and prewar plans of the American air force. Before Pearl Harbor the Air Corps school had taught the principle of forcing the enemy to do one's will, and had emphasized that civilians were part of the enemy war machine and must be made to suffer. The authors of AWPD-1 had imagined in 1941 that when Germany had reached the verge of defeat it might be profitable to deliver a "large scale, all-out attack on the civil population of Berlin." These ideas reemerged in the Weicker plan and similar proposals for psychological air warfare.

Hopes for air force supremacy in America's postwar security system influenced the move toward Douhetian warfare, but the influence ran in opposite directions. David Griggs observed that it would be very advantageous to the AAF if the Germans appeared to surrender exclusively to air power, say in response to Quesada plan attacks. Yet as Secretary Lovett and Colonel Hughes admonished, and as General Arnold and other AAF leaders recognized, if the American people came to believe that the AAF was terrorizing German women and children the interests of AAF would suffer.

At the same time American public opinion, as AAF leaders understood it, increased the pressure to bomb enemy civilians. General Arnold believed, no doubt correctly, that the people at home wished to employ U.S. technology to limit U.S. casualties. This came to mean using warplanes against the German populace in an effort to end the war as quickly as possible.

A desire to influence the postwar settlement also produced opposing effects. Some American and British officers wanted to impress the Russians with Western air strength by devastating German cities. Other persons in the AAF, on the Joint Chiefs of Staff, and in the State Department recognized that overwhelming AAF attacks on Axis cities could help the Russians politically while hurting the United States.

Elements of the Royal Air Force and the British government influenced the way American air strategy evolved. Whatever their suspicions of British motives, some U.S. officers like Spaatz and Eaker, who associated personally with leaders of the RAF, were affected by and often sympathetic to the views of their British counterparts. RAF officers enjoyed a psychological advantage because they could convey to the Americans the feeling that the AAF ought to share more in the dirty work of bombing cities. This was something the Americans found it difficult to oppose without appearing excessively "pure," to use General Cabell's term.[59]

Advocates of urban raids and terror bombing also pressed their case with the AAF itself. These men included relatively low-ranking officers such as Colonels Berliner and Weicker, civilian-soldiers recruited from industry. They also included AAF professionals at or near the top.

Some officers who had doubts about the wisdom of moving toward Douhetian warfare chose not to make a really strong stand against it. General Kuter disapproved of terror attacks but, following the usual procedures for his office, helped develop them anyway. General Spaatz was ambivalent about attacking enemy civilians. He favored some forms of terror raids—the fighter sweeps across Germany—but disliked others, feeling it was better to hit oil refineries than cities. Still, Spaatz always went along, hitting towns behind the lines so long as the Army took responsibility, ordering THUNDERCLAP to proceed, despite considerable doubts, because his job required him to do what his superiors ordered.

It might be said that the air force undertook THUNDERCLAP and CLARION because the people who strongly opposed morale and area bombing lacked the power to impose their views. Some of the civilians working with USSTAF, like Pincus and Barnett, disciples of the selective bombing theory, had far less influence than scientific advisor David Griggs, who wished to terrorize the German people. This was because Griggs had direct access to high-level people in Washington who agreed with his point of view. Colonel Hughes, General McDonald, and General Cabell condemned Douhetian war, but even though they could support their position by referring to the selective bombing theory and by reminding other officers of what might happen to the AAF if it violated the moral sentiments of the American people, they presented their opinions only at a regional headquarters of the AAF and could not affect national policy.

These three officers had to overcome a special disadvantage. Hughes and Cabell had both served on Spaatz's Special Planning Committee when it considered adding morale as a target system. Both felt that bombing civilians to break their will involved serious moral questions. Yet the report of that committee makes no mention of moral issues. This was because in the U.S. Army Air Forces of World War II it was more persuasive to employ pragmatic arguments and not show too much concern for the welfare of the enemy—to be "realistic" and tough. Colonel Hughes alluded to this situation when he said that "silly as it may seem to some of us realists here [in USSTAF]," there was concern at home "about the inhumanity of indiscriminate area bombing."[60] General Chidlaw reflected the prevailing climate when he denied that squeamishness had led him to oppose General Arnold's booby trap scheme. "We must not get soft," wrote General Arnold. AAF officers were trained to consider practical issues, not the morality of certain types of warfare. Thinking about the morality of what you were doing could drive you crazy, as General LeMay observed.

The people who favored hitting populated areas drew on moral arguments of their own. One reason why strategic bombing theory had developed in the first place was to prevent the slaughter of ground troops. Douhet and others believed there was a moral point to keeping young soldiers, the "'flower" of society, from butchering one another, even if it meant that airmen would have to bomb civilians and attack the structure of societies. Besides, if General Arnold was right, air power, used with "understanding," could end war more rapidly than would otherwise be possible, saving countless lives. That was General Anderson's belief when he wrote in July 1943 that his VIII Bomber Command would devastate the German economy so badly there would be no need to invade the continent, "with consequent loss of thousands and possibly millions of lives."[61] Events did not turn out as Anderson wished, however. General Cabell claimed that this kind of argument was only a rationalization. Still, the case could be made that U.S. airmen joined in terror attacks and area raids to save lives as well as to take them.

People invoked other moral concepts to justify bombing civilians. General Eaker regarded the European war as a conflict against evil in which the entire German nation was the enemy; he thought it necessary to attack bad people to save the good, the righteous, and the just.[62] Lowell Weicker suggested that enemy lives and Allied lives had wholly different values, for he maintained that if terror attacks saved just a few British and Americans, the price paid by the enemy should not be an object of serious consideration.

The most important factor moving the AAF toward Douhetian war was the attitude of the country's top civilian and military leaders. The chief movers, some of them moved at times by other leaders and by circumstances, were Arnold, who, despite his preference for selective bombing, sometimes promoted less discriminate forms of attack; Eisenhower, who would do anything to bring a speedy end to the conflict; Marshall, who wanted to put on CLARION and THUNDERCLAP and to show the Germans fleeing to Munich that their situation was hopeless; Lovett, who felt the war should be painful and unforgettable to German civilians; Stimson, who found the Quesada plan intriguing and defended U.S. participation in the eastern German raids, yet did not inquire carefully into the way American air power was actually used; and Franklin Roosevelt, who, recalling what had happened after the First World War, believed the German people must be compelled this time to recognize their defeat and accept responsibility for the horrors their country had inflicted on the world.

— 6

The Bombing of Japan:
Preparing for the Fire Raids

The detonation of nuclear weapons over Hiroshima and Nagasaki culminated an effort by American strategic air forces to lay waste almost every important city in Japan. The chief instrument of this campaign, which began with the great Tokyo raid of March 9–10, 1945, was fire. The men who directed it hoped that incendiary air attacks, together with precision bombing of industrial and military targets and the explosion of nuclear devices, would shatter the will of the Japanese people and destroy their nation's ability to fight. Optimistic that a Douhetian kind of warfare, which had not achieved the results its proponents had anticipated in Europe, would succeed in Asia, yet never entirely agreed about what it would take to make the Japanese surrender, American planners devoted intellectual and physical resources to determining how to obliterate Japan's cities. Some of the men who were privy to these deliberations wondered at the time about the morality of what was being planned, but for the most part controversy about the moral issue in the American bombing of Japan awaited the end of the war.

The Development of American Incendiary Warfare

Long before the attack on Pearl Harbor, American air force officers had begun to think about using fire weapons against Japanese population centers. This approach, which Billy Mitchell had suggested years earlier, was discussed at the Air Corps Tactical School. During the spring of 1939 one of the school's instructors,

Major C. E. Thomas, delivered a lecture on air operations against Japan, a subject, he noted, "of considerable practical importance." He described Japan, a compact, highly integrated modern industrial state, as an ideal objective for aerial bombing. The earthquake and fire of 1923 had demonstrated the "fearful destruction" incendiary bombs could inflict on Japan's cities, and Thomas speculated that direct attack against Japanese civilians might prove highly effective in breaking their morale. But "humanitarian considerations," he said, ruled out this kind of warfare.[1]

Humanitarian considerations did not, of course, prevent other powers from using incendiaries against civilians during World War II, and after hostilities began several American agencies hastened to develop their country's capacity for fire bombing. Army Air Corps officers went to England and studied the Nazi blitz. The Chemical Warfare Service, which had been urging the Air Corps to adopt incendiary weapons, sent one of its experts, Colonel J. Enrique Zanetti, a Columbia University chemistry professor on active duty, to London in June 1941 to analyze fire raids, then put him in charge of its own incendiary program. A few days after Pearl Harbor it set up an incendiary laboratory at the Massachusetts Institute of Technology. The National Defense Research Committee, established in 1940 to coordinate the military work of American scientists, created an incendiary weapons section. NDRC specialists worked with the Arthur D. Little Company, the E. I. du Pont Corporation, Eastman Kodak, the Standard Oil Development Company, and other chemical suppliers and users to develop fire weapons. The Standard Oil group soon devised a small, extremely efficient bomb, designated the M-69, which ejected napalm from its tail. This was the jellied gasoline product created chiefly by Harvard University chemist Louis F. Fieser, a leading figure in the NDRC incendiary program.[2]

Some of the most realistic information about the effects of incendiary weapons came from the ruins of English and German cities. In September 1942, after surveying this data, the chemist Robert P. Russell, vice-president of Standard Oil Development and an NDRC executive, prepared a highly optimistic account of the potential of fire bombing. "The possibilities inherent in incendiary bombing," he wrote, "have greatly brightened in recent months. The mass raid has made its first appearance; its practicality as a destructive offense is now clear. Better and better incendiaries are becoming available—though not yet in full production. . . ."[3]

The most vigorous advocates of fire attack were neither scientists nor military people but insurance experts, led by Horatio

Bond, chief engineer of the National Fire Protection Association. These men did not simply advise the AAF. They pushed it as hard as they could to make it wage incendiary warfare against factories and cities. Bond later explained that "it was necessary for those of us familiar with fire destruction to try to keep a constant pressure on the air force and their scientific advisors to get on with the business of exploiting fire attack to bring about the end of the war."[4]

Dispatched to England by the Office of Civil Defense, Bond urged the Eighth Air Force to use more incendiaries against German targets. He prepared a long treatise on how to propagate fires, discussing the potential for fire spread of different kinds of structures, such as homes of various sizes and constructions, chemical factories (actually a better target for high explosives, Bond felt), and churches (quite vulnerable to small incendiaries, which lodged in a hard-to-get-to space between the roof and interior ceiling.) Bond pressed his ideas on Colonel Richard D. Hughes. Some of the latest devices were "humdingers," he said, and he urged Hughes not to overlook them. Hughes thought Bond's ideas worth investigating, but the Eighth Air Force continued to rely on high explosives until the British incinerated Hamburg. Then it started to employ greatly increasing quantities of fire bombs. From 250 tons in July 1943, before the Hamburg fire storm, the weight of incendiaries delivered by the Eighth Air Force rose by the end of 1944 to 5,000 a month and peaked at 7,726 in March 1945.[5]

American fire experts explored the economic and military effects of incendiary air attacks. The first full-scale study of the prospect for mass incendiary raids on enemy cities, a report from the Foreign Economic Administration, appeared in February 1943. Its author, Seymour Janow, a UCLA- and UC Berkeley–trained analyst, examined English data about the effects of fire attacks and reviewed information provided by British insurance companies that had covered property in Japan before the war. He concluded that Japanese urban areas were highly vulnerable to firebombing and that fire raids would hinder Japanese production seriously by "dehousing" workers. They would profoundly dislocate Japan's entire economy.[6]

Soon after Janow's report appeared, AAF Air Staff ordered its intelligence division (A-2) to investigate bombing objectives in Korea, Manchuria, and the Japanese home islands. On March 20 Air Staff Intelligence produced a study that listed eight leading target systems and fifty-seven key targets essential to the Japanese economy. It did not describe the cities per se as primary target

systems,[7] but its civilian advisors did, and some of them recommended that the AAF launch incendiary bombing raids against
Japanese urban areas.

Raymond H. Ewell, a protégé of Horatio Bond, offered a particularly expansive proposal. Ewell was a thirty-five-year-old chemist with a doctorate from Princeton who, after teaching at Purdue
for a few years, had joined Division 11 of NDRC, the incendiary
section. By the spring of 1943 he had begun to worry that the Allies
might attempt to meet Japanese threats to Australia and other
places in the Pacific by transferring forces from the European
theater. This, he believed, would be a cardinal error of grand
strategy, and he proposed to avert it by firebombing the major cities
of Japan.

In a memo to NDRC, Ewell estimated that ten tons of M-69
incendiaries, dropped on any of those cities, would cause 2,000
destructive blazes, half of which would be "appliance fires," impossible to contain without professional equipment. Since no municipal
department in the world could cope with that many fires, they
would get completely out of hand and the resulting conflagrations
would cripple Japan so badly that for six months to a year it would
be incapable of threatening vital areas in the Pacific. Ewell thought
American military planners did not understand the potential of the
M-69, which he claimed put it "almost in the class of the oft-
mentioned 'secret weapon.'" That was why people in research and
development (such as himself) had to bring the matter to their
attention.[8]

General Arnold was always looking for new "secret weapons,"
and Ewell's proposal found a receptive audience in AAF headquarters. It was also characteristic of the AAF chief to assign overlap-
ping task forces to important projects. In March 1943 Arnold arranged to have the Committee of Operations Analysts supplement
the work of his intelligence staff by doing its own study of bombing
objectives in Japan.[9]

The Committee of Operations Analysts

Founded the year before to appraise European target systems for
the AAF, the Committee of Operations Analysts brought together
military specialists and a group of civilians with considerable experience in analyzing large, complex problems. Its members and consultants included the banker Thomas W. Lamont of J. P. Morgan
and Company; corporation attorneys Guido R. Perera and Elihu

Root, Jr.; W. Barton Leach, onetime professor at Harvard Law School; Edward S. Mason of the Office of Strategic Services, formerly professor of economics at Harvard; and Edward Mead Earle of the Institute for Advanced Study, chairman of a Princeton faculty military studies group and an expert in the history of strategic thought. Another member, Fowler Hamilton of the Board of Economic Warfare, had served in the U.S. Department of Justice during a period of intense anti-trust activity, developing a knowledge of economic structures which could be very useful to a committee that was seeking ways to make economic structures collapse. Francis Bitter, a physicist from MIT, worked in the Naval Ordnance Laboratory on mines, torpedoes, and countermeasures against them, crucial subjects for a war against an island power. Some of these men held commissions: Perera and Leach in the AAF, Bitter in the U.S. Naval Reserve. The career military officers who took part included General Clayton L. Bissell, the assistant chief of air staff for intelligence; Colonel Malcolm W. Moss, also of A-2; Captain H. C. Wick from the office of the Deputy Chief of Naval Operations, Air; and Colonels Thomas G. Lanphier and Moses W. Pettigrew of Army Intelligence. The chair was General Byron E. Gates of Air Staff Management Control.[10]

From the spring through early November 1943 the COA worked on the Japanese bombing project using a system of subcommittees to examine potential target systems. For data and ideas it consulted the Foreign Economic Administration, the Office of Strategic Services, Air Staff Intelligence, Army G-2, and the British Ministry of Economic Warfare. Reliable information was difficult to obtain, since the Japanese had done a good job of concealing important data about their economy, particularly about industries contributing to their war effort. The COA did not even know where some of the important installations were, and at this stage of the war good aerial reconnaissance photographs were almost impossible to come by. But by using economic and technical journals and other Japanese-language publications, radio intercepts, and the recollections of American and Allied engineers and businessmen who had built plants in Japan or lived in the Far East, the committee pieced together information about the target systems and on November 11, 1943, reported to General Arnold that the most important targets appeared to be merchant shipping, aircraft plants, steel, and urban industrial areas.[11]

The committee believed that a series of massive firebomb attacks on urban areas would produce a major disaster for Japan. Air raids would burn out great numbers of small subcontracting operations in homes and workshops scattered through the highly flammable cities and would damage some large plants. Incendiary destruction of workers' homes and dormitories surrounding the bigger factories would reduce output of Japanese heavy industry. Fire raids would destroy food and clothing, interrupt public services necessary for production, and, through death, injury, and destruction of homes, dislocate war workers, forcing survivors to migrate and diverting them to relief and repair. The COA recommended staging the fire raids between December and May, when wind conditions and humidity would most effectively promote the spread of fire. Until then the air force should avoid sending out small forces, so that the Japanese would be given no clues to what awaited them and no time to prepare. The committee preferred to delay, build up American airpower in striking distance of the main islands, and then destroy the cities and their factories with a storm of incendiary bombs.[12]

Early in 1944 the Joint Chiefs of Staff decided that the AAF should attack Japan with a bombing offensive aimed at industry and morale as well as at military forces, and in April they issued a series of target priorities which essentially paralleled the committee's recommendations, including its proposal to bomb urban areas. But other experts challenged some of the data that underlay the COA report, information developed by Air Staff Intelligence in consultation with Raymond Ewell.

A-2 had suggested that 1,690 tons of M-69 bombs, properly placed in flammable zones of twenty Japanese cities, would devastate 180 square miles, render twelve million people—70 percent of the population of those cities—homeless, disrupt essential services, engulf administrative agencies with overwhelming relief and repair problems, and cause production to fall about 30 percent, with a four- to six-month recuperation period. But according to British and American analysts who had studied the fire raids on German and English cities, these estimates were far too optimistic. James K. McElroy, an American fire protection engineer working with the British Ministry of Home Security, considered A-2's findings "totally unrealistic." His comments, and criticisms by his colleagues, induced the Committee of Operations Analysts to reopen its investigation of urban incendiary bombing.[13]

In June 1944 the COA established a Joint Incendiary Committee (also known as the Incendiary Subcommittee), staffed with economists, fire experts borrowed from the British Ministry of Home Security, and analysts from OSS, the Foreign Economic

Administration, the National Defense Research Council, the navy, and the AAF. The Twentieth Air Force, which the Joint Chiefs had created in April to direct long-range bombing operations against Japan, was represented by the chief of its operations analysis section, Robert L. Stearns, president (on leave) of the University of Colorado. The chairman was a naval air intelligence officer, Commander John Mitchell, USNR.

The central tasks of the subcommittee were to determine the forces it would take to burn down six major Japanese urban areas, all located on the island of Honshu—Tokyo, Yokohama, Kawasaki, Nagoya, Osaka, and Kobe—and to estimate the probable economic and military consequences of incinerating them. These determinations required the subcommittee to answer several highly complex questions based on data it could not always obtain and involving judgments that could not be verified until the air force actually burned the cities down.[14]

It was crucial for the Incendiary Subcommittee to estimate the forces needed to destroy the cities, since that calculation would determine how many planes, men, bombs, and supplies the air force would have to assemble at its Pacific bases. It would also permit a prediction of when the raids could begin. The force estimate hinged on the density of firebombs needed to create a holocaust. But experts had disagreed for months about this density, which itself depended on several chains of subsidiary estimates and calculations.

For example, since the more difficult it was to burn down these cities, the larger the number of bombs needed, it was essential to find out how far the fires set by incendiaries could be made to spread. Fire spread, in turn, was a function of several variables, including the construction of buildings, weather conditions, and the will and competence of fire fighters. An analyst for the Foreign Economic Administration had deduced, from fragmentary reports about the Japanese civil defense program, that the entire populace would be mobilized to put out fires and that the incendiaries must therefore be combined with anti-personnel devices to kill or injure people who tried to extinguish the flames before they became uncontrollable. What kind of anti-personnel weapon would work best: Fragmentation bombs? White phosphorus that caused blinding smoke? Delayed-action bombs that exploded after people entered burning areas? High explosives? Perhaps some combination? If high explosives were used, would they blow out the fires or flatten buildings, making it more difficult for the fires to spread? Or would the damage they did to water mains and firefighting equipment compensate for their anti-fire effects? How many incendiaries and how many high explosives had to be dropped on each target to ensure that fires would blaze out of control? Where were the best places to drop them? At what time of day should the bombs be dropped? Should the planes release their loads singly or in patterns? From what altitudes?[15]

Even if the planners could determine how to set uncontrollable conflagrations, there remained the question of how much good it would do to incinerate the cities—that is, how effective, compared with other kinds of bombing, incendiary area raids would be against Japan's ability to make war. The AAF expected to have almost unlimited resources to use against Japan after Germany surrendered, but in the meantime it had to base its strategy on scarcity, determining whether to direct the bulk of its number of warplanes against cities, or critical military and industrial targets, or both.[16]

Here the subcommittee faced significant unknowns. It did not know if the Pacific war would be ended through blockade and air attack or by an early invasion. The choice of strategy would make some targets more important than others, and the subcommittee would have to decide if the six major cities contained enough of the appropriate objectives to make them worth eliminating before other target systems were attacked. If, for instance, there was to be an invasion of Japan, was it better to bomb steel plants, tank factories, and artillery works, or to burn out Tokyo?[17]

In order to assess the military and economic value of destroying the cities, the subcommittee needed to estimate how burning out workshops in flammable areas would affect the flow of finished products. It did not know how many of these shops there were or where they were located. It could consult old maps and prewar insurance data, but it lacked adequate reconnaissance photos or other recent information. Presumably destroying residential districts would affect production in the usual ways—by killing and wounding workers, burning down their homes, forcing them to evacuate, and diverting them to relief and repair activities. Yet the Incendiary Subcommittee could not quantify these effects with any confidence. Large war factories generally were located outside the workers' housing areas. Fire storms, for which the workers' homes would serve as kindling, might spread to those factories and burn them down. But how many factories would be affected the subcommittee really did not know.[18]

In an effort to make intelligent surmises, its members analyzed data gathered at American testing grounds where the Standard Oil

Development Company and the Chemical Warfare Service had been using incendiaries on structures since 1942. Early in 1944 NDRC and the Army Air Forces board constructed a few small villages at Eglin Field, "little Tokyos" designed to represent Japanese buildings. They were supposed to enable experts to evaluate fire spread in groups of buildings and to estimate the most destructive ratio of high explosives to incendiary bombs.[19]

General Kuter and Colonel Joe L. Loutzenheiser reported to General Arnold about an experiment using M-69 jellied gasoline bombs against replicas of Japanese workers' homes. A B-17, flying at 10,000 feet, dropped three incendiary clusters, each containing thirty-eight bombs, on a simulated dwelling area of eighteen houses—six or seven individual units separated by wooden partitions. Fifteen incendiaries landed in the building area. Firefighters with modest equipment appeared, tried to extinguish the flames, then estimated the forces needed to put them out.

Several of the fires could not be controlled. An observer from the AAF Operational Plans Division and other witnesses concluded that the Japanese would be able to extinguish most incendiary fires if they could get to them in two minutes, but if the bombs landed between the ceiling and roof, say, where they could not be reached that quickly, only the most modern firefighting equipment could handle the blaze. After five minutes it would be difficult to limit the fire to one area. The AAF observer thought fragmentation bombs interspersed with incendiaries would keep firefighters away long enough to allow the flames to become uncontrollable and, with any appreciable wind, sweep an entire community, probably inflicting "tremendous casualties" on the inhabitants, at least 60 percent.[20]

To estimate how this kind of attack would affect production in the burned-out areas, the Office of Strategic Services did a series of studies based on prewar data. While it believed that about half of Japanese manufacturing employees worked in shops of five people or less—the kind of shops scattered through the flammable districts—it considered these enterprises relatively unproductive. It also stated that the proportion of workers in the small establishments varied greatly from city to city, ranging from about 50 percent in Hiroshima and three other cities to about 10 percent in Tokyo. But OSS believed the small workshops made parts for other war items and served as feeder plants for larger factories, and that destroying them would yield economic results out of proportion to what they produced directly.[21]

The subcommittee realized that this kind of statistical analysis and the studies of simulated firebombing might lead to erroneous conclusions. To make its investigation more realistic, it tried to learn what had happened to large cities in actual catastrophes, extracting ideas about fire spread and production loss from the results of bombing in Europe and from the history of Japanese earthquakes, particularly the earthquake and fire of 1923. Naval Air Intelligence prepared a study for the Incendiary Subcommittee of the effects of area bombing in Germany, drawing implications for Japan.[22]

In early September the subcommittee submitted its findings to the COA, then elaborated on them in a series of meetings with the full committee. It estimated that the fire raids would do far more damage in Japan than in Germany, where workers were less concentrated in urban centers and cities were not as flammable. An attack on the six major cities of Honshu would harm the Japanese economy substantially, destroy 70 percent of housing in the affected area, and kill more than a half million civilians. The raids would cost Japan 15 percent of its total manufacturing output and possibly an additional 5 percent for tank and truck parts and aircraft components. The attacks would do little immediately to reduce Japanese front-line military strength, since they would damage or destroy only a few of the highest-priority war plants, and other factories and existing stocks would replenish what was lost. Still, over the long run the military consequences would be substantial. For the greatest impact on the Japanese war economy, the subcommittee recommended that the AAF bomb the six cities in a short space of time with overwhelming force.[23]

Subcommittee members made no effort to conceal their uncertainty about crucial points. Colonel John F. Turner of A-2 explained that while the possibilities of successful incendiary attack had intrigued his group, many problems remained to be resolved. "The subcommittee considered an optimum result of complete chaos in six cities killing 584,000 people." If the raids were that successful, they might affect more than a fifth of Japanese output. Yet it was also possible, Turner acknowledged, that "our expectations will never be realized." There were so many intangibles. Turner wondered how the effects of bombing Tokyo would travel through the Japanese economy. "Would it prevent 15% of industry from going on if they do not have machine tools, if people who worked in the factories are dead? What effect would it have on the other 85%?" Another spokesman for the incendiary group, Lieutenant Charles Hitch of the OSS, explained that considerable doubt remained about vital data underlying the estimates: "We do not know how effective these available incendiary bombs are in starting fires in Japanese cities. It is possible the force requirements may be as estimated by us, or twice, or half."[24]

Hitch explained that the incendiary subcommittee had examined the vulnerability of 320 important plants to conflagrations, but that when they analyzed the data for Tokyo, they concluded that for one major industry, machine tools, only a fifth of the most important plants would be in the fire zones. For Japanese manufacturing as a whole there were still no data about smaller, medium-sized, and newer plants, including the shops in working-class residential areas, so the subcommittee had made an arbitrary guess as to where they were located with respect to the areas to be ignited. It would take two or three months to develop more accurate information about factory and workshop sites.[25]

Lieutenant Hitch felt reasonably confident about some things. He was sure that if the AAF carried out the attacks during a six-week period it would damage machine tool manufacturing severely. He thought the attacks could harm large industrial plants seriously, but only if the attacks produced fire storms that spread to nearby factories. He did not feel that information currently available allowed an accurate quantitative estimate of the effects of urban area bombing.[26]

Some of the most essential information seemed to defy precise measurement. Colonel William M. Burgess of A-2 observed that the Incendiary Subcommittee's whole presentation had been "from a mathematical precision point of view." Yet one of the largest factors to be considered, he told the COA, was the effect the fire raids would have "on leadership, on the ability of the Japanese people to be led into doing something. . . . Would bedlam be created?"[27]

Burgess had touched on the persistent question of whether morale bombing worked, the issue Colonels Hughes and Weicker and other air force planners had been debating as they weighed proposals for terror bombing in the European theater. Members of the COA and the Incendiary Subcommittee had some general ideas about this subject. Charles Hitch thought there was a relationship between morale and the ability to recuperate from attacks on industrial targets, since a spirited populace could nullify many of the economic effects of bombing by gathering materials and rebuilding.[28] Other experts believed that heavy morale attacks might cause wholesale administrative, psychological, and economic collapse, breaking the backbone of the enemy society. Fowler Hamilton told the committee that social disintegration and terror in the aftermath of fire raids might produce a "national catastrophe," though he regarded this as too speculative to influence planning. Still, the possibility intrigued the committee, which attempted to determine how bombing might affect Japanese morale.[29]

It called in Commander William M. McGovern of OSS, a political scientist, explorer, and war correspondent who had written about the Japanese and their language.[30] Lieutenant Hitch told him how the COA had been unable to come to grips with the psychological effects of fire raids and asked how far incendiary attacks could be expected to demoralize the Japanese and break down their administrative machine. Hitch explained that the committee was thinking about two alternatives: a series of light attacks spread over six months, or heavily concentrated bombing of the most congested sections of Japan's chief cities aimed at destroying every target area in the first few weeks.

McGovern told the committee he was "all in favor of Japanese area bombing," though not to the exclusion of precision attacks. He felt the AAF should "raise Hell" with Osaka and with Tokyo-Yokohama, which he described as the country's two psychological centers, more important to the Japanese than New York was to the Americans or Berlin to the Germans. "Knock out Tokyo," he declared, "and the Japanese throughout the country would say we have been hit."

The Japanese people, he explained, though extraordinarily brave, had a tendency to panic. "The panic side of the Japanese is amazing," he declared. "It is what I call internal panic." In 1931 he had witnessed Japanese troops advancing "magnificently" against machine-gun fire in Peking and dying "without hesitation." But the next day, when a sentry accidentally discharged his rifle, the same troops became hysterical.

Fire was a powerful incitement to panic in Japan. It was "one of the great things they are terrified at from childhood." McGovern described how he had been present several times when a real or imagined fire had broken out in a theater. People utterly lost their heads. He thought mass fire raids would panic the Japanese populace. The United States should warn them that it was going to attack Tokyo on a specific date, tell the inhabitants to leave, wait until they had cleared out and then begun to dribble back to their houses, then "raise Hell." After that it should start the whole procedure again.

Colonel Guido Perera asked McGovern if destroying Tokyo and Osaka would lead the Japanese army and navy to call for surrender. McGovern did not think this would occur during the first attacks, but by the second or third raid the Japanese would begin to panic, demand a revolutionary change in government, and call for a nationalist group of the extreme right. By the third major attack there would be a demand for surrender, though he doubted Japan would surrender unconditionally until Allied troops had landed on the home islands.

Proposals for Experimental Fire Raids

Expert testimony and weeks of analysis had still not answered all the important questions about incendiary attacks. To verify their hypotheses about what it took to set urban areas on fire and to estimate more precisely the effects of conflagrations on the Japanese war economy, expert consultants proposed that the air force launch "experimental" raids against cities in range of air force bases in China. American B-29 Superfortresses, very long-range bombers recently delivered to the Pacific theater, had already staged one test raid against Nagasaki on August 10; only twenty-four planes actually bombed the city, all but eight of them by radar. This effort had produced almost no significant information.[31]

Just before the B-29s took off for Nagasaki, fire expert Raymond Ewell sent the National Defense Research Council a proposal for massive test attacks against several cities—Nagasaki, Sasebo, Tobata-Wakamatsu, Kokura, and Yawata, all of them on the island of Kyushu. Ewell intended these raids solely as experiments in establishing conflagrations in large congested urban areas. Any damage to industrial or military targets would be incidental. For instance, Ewell described a section of Yawata he proposed to hit, south of a steel mill and the main railroad tracks, as "very densely populated and thickly covered with inflammable dwellings, including large areas of workers dormitories." An attack that burned this area would probably leave the steel works and other industrial plants north of the railroad untouched, Ewell observed, though it might seriously damage the railroad line itself.[32]

While the COA Incendiary Subcommittee agreed that there ought to be a realistic test of its area bombing theories and felt a single raid should be launched against a Kyushu city, it preferred to delay additional incendiary attacks until all the designated Honshu cities could be destroyed in rapid succession. It was vital, the subcommittee insisted, to learn as much as possible with a minimum of experimentation, so the enemy would not learn too well how to limit the effects of firebombing. The full committee accepted this view, including the idea of a single added test raid, from which it felt the Americans would learn more than the Japanese. In its final report, delivered October 11, 1944, the COA recommended that until the AAF was ready to obliterate the Honshu cities it should send its B-29s against vital precision targets like aircraft plants.[33]

Ewell disagreed with these priorities. Two days later the fire expert sent a memo to Vannevar Bush, head of the NDRC Office of Scientific Research and Development, recommending that the air force suspend plans for precision attacks on aircraft factories and start firebombing Tokyo, Osaka, Nagoya, Yokohama, Kobe, and Kawasaki.[34] By now Ewell had raised his estimate of the amount of incendiaries required, but it was still a mere 6,065 tons to destroy the six major urban centers and 3,000 additional tons to burn down the sixteen next most important cities. He claimed that these raids would damage the airplane industry more severely than would directing the same weight of bombs at airplane factories.

The fire expert offered several other reasons for launching incendiary raids as soon as possible. Besides destroying hundreds of large and thousands of small workshops and wrecking eight high-priority war industries and several lesser ones, the attacks would disrupt transportation and ruin storage facilities, make casualties of one out of ten workers, depress the will to go on with the war, cause general social disorder, and achieve the cumulative effect of a "major disaster." Bad weather, which he expected the AAF to encounter over Japan, would hinder precision bombing much more than area attacks. Area raids would destroy many of the precision targets, simplifying the tasks of flyers coming in later for selective bombing, and reduce the efficiency of plants that had not been damaged, making it harder for the Japanese to repair damage later inflicted by precision raids.

Ewell wanted the people in charge of the war—AAF Air Staff, the War Department, the General Staff, the secretaries of war and the navy, and the president—to recognize that incendiary bombing of Japanese cities could be "the key to accelerating the defeat of Japan, and if as successful as seems probable, . . . might shorten the war by some months and save many thousands of American lives." He recommended a series of actions. The air force should give top priority to determining the actual density of bombs needed for a successful fire raid. It should stage at least two carefully planned test raids in daylight, preferably with precision bombsighting and before-and-after photoreconnaissance, so that the extent of damage to housing, utilities, and industry, the ways fires had spread, and the possible magnitude of civilian casualties could be determined. A decision should be made at the highest level "re the humanitarian and political question." Then, if prospects looked good, the AAF should go "all out," dropping incendiaries on fifteen to thirty major Japanese cities until it had eliminated every important target that could be destroyed by fire. Afterwards precision bombers should hit the objectives that remained.

Bush sent Ewell's proposal to General Arnold, explaining that it represented the line of thought of some of "my group" in NDRC. Two of Dr. Ewell's ideas stood out in his own mind, he added: that it would be readily possible to test the plan with a moderate effort, and that "the decision on the humanitarian aspects will have to be made at a high level if it has not been done already."[35]

Without commenting on the "humanitarian aspects," Arnold forwarded Ewell's memo with Bush's remarks to the chief of staff of the Twentieth Air Force, General Lauris Norstad. He told him to note what Ewell had written and to have his staff study it. Norstad's aides sympathized with Ewell's approach but were not yet agreed that the time for an all-out incendiary offensive had arrived. The Twentieth Air Force did agree to launch more test raids. On November 29–30, B-29s based on the Marianas Islands attacked a section of Tokyo with incendiaries. Another experimental bombing followed a month later, against Nagoya. Both proved inconclusive. The questions still persisted of how to establish an uncontrollable fire in a large Japanese city and what the effects of urban area attack would be against the war effort of Japan.[36]

The Joint Target Group and Urban Area Bombing

These questions were taken up by the Joint Target Group, which assumed responsibility for advising the AAF on air strategy for Japan after the COA ceased operations. Established in the fall of 1944 in the Office of Air Staff, Intelligence, the JTG analyzed targets, set priorities for attacking them, prepared detailed information for other planning agencies, such as the Twentieth Air Force and the XXI Bomber Command, and investigated the results of air attacks. Like the Committee of Operations Analysts, it drew its members and advisors from several organizations: the Army Air Forces, the U.S. Navy, the Office of Strategic Services, the Foreign Economic Administration, the Office of Scientific Research and Development, Army Chemical Warfare Service, and the Royal Air Force. Several of its people simply moved over from the COA.

While the Joint Target Group took particular interest in the effects of bombing on factories, shipping, rail facilities, military storage depots, and airfields, it also tried to understand what had happened inside cities that Allied planes had struck in earlier raids. It asked the usual questions about area attacks: How many people lost their homes? How many buildings had bombing damaged or destroyed? How many casualties were there? What were the effects on public utilities? How effective had firefighting equipment been? Did air attack produce general administrative and social disorganization? The JTG looked into the impact of bombing on morale. It wanted to know if incendiary bombing could bring the Japanese people to a "breaking point," a state of mental paralysis which would stop them from fighting fires.[37]

Toward the end of November, Commander Francis Bitter of the JTG asked a Twentieth Air Force operations analyst, William J. Crozier, to investigate the breaking-point question. A professor of physiology at Harvard before the war, Crozier had no special knowledge about morale, but he spent a week in Cambridge, Massachusetts, talking with experts who might help him respond to Bitter's inquiry. He spoke to people who had lived in Japan and had studied Japanese behavior, and interviewed survivors of the London blitz. Naturally, he called on Professor Allport, but since the psychologist had only recently begun his study on the morale effects of bombing, he could offer little help. (Besides, Allport's respondents could not have contributed much anyway, since, as some of them admitted, they knew little about Japan or the Japanese people.) However, other Cambridge sources and published works gave Crozier enough information to make some generalizations.[38]

He concluded that if the AAF were to break Japanese morale with air strikes, it would have to employ new weapons and techniques on a vast scale, delivering heavy attacks continuously, concentrating them in time and space, staging the climactic raids at irregular intervals. To emphasize social cleavages, American planes should avoid hitting upper-class neighborhoods while destroying the homes of workers. Bombing could debilitate a population slowly, reducing the vigor of its civil defense, but widespread psychological breakdown was not likely to occur, and there really was no evidence that air raids could crack the morale of an urban populace. While extreme conflagrations might affect the Japanese profoundly, it would not be wise to assume they would panic or become immobilized.

This analysis was, of course, only one of several views about the effects of morale bombing. Commander McGovern of OSS saw the matter differently, and so did General Norstad of the Twentieth Air Force, one of the AAF generals who consulted with McGovern. Norstad believed that aerial attack directed at central institutions of Japanese society could shake the Japanese. He proposed to General Arnold, late in November 1944, that the AAF commemorate Pearl Harbor by launching a huge strike against the emperor's palace in Tokyo. He had discussed the idea with experts in Japanese psychology, who felt that even partial destruction of the palace would "directly attack the Emperor's position of the invulnerable deity."[39]

Norstad recognized that an operation of this kind entailed certain risks. Commander McGovern, who agreed strongly with the idea of striking at Japanese society by bombing the imperial palace, had warned Norstad that the Japanese might retaliate violently against U.S. prisoners, and Norstad himself expected "the grossest mistreatment and perhaps the death of . . . many of our prisoners of war," but he was willing to take that chance. However, since many of the POW victims would be men from the other services, he recommended that Arnold discuss his proposal with the chiefs of the army and navy.

Arnold considered Norstad's idea premature. "Not at this time," he wrote on Norstad's memo. "Our position—bombing factories, docks, etc. is sound. Later destroy the whole city."

By now some of Arnold's staff officers no longer wished to delay the incendiary offensive. While they realized it would take additional time to assemble enough B-29s to burn out the six major Honshu cities in one set of operations, they did not feel it was essential to wait until all six could be destroyed. In mid-January 1945 Major Philip G. Bower suggested that it would not even be necessary to collect all the planes needed to incinerate Tokyo in one raid before attacking the Japanese capital. Bower proposed to burn out a section at a time, with the B-29s flying back to their bases, reloading, and bombing again while Japanese firefighters struggled to control the flames spreading through areas already hit.[40]

LeMay Takes Command

The Joint Target Group disagreed with Bower. It preferred to continue concentrating forces on the Marianas Islands from which the raids would be launched. This was also the view of the field commander whose planes would have to deliver the attack, General Haywood S. Hansell, Jr., head of the XXI Bomber Command. Hansell wanted to eradicate the Japanese aircraft industry before burning down the cities. A founder of the selective bombing strategy, he still believed in it, though he was finding it extremely difficult to apply against Japan.

Serious problems continually hampered General Hansell's command. As Dr. Ewell had foreseen, weather conditions over Japan made precision bombing extremely difficult. An almost constant cloud cover interfered with reconnaissance and forced the airmen to bomb with inaccurate radar devices. Off the Japanese coast towering fronts, sometimes solid with clouds from 1,500 to 30,000 feet, stood between the designated assembly points and the targets. Since the B-29s might collide if they entered these clouds in large formations, they had to pass through one at a time, then assemble over land, well within range of Japanese interceptors. Winds at bombing altitude sometimes blew at over 200 knots, forcing the big planes to drift as much as forty-five degrees, though their bombsights could only correct for a thirty-five degree drift, and even fifteen degrees reduced their accuracy. If a Superfortress flew with the wind behind it, it would pass over the target at 500 to 600 miles an hour, much too fast for precision bombing. But if it turned into the wind its speed could drop to 125 miles an hour, making it an easy target. On December 13, 1944, during a raid on Nagoya, antiaircraft fire damaged thirty-one of a little more than seventy B-29s and probably hit four others that never returned. As the survivors approached their bases hours later with fuel tanks nearing empty, a tropical storm began, with sheets of rain, reducing visibility to zero and making landing impossible until it passed. Adding to these natural difficulties were the human problems of Hansell's new command: inexperienced flyers and crews trained for night radar bombing who had to learn the technique of precision daylight attack.[41]

The ineffectiveness of so many of Hansell's operations stretched General Arnold's patience and strengthened the position of those in AAF headquarters who wanted to start burning the Japanese cities at once. On December 18 General Norstad told

Hansell to go after Nagoya again, this time with a full-scale incendiary assault. Hansell protested. He was beginning to do real damage to the Japanese industry, he said, and pressure to divert his command from precision area raids threatened to undermine progress already made. Still, he ordered the raid as a daylight incendiary mission, although he made the target the Mitsubishi aircraft works rather than the flammable district. Only forty-eight planes bombed the plant and since clouds covered it, they had to use radar. They made no detectable impact on production.

Hansell sent Arnold long explanations of the problems that afflicted his command, but it did no good. General Curtis E. LeMay relieved him on January 20, 1945, and began to prepare the XXI Bomber Command for fire attacks on Japanese urban areas.[42]

For the next few weeks LeMay's airmen perfected their bombing techniques. While they continued precision assaults on industrial targets, particularly airplane factories and aircraft engine plants, they launched another series of experimental fire attacks. AAF planners had concluded that the earlier test raids had failed to set uncontrollable fires because the planes had scattered their incendiaries. They recommended bombing on specific aiming points, suggesting Kobe, Japan's sixth largest city, as the site for the next experiment. On February 4, sixty-nine Superfortresses dropped nearly 160 tons of incendiaries on the city's highly flammable residential areas and on adjacent factory and commercial districts, along with several tons of fragmentation bombs to discourage firefighting. Reconnaissance photographs showed severe damage to the industrial area. Two weeks later General Arnold moved urban area attacks up to second priority, behind aircraft engine plants, and specified particular cities for daylight test raids when engine factories could not be hit.[43]

A section of Tokyo was one of the test raid areas. On the afternoon of February 25, 172 B-29s dropped more than 453 tons of bombs onto the snow-covered capital, destroying 27,970 buildings, devastating about one square mile, setting whole districts on fire, causing the snow to fall black with ashes. The bombers returned March 4, diverted from the visual attack on Musashino-Tama. Robert Guillain, an interned French journalist, described how they unloaded their cargo through a snowfall:

> The raiders were probably above the clouds and operating on radar. Falling endlessly in the absolutely still afternoon air, the flakes smothered the throbbing of the B-29s in a plume of white, muffling the shrouded whine of the bombs. Suddenly, the slowly descending snow was lit up by a myste-

rious inner light—huge, invisible fires that I judged to be near my neighborhood. The half-light veiling the city gradually took on a luminous yellow tint
shot with a wondrous pink gold that pulsated weirdly, fading slowly, then
flaring anew. At last, in the total silence that returned at the end of the day,
everything bathed in a final rasberry-colored glow that flickered and
dwindled, disappearing in the snow-filled air behind a curtain of bluish
twilight.[44]

It was now clear to LeMay and the planners in Washington
that Hamburg-type fire storms could be started in the cities of
Japan. The question remained, how soon? It would take a heavy
density of firebombs to set up a holocaust. LeMay, pressed for
results by General Arnold, did not want to wait for good weather
and hundreds of additional planes to carry the required loads. He
decided to make more room for bombs by stripping his B-29s of
guns and ammunition and sending them over the targets at low
altitude. Since this would save the fuel ordinarily needed to reach a
bombing height of 25,000 or 30,000 more feet fully armed, it
enabled the planes to carry less gasoline and more bombs. By flying
underneath the tremendous jet stream winds, the bombers could
approach their objectives from any direction without excessive drift
and land their incendiaries, which the wind tended to scatter, closer
to the aiming points. Low-level attack would also place less strain
on the engines. That would reduce maintenance problems, keeping
more aircraft in service and more bombloads in the air.

LeMay realized that low-level bombing posed certain hazards.
In Europe it had sometimes proved tremendously expensive to the
attackers. But from reconnaissance photographs and information
acquired on test raids, he estimated that the enemy did not have the
right kind of searchlights and enough fast-moving, radar-controlled
twenty- and forty-millimeter anti-aircraft weapons to do U.S.
planes serious harm at low altitudes, especially if they flew singly
rather than in formation. Though LeMay's staff believed that
nearly three hundred fighters might rise to defend the capital, he
knew the Japanese had no really good night-fighting craft and he
expected to surprise the defenders. The probable results, as LeMay
calculated them, amply justified the risks.[45]

Not all the ideas behind this tactic originated with General
LeMay. Other officers had considered the advantages of using
heavy bombers at low altitude. General Spaatz had employed them
that way in the CLARION raids against the Germans. Dr. E. L.
Bowles, Secretary Stimson's scientific advisor, had recommended

stripping the B-29s and sending them with an extra-heavy load of bombs on night radar attacks. But LeMay and his staff put these ideas together, and it was he who gave the order for the most catastrophic fire raid of the Second World War, the attack on Tokyo of March 10, 1945.[46]

7

The Bombing of Japan: From Tokyo to Nagasaki

Just after sunset on the 9th of March, 1945, fifty-four graceful silver-colored B-29s of the XXI Bomber Command's 314th wing began taking off from the American air base on Guam. Led by General Thomas S. Power, the very long-range bombers, three stories high and almost 100 feet long with wing spans of slightly more than 141 feet, climbed to altitudes of a thousand to five thousand feet above the water and headed toward Tokyo, 1,650 miles away. About three-quarters of an hour later the 73rd and 313th wings, closer to the target, started down the runways on Saipan and Tinian. The mission of these planes was to reduce the enemy capital's most congested residential areas, nearby factories, and transportation centers to rubble and ashes.[1]

Some time after the bombers had left, General LeMay discussed his hopes for the raid with St. Clair McKelway, press censor and public information officer for the XXI Bomber Command and a writer for the *New Yorker*. LeMay wanted Tokyo "burned down—wiped right off the map," every industrial target in the area destroyed and the city devitalized. "If this raid works the way I think it will," he said, "we can shorten the war." McKelway agreed. "LeMay and his people," he told the *New Yorker*'s readers, "are shortening the war." The "mass effect of LeMay and all of his people," he declared, "all those men on the islands of Guam and Tinian and Saipan, working for a high and common purpose, with leadership based on brains and goodness and faith in human endeavor, was something nearly tangible, something you felt all around you and inside you when you woke up after a few hours' sleep, those tense days and nights."[2]

Destroying Japan's Cities with Conventional Bombing

Despite all the earlier raids on Japan, the inhabitants of Tokyo were remarkably unprepared to defend themselves against the armada that approached them. To protect one of the world's largest and most flammable cities Tokyo had fewer than 8,100 professional firefighters and about the same number of auxiliaries. It had very little modern equipment—just three aerial ladders, for instance, only one of them working. The government expected ordinary citizens, in neighborhood groups of about ten families apiece, to form most of the resistance to American fire-making technology.[3]

The neighborhood groups had been fighting fires and natural disasters for decades. During the war, they supervised blackouts and saw to it that each household had prescribed equipment for extinguishing incendiary fires: shovels, grappling hooks, buckets or small paper bags of sand, straw mats or brooms to be soaked in water and used to beat out flames, hand pumps that sent out a jet of water the thickness of a finger, cisterns and buckets to be carried in chains by the women, elderly men, and girls who served as local firefighters. Depending more on morale than on physical resources, group members took an "air defense oath of certain victory." They pledged to follow orders and cooperate in air defense, and to "refrain from selfish conduct."[4]

Government officials had tried to limit the threat of fire spread by ordering construction of firebreaks, sections 45 to 110 yards wide cut through flammable areas with regularly spaced observation posts and reservoirs placed 80 to 100 yards apart. In the summer of 1942, after General James Doolittle's fliers dropped the first American bombs on Japan's cities, people living in places designated for firebreaks were told to evacuate their homes. Then troops appeared, lined up for miles. Accompanied by schoolboys and older students, they smashed buildings with battering rams, chopped them down with axes, and pulled them apart with ropes. Neighborhood associations carried away the rubble, though in some places piles of wood still remained when the B-29s appeared.[5]

Most of Tokyo's inhabitants depended on small, primitive air raid shelters. The government wanted people to stay in their neighborhoods during air attacks so they could rush out and extinguish fires before they spread. Early in the war it had told residents to build dugouts under their houses or, if necessary, to take cover in closets, but in September 1943, on official command, citizens began constructing outdoor shelters in gardens, empty lots, streets and

sidewalks. Wearing iron helmets, chanting rhythmically, they exca-
vated trenches in varying shapes, some six feet square, others
about six to sixteen feet long, three feet wide, and a foot and a half
to six feet deep. Housewives tried them out, squatting with their
knees against their collarbones. The inhabitants planted flowers
around the excavations. Later they used bamboo, one-inch boards,
or corrugated sheet metal from the firebreak areas to reinforce the
trenches and constructed flimsy roofs which they covered with a
foot or two of earth; these shelters contained no food supplies or
sanitary facilities and they tended to fill with rainwater.

There were also some spartan community shelters, dug twenty
to thirty feet underground in hillsides or under elevated park areas
a considerable distance from residential zones. Eighteen private
concrete shelters with ventilation, electricity, seating and sanitary
facilities, and a capacity of less than 5,000 were reserved for old
people, children, and the sick. A few basements in Western-style
buildings, which had been built to resist earthquakes, contained
shelter areas. Since the buildings were in the commercial districts
they provided little protection against nighttime bombing.[6]

In October 1943 the Japanese cabinet decided to evacuate
urban dwellers who did not work in war plants. Official suggestions
failed to get them to move, so the authorities tried to frighten them
into leaving by showing propaganda films like *Evacuation*, which
depicted neighborhoods on fire. A large number of schoolchildren
went to live with relatives in the country. Then in August 1944, as
the Americans approached within bombing range, having captured
the Marianas, several hundred thousand more children left on
government orders, moving into resorts, meeting halls, inns, and
temples in the outlying districts. By March 1945 over 1.7 million
people had evacuated Tokyo. This left about 5 million in the capital
a few minutes past midnight on the 10th when General LeMay's
bombers arrived.[7]

Radar stations about 600 miles away in the Bonin Islands
detected the B-29s. Following customary procedure, the first warning sounded when the planes were approximately one hour's flight
from the city. Observers thought they were turning out to sea.
Instead, navigating by radar and making visual corrections, 279
bombers proceeded toward the darkened capital, spread out before
them under a clear sky.[8]

The B-29s were expected to bomb an area shaped like a crude
rectangle, three miles east to west and almost four miles north to
south. The lakes and gardens of the imperial palace grounds

marked the outside of the southwest corner and the northwest boundary fell at the southern edge of Ueno Park. From there the perimeter ran eastward along the Joban railroad to the Sumida River, then southeast to a north-south line roughly paralleling the river as it meandered through the Tokyo flatlands. From the Sumida's Y-shaped mouth the boundary ran due west, then turned south to the Tokyo railroad station. The southeast segment, near the river mouth, was largely industrial. A commercial district, with shops, large stores, and warehouses, bordered the western edge of the target zone. According to a target information sheet supplied to AAF officers before the raid, most of the bombing zone was residential, with flimsy housing and an average density of 103,000 people per square mile, a figure which the sheet described as probably unsurpassed in any other modern industrial city. It estimated the population density of Asakusa ward near the center of the target zone at about 135,000 per square mile.[9]

At the head of each squadron moving toward the target area, one wing of bombers carried M-47 incendiaries, each containing enough napalm to generate 600,000 British thermal units and produce a blaze that could tie up an entire fire engine company. The M-47s were to mark out patterns of equal size, enabling the planes that followed to distribute their bombs evenly, covering all sectors with more than sixty tons per square mile. Air force analysts had calculated that this density would produce an uncontrollable conflagration.[10]

A few minutes after midnight, Tokyo time, the lead Superfortresses began to drop their marking bombs using precision bombsights. Planes following behind them circled and crisscrossed the target zone individually. Flying at altitudes of 4,900 to 9,200 feet, they unloaded clusters of M-69s which created giant rings of fire. The remaining bombers filled the rings with showers of incendiaries.[11]

During the raid General Power flew back and forth for nearly two hours taking photographs of the city, which changed beneath him to a sea of flame. "True there is no room for emotions in war," he later wrote. "But the destruction I witnessed that night over Tokyo was so overwhelming that it left a tremendous and lasting impression on me."[12]

As the fire grew, rising thermal currents bounced the huge bombers like paper airplanes. Rising smoke lowered visibility to zero, forcing the later planes to bomb blind. Finally, at approximately 3:45 A.M., the last B-29s completed their runs and roared out toward the Pacific. People on departing bombers eighty-five miles away could still see smoke and fire. Planes from the later waves smelled like the insides of burned buildings. Their fuselages were coated with soot.[13]

When the 314th Wing returned to Guam, General LeMay was there to greet it with General Norstad at his side. LeMay told his flyers that if they had shortened the war by "only one day or one hour," they had "served a high purpose." Hap Arnold wired him, "Congratulations. This mission shows your crews have got the guts for anything."[14]

Altogether, LeMay's command had dropped 1,665 tons of bombs on Tokyo. An estimated seventy-four Japanese fighters had attacked the B-29s without bringing down a single bomber, though intense anti-aircraft fire had brought down two planes and damaged forty-two before the spreading web of flames extinguished the gun batteries. Reconnaissance photographs disclosed that the firebombs had incinerated 15.8 square miles of the city, much of it east of the target zone in the flatlands beyond the Sumida River. They had burned out 18 percent of the industrial area, 63 percent of the commerical district, and the entire working-class residential zone, consuming 250,000 buildings. The United States Strategic Bombing Survey estimated that 87,793 people died in the March 10 raid, 40,918 suffered injuries, and 1,008,005 lost their housing. These were very rough estimates. General Power later called the Tokyo raid "the greatest single disaster incurred by any enemy in military history. . . . There were more casualties than in any other military action in the history of the world."[15]

Numbers are not much help in describing what happened in the Japanese capital. To grasp the effects of the March 10 bombing raid one has to view it from the vantage point of people on the ground.

For some of the inhabitants the first sign of the raid was the low-pitched throbbing of hundreds of engines as the B-29s moved over the city. Flying in and out of searchlights and through anti-aircraft fire, the planes unleashed clusters of incendiaries that seemed to drop slowly, in silvery cascades. The incendiaries made rattling and crashing sounds. When they landed napalm spurted out of their cases. There was a smell of gasoline, then yellow, white, and red flames appeared everywhere. Within fifteen minutes the cold night turned intensely hot, and as the bombs implanted themselves residents began to hear crackling like that of a bonfire and the thud of falling roofs and walls.[16]

In a hilly section of the city, miles away from the targeted districts, people peering out of their shelters toward the flatlands uttered cries of admiration as they watched lights like Christmas decorations flashing under the incandescent smoke, B-29s like shiny winged fish glinting with reflections from below, and bomb blasts that resembled flaming strands of hair or long shreds of tinsel. Then less than thirty minutes from the start of the raid they saw the flames lit by the bombers and driven by the wind coalesce into a mass of fire.[17]

The morning before, in a first sign of spring, a breeze had started to blow across Tokyo. It rose during the day and became gusty, sometimes violent. When the American planes began to drop their incendiaries, the wind whipped the fires they set, driving flames down alleys and through buildings, forcing them across streets and firebreaks, creating huge vortices of swirling, glowing gases that flattened and devoured whole blocks. Tongues of fire like solar flares leaped into a sky filled with clouds of burning paper and wood. Flaming planks soared overhead. Above the target area a towering wall of fire appeared and began to move across the lowlands of the city, preceded by a turbid mass of heated vapors.[18]

The neighborhood firefighting system crumbled as groups of homeowners, after brief attempts to oppose the inferno, began to break and flee. The Tokyo Fire Department found itself unable to deploy its own forces in an orderly way. The holocaust attacked the firemen. It burned their equipment, destroying 95 engines, 150 hand-drawn, gasoline-driven pumps, and 65,000 feet of hose. It swept through fire stations and killed a hundred professional firefighters and hundreds of their auxiliaries. Eight months later scorched fire equipment still remained in one station where the firemen had died attempting to move it out.[19]

An hour and a half after the beginning of the raid the Tokyo fire chief left his headquarters to investigate the situation in person. When he arrived at the Kanda district, flames were creeping along the ground and bits of the tin sheeting from roofs were flying through the air like snowflakes. His car caught fire but he was able to have the flames extinguished and drove on to Ueno and then to Honjo, where it reignited. At the Shitaya fire station the wind almost knocked him over. At Asakusa, the roof of the fire station was in flames. By the time he reached the station house at Hoza it had burned down completely. Near Tokyo Bay, at Fukagawa, corpses littered the road for over a mile and he had to wait until it was cleared before proceeding. When he entered the Ryogaku district he found everything destroyed except for a few homes near the fire station.[20]

By now crowds of people, some of them screaming, were plunging through the city. The fire storm quickly roasted those who stayed in under-house shelters. Alleys and small gardens filled with flaming debris. Shifting flames blocked exit routes. Abandoning their efforts to check the inferno, firemen tried to channel people across already burned areas, and where there was still water pressure they drenched people so they could pass through the fire. Some inhabitants ducked themselves in firefighting cisterns before moving. A messenger boy for the Domei news service ran around blindly until he found a small firefighting reservoir; he survived by immersing himself in it all night.

Choking inhabitants crawled across fallen telephone poles and trolley wires. As superheated air burned their lungs and ignited their clothing, some burst into flames, fire sweeping up from the bottoms of trousers or starting in the cloth hoods worn for protection against sparks. Residents hurried from burning areas with possessions bundled on their backs, unaware that the bundles had ignited. Some women who carried infants this way realized only when they stopped to rest that their babies were on fire.

Thousands fled toward parks, crossroads, gardens, and other supposedly safe areas, but safety was often an illusion. After one group stopped in an open space and deposited their bundles in a pile, the bundles suddenly caught fire, igniting the people around them. Crowds packed into untouched, substantial-looking schools and theaters which burned, trapping those inside. Others headed toward water, to the canals dug through the Tokyo flatlands, to the Sumida, and to the frigid waters of Tokyo Bay. A woman spent the night knee-deep in the bay, holding onto a piling with her three-year-old son clinging to her back; by morning several of the people around her were dead of burns, shock, fatigue, and hypothermia. Thousands submerged themselves in stagnant, foul-smelling canals with their mouths just above the surface, but many died from smoke inhalation, anoxia, or carbon monoxide poisoning, or were submerged by masses of people who tumbled in on top of them, or boiled to death when the fire storm heated the water. Others, huddling in canals connected to the Sumida River, drowned when the tide came in. In the Honjo and Asakusa districts people jammed onto steel bridges. As the metal became unbearably hot, those who clung to the rails started to let go, falling off in waves, and were carried away by the waters below. Huge crowds lined the gardens and parks along the Sumida, and as the masses behind them pushed toward the river, walls of screaming people fell in and vanished.[21]

Before dawn Dr. Kuboto Shigenori, who headed a military rescue unit, drove to the Ryogoku Bridge. "In the black Sumida River," he recalled, "countless bodies were floating, clothed bodies, naked bodies, all as black as charcoal. It was unreal. These were dead people, but you couldn't tell whether they were men or women. You couldn't even tell if the objects floating by were arms and legs or pieces of burnt wood."[22]

At about 5:00 A.M. the all-clear sounded, but for twelve hours the city continued to burn. Coal piles, some fire-resistant buildings, and areas outside the conflagration smoldered for days. Government agencies dispatched officials to survey the damage. An official of the Home Affairs Ministry Police Bureau later told American investigators, "We were instructed to report on actual conditions. Most of us were unable to do this because of horrifying conditions beyond imagination. . . . After a raid I was supposed to investigate, but I didn't go because I did not like to see the terrible sights [laughing]."[23]

Corpses, scattered or in heaps, lay in streets, vacant lots, public shelters, and the spaces under railroad viaducts. Many were huddled together, apparently for mutual protection. While several bodies showed signs of agony or of a struggle to escape, unburned occupants of the more secure shelters appeared to have died peaceably from carbon monoxide poisoning. Elsewhere, remains of the dead looked like irregular pieces of charcoal, or consisted only of skeletons with here and there some charred bits of soft tissue and clothing. Most of those who had died in the shelters beneath houses or in the midst of burned buildings were unrecognizable. Some people had turned into ashes that scattered like sand in a light wind.[24]

Soldiers and civilian volunteers removed the dead. While official plans called for identification by relatives or authorities, followed by cremation or burial in individual graves, the scale of the disaster made this unfeasible. Bodies were carted to temples and parks, identified if possible, then cremated without delay or, in the case of very charred corpses, placed in mass graves with the intent of exhuming them later for a more orderly burial. Of these, only sixty-four were claimed by families. Sixty-nine thousand one hundred remained unidentified and were buried in temporary plots in groups of twenty or more. For over two weeks traces of a sickly-sweet odor lingered in parts of the city where corpses remained tangled in the ruins.[25]

During the day that followed the raid, dirty, worn-looking survivors wandered through the smoldering landscape. The fire had covered a much larger area than the target zone, for the wind had blown it far to the east of the Sumida. Parts of the city showed no signs of life at all. Of the automobiles that had been parked in the streets the night before only shells remained, along with the skeletons of streetcars and buses, fallen wires, and twisted steel poles. Homes and factories were reduced to bits of corrugated metal, piles of bricks or concrete blocks, and ashes. Even modern fire-resistant buildings had turned into hulks of concrete and warped steel. The raid, which had destroyed 449 first aid stations, left surviving medical facilities overwhelmed. There was no gas, water, electric power, or public transportation for days, partly because demoralized public authorities could not bring themselves to rebuild services for neighborhoods that no longer existed.[26]

The government provided twenty-nine trains—not nearly enough—to remove refugees to the mountains, giving preference to the aged, the disabled, the sick, expectant mothers, children, and workers in the building trades. Thousands headed out by road, loading kitchen utensils, bedding, and other belongings on bicycles, tricycles, oxcarts, horsecarts, and truck beds. Small babies and exhausted women sat or lay on top of the piles, while the larger children and most of the adults pushed or walked alongside. By August some 2,807,000 had left.[27]

Back in the fall of 1944, when the Joint Target Group was planning the firebombing raids, Professor Crozier had suggested that the air force could intensify class hostility if it destroyed slum areas while leaving wealthier districts intact. This may have occurred to some extent. One group of tough slum residents, evacuated from their burned-out homes to a wealthy residential area, began to loot the neighborhood. But sympathy, cooperation, and stoic acceptance of new burdens were much more common. People in the unbombed parts of the city and in nearby prefectures opened schools, temples, and theaters to feed and shelter the homeless. Several communities allowed them free use of bathhouses. Bankers raised relief funds. The Hokkaido-Aomorai area sent Tokyo forty carloads of fresh and canned fish. The government distributed food. Temporarily, rules requiring people to document their need for relief were ignored.[28]

The March 10 fire raid helped drive home to the Japanese the vulnerability of their cities. Together with other recent military disasters, like the fall of Saipan, it depressed people badly. Yet dispiriting as it was to those directly affected by it, it did not bring the morale of the Japanese civilian population to a "breaking point." This was not altogether unexpected. American experts like Commander McGovern had imagined it would take more than a single raid.[29]

During the next months the B-29s came back to Tokyo, systematically destroying undamaged areas. On April 13 and 15 they dropped thousands of tons of incendiaries on the northern sections of the city and in areas along Tokyo Bay. On the nights of May 23–24 and again on the 25th–26th they struck the center and western sections. During the last of these raids the wind was blowing hard again and the resulting fire storm burned the homes of about 570,000 people. Altogether American bombers gutted 56.3 square miles of Tokyo, a little more than half the city. Meanwhile they attacked other large Honshu cities—Nagoya, Osaka, Kobe and Yokohama—sending weary air crews day after day to saturate the most flammable areas with firebombs. Casualties were much smaller in these raids than in the March 10 conflagration because so many people had evacuated to the countryside.[30]

When it analyzed the effects of the Honshu urban area raids the Joint Target Group found evidence that both supported and modified the theories of area bombing advocates. Fire attacks on the cities had badly damaged Japan's overall economy. They were reducing the ability of its military forces to resist an invasion of the home islands. But the tinderbox theory—that firebombing residential districts would ignite industrial concentrations—had generally proved incorrect. The most flammable zones did not contain the most important war plants. Some of the workshops and factories that were destroyed could not have contributed to the Japanese military effort in any case, since American attacks on transportation had shut off their supplies and made it impossible to ship what they produced. While area raids set back production for a while, they could not interfere quickly and decisively with Japan's ability to fight—which meant that despite all the damage the fire raids had done, Allied troops could anticipate severe casualties if they landed on the Japanese main islands.

The Joint Target Group felt the AAF should concentrate more on direct attacks against industrial sites and less on attempts to disrupt production indirectly by burning out workers' housing. It recommended, and the air force pursued, a policy similar to the Combined Bomber Offensive in Europe: complementary attacks on factories and urban areas which, along with destruction of Japanese shipping and internal transportation, would soften the enemy for invasion.[31]

But would an invasion be necessary? Leading air force officers thought not. They were convinced that bombing alone would finish the war. General LeMay wrote General Norstad that the evolution of the air war against Japan had presented the AAF for the first time with "the opportunity of proving the power of the strategic air arm." LeMay was sure that if he pushed his command to its limits, within six months he could destroy Japan's capacity for war.[32]

But there was also the matter of will to fight, which air force doctrine had long maintained must be destroyed along with the ability to make war. Recent battles in the Pacific, where Japanese troops committed suicide rather than give up and Japanese kamikaze pilots crashed their planes into American vessels, suggested it would not be easy to make their nation surrender. Still, LeMay and his colleagues felt air power could do it. General Norstad, who thought bombing had damaged German morale gravely and that the success of the fire raids on Japan had been "nothing short of wonderful," told LeMay in April that if the AAF destroyed the next group of targeted areas within a reasonable time, "we can only guess what the effect will be on the Japanese. Certainly their warmaking ability will have been curtailed. Possibly they may lose their taste for more war." More than any other branch or service, he told LeMay, the XXI Bomber Command was in a position to strike a decisive blow.[33]

Norstad's deputy for combat operations, Colonel Cecil E. Combs, agreed, and he sent General Norstad a plan for using the very long-range bombers to finish the war. Combs granted that there was no way to perform a statistical evaluation of the effects of the firebombing on Japanese morale. Yet he believed incendiary attacks alone might break their will to fight. With Germany on the verge of collapse, Allied land forces approaching through the Philippines, and the Soviet Union poised to attack from the north, the threat of further air attacks might cause the people of Japan and their leaders to see the futility of resistance. For instance, Japanese manufacturers, realizing that further destruction of their plants threatened the industrial basis of their nation's postwar power, might induce government leaders to sue for peace. Combs recommended that the AAF undertake a new series of very large-scale incendiary attacks on the most vulnerable sections of remaining key industrial areas. The aim of these raids would be chiefly psychological: to "affect directly the largest number of Japanese people . . . in the shortest period of time." Their "secondary purpose" would be to eradicate Japan's industrial system.[34]

Leaders of the other branches were less sanguine than Colonel Combs and the air force generals. General Marshall did not believe conventional air attacks, even combined with sea blockade, would end the war in an acceptable amount of time. He insisted that there would have to be an invasion. Officially the other Joint Chiefs agreed with him—though Hap Arnold and Admirals Leahy and King privately disputed his view. General MacArthur, who would command the Allied army on the plain of Tokyo, was confident that with or without a bombing offensive he would still have to land on the shores of Honshu Island.[35]

The directors of the United States Strategic Bombing Survey doubted that urban area bombing could end the war. While they eventually concluded that the right kind of conventional bombing would have forced Japan to surrender without an invasion by November 1945, they felt that the kind of attacks Combs and other AAF officers advocated would neither break Japanese morale nor administer a conclusive blow to the Japanese economy.

After spending several months analyzing the effects of strategic bombing in Europe, Strategic Bombing Survey leaders, including Paul Nitze, George Ball, General Orvil Anderson, and Henry Alexander, were called to Washington. At a series of meetings in June and July they told the secretaries of war and the navy, the chief of staff, General Norstad, and the Joint Target Group how what had been learned in Germany might be applied to Japan. Area bombing was far down their list of priorities. They thought the AAF should concentrate on destroying Japanese land and water transportation. They placed considerably less emphasis on all the remaining target systems, including ammunition reserves, coke- and gasoline-producing plants, and factories that produced certain types of military equipment. Survey directors were not trying to be easy on Japanese civilians. They recommended a program to starve them. They proposed to reduce their food supply through blockade, to deprive them of fertilizer by blowing up their nitrogen plants, and to destroy their rice crop with the chemical defoliant TN-8. But they believed the air force should attack urban industrial areas only when that seemed more likely than precision raids to destroy specific targets, a situation they doubted would occur very often.[36]

Using the argument Colonel Hughes, General Cabell, and other USSTAF officers had presented a year and a half earlier, the Strategic Bombing Survey directors challenged the view that the air force could end the war by breaking Japanese morale. George Ball and Henry Alexander told the Joint Target Group that even if air raids depressed the morale of German industrial workers, Nazi leaders were still able to force them to produce. "Whatever the state of mind may have been," Alexander observed, "their behavior was not such as to seriously affect the rates of production." General Anderson, the AAF representative on the bombing survey, told of evidence that air raids had made Russian, French, and Polish workers in German factories more productive by leading them to join in "as a common herd against a common enemy."

General Norstad found Anderson's remarks "astonishing." He would have expected productivity to decrease greatly, not rise. But he did not think that area attacks should stop, and neither did the Joint Target Group. It reported to the War Department that although it agreed with Strategic Bombing Survey experts that transportation ought to have top priority, it placed much higher value than the survey leaders did on incendiary attacks against military products, flammable raw materials, and workers' housing. These were among the targets U.S. warplanes continued to attack.[37]

Throughout the summer of 1945 American air forces, joined by navy aircraft, devastated Japan. Warplanes of the XXI Bomber Command, the Fifth and Seventh Air Forces, and the VII Fighter Command attacked naval and military installations, economic targets, and towns of all sizes throughout the Japanese home islands. As one of its staff officers explained, the object of the Twentieth Air Force was to lay waste the main Japanese cities "with the prime purpose of not leaving one stone lying on another."[38]

That was the immediate object. The longer-term purpose of American strategic bombing in the Pacific was changing, just as it had changed in Germany. Having eliminated most targets of military and economic significance, the AAF moved increasingly into political and psychological warfare. In May 1945 the Combined Chiefs of Staff adopted a program for creating doubt, confusion, hopelessness, and defeatism among both civilians and military personnel in Japan and for alienating the citizens from their government. In support of this plan General LeMay inaugurated a series of morale bombing attacks, describing them as "a powerful psychological weapon" which could be used to convince the Japanese and "certain articulate minority groups" in the United States that the air

force policy was attempting to destroy Japan's war-making industry, not the people of Japan.[39]

The campaign began July 27, when American aircraft dropped
60,000 leaflets on each of eleven cities warning the Japanese that an
unspecified number of those cities were about to be destroyed. The
next day 471 superfortresses firebombed six of them. Twelve cities
were warned on the 31st and on August 1 four were bombed by
627 B-29s. Three days later a third group of towns received the
message and the XXI Bomber Command saturated four of them
with incendiaries the following night.

These attacks exemplified the approach that people like Lowell
Weicker and Commander McGovern had long advocated, and that
the air force had conducted in Germany six months earlier; only
now American planes carried even greater firepower and their
commanders no longer had to take enemy resistance seriously.
Some of the Japanese towns LeMay's B-29s obliterated were as
devoid of military significance as certain targets of Operation CLAR-
ION had been. Some were important only as transportation centers,
though earlier raids had shown that incendiaries had little effect on
transport. Still, the July and August missions provided some support for the views of morale bombing advocates. Especially among
people whose morale was already low, the bombing missions emphasized how helpless Japan was to resist air attack. They proved to
the Japanese that the Americans would do what they said they
would, and according to Japanese citizens interviewed after the war,
they produced amazement, defeatism, and, above all, terror. The
target, as an American air commander observed, had become "the
Japanese mind."[40]

Several of the leaflets used in this operation were printed on
blue paper, six inches by eight inches. On one side they showed the
characters for twelve Japanese cities inside of twelve small circles
and a photograph of B-29s dropping firebombs. On the reverse,
under the heading "Appeal to the People," they asked their mostly
female recipients,

> Do you wish to save the lives of your parents, brothers and friends? If you
> do, read this leaflet very carefully. Within a few days military establish-
> ments in the cities mentioned on the back of this sheet will be bombed by
> the American Air Forces. In those cities there are military establishments
> and arms factories. The American Air Forces must destroy all armaments
> that the Japanese militarists are using in order to prolong a war that has no
> chance for victory for Japan. However, bombs have no eyes, and there is no
> knowing where they may fall. As you know, America, which stands for

humanity, does not wish to injure the innocent people, so you had better evacuate these cities.

You are not the enemy of America. Our enemy is the Japanese militarist who has dragged you into the war. We believe that peace will make you free from the oppression of the militarists, and a better Japan will then be born anew.[41]

At about the time General LeMay began to direct this combination of propaganda and vast yet controlled violence at the Japanese public, the Fifth Air Force issued a message to its flyers calling for violence without restraint. In its *Weekly Intelligence Review* Colonel Harry F. Cunningham complained about people who said it was "wicked and inhuman—therefore un-American" to bomb Japanese civilians. The war, Cunningham asserted, was exclusively the province of the military, except insofar as results were concerned, and the methods it used to secure the national interest were no business of either the critics or of the public in general. To prove how misguided these "professional pious persons" were, Colonel Cunningham noted that the Japanese government had ordered all men, women, and children into a Volunteer Defense Corps. As a result, whether they liked it or not they were no longer civilians but members of their country's armed forces, commanded to bear arms against Americans. The entire population of Japan was therefore "a proper military target."

We military men [Cunningham concluded] do not pull punches or put on Sunday School picnics. We are making War and making it in the all-out fashion which saves American lives, shortens the agony which War is and seeks to bring about an enduring Peace. We intend to seek out and destroy the enemy wherever he or she is, in the greatest possible numbers, in the shortest possible time. For us, THERE ARE NO CIVILIANS IN JAPAN.[42]

The AAF and Atomic Warfare

The nuclear bomb raids of August 1945 are of course the most famous American area bombing attacks. The air force had played only a minor part in the nuclear program until the spring of 1944, when General Leslie A. Groves, director of the Manhattan Engineer District,* gave General Arnold the responsibility for modifying B-29s to carry atomic weapons, for testing the ballistic qualities

---

*This organization ran the U.S. atomic bomb program, and was generally referred to as the Manhattan Project.

of proposed nuclear bombs, and for training a special organization to deliver them. This was the 509th Composite Group, a self-contained unit within the Twentieth Air Force. The AAF also helped choose targets for nuclear attack. General Norstad consulted with Groves about criteria for the objectives. Civilian air force advisors sat with Manhattan Project scientists and representatives from Groves's office on a target selection committee that advised the secretary of war.[43]

The criteria the committee proposed guaranteed that the bombs would be dropped on cities. Targets were to be important militarily and were to include troop concentrations or centers of military production. Any small or strictly military objective had to lie within a much larger area susceptible to destruction by bombing. Yet the city that contained it must be relatively free from conventional bombing damage and susceptible to destruction by an A-bomb. This would assure that the new weapon's effects could be measured. Psychological and political factors were extremely important. The first atomic explosion would have to deliver a tremendous psychic shock to the Japanese and be sufficiently spectacular for the importance of the weapon to be recognized internationally.[44]

Secretary of War Henry Stimson agreed with the thrust of these recommendations, as did his Interim Committee, a group of military and scientific advisors, officials of the State and Navy Departments, and Stimson's personal assistants that examined questions of nuclear policy. In order to make as profound an impression as possible, Stimson and the Interim Committee members felt there should be no warning. And though they thought the air force should not concentrate specifically on a civilian target, they agreed that the most desirable objective would be a vital war plant, employing a large number of workers and closely surrounded by workers' homes.[45]

The Saving of Kyoto

The target selection panel recommended as its first choices, for nuclear bombing the cities of Kyoto, Hiroshima, Yokohama, and an arsenal in the city of Kokura. General Arnold particularly favored Kokura, situated at the north end of Kyushu, because a tunnel connected it to the island of Honshu and Arnold was anxious to see what effect the bomb would have on the tunnel—whether the tunnel would fill up with water, how badly it would leak, and whether any of the bomb's effects would travel through to the northern entrance. Later, Niigata and Nagasaki were added to the target list and Yokohama and Kyoto struck off.[46]

A remarkable series of circumstances combined to save Kyoto, the ancient capital of Japan. A religious and cultural center with exquisite palaces and gardens and great art treasures, Kyoto was the site of numerous colleges and universities, temples, monasteries, and shrines. Its workshops, which in peacetime produced fine embroidery, porcelain, enamelware, bronzes, brocades, and fans, had turned to war production. With a population that had grown to over 800,000, it was one of the largest urban centers on Honshu. Nevertheless, the AAF did not attack it in the first series of fire raids. To achieve the proper concentration of incendiaries for a fire storm the XXI Bomber Command had to send its planes to the targets of highest importance, and Kyoto's contribution to the Japanese war effort was not large enough at that point to win it a place on the target list.[47]

This consideration would not have saved the old capital indefinitely, for after LeMay's forces replenished their incendiaries and added more very long-range bombers they devastated places with far less military and industrial significance. War industries from the burned-out cities began to relocate in Kyoto's outskirts, and it became a promising target for morale bombing. On April 10, 1945, Colonel Combs told General Norstad it should be considered for incendiary attack "if large numbers of people from the burned-out areas migrate to Kyoto," which is exactly what happened. Thousands of refugees migrated there, encouraged by a rumor that the United States had not bombed the city because it contained the grave of General Douglas MacArthur's mother.[48]

From a technical point of view Kyoto was the perfect target for fire attack. It spread across a saucer-shaped area, and though it contained the usual firebreaks and had thoroughfares larger than those of most Japanese cities, the buildings in its core were old and constructed of wood and paper, with roofs covering a large percentage of the built-up area. Standard incendiary techniques could have destroyed it easily with a fire storm.[49]

Yet the characteristics that made it such a desirable target for conventional firebombing also made it suitable for nuclear attack. Since it was large enough to contain an A-bomb explosion, scientists would be able to measure the bomb's effects. Its factories had growing military importance. And destroying one of Japan's leading cultural and religious centers would certainly have made an impression on the Japanese government and people and offered the world a spectacular display of nuclear power. Secretary Stimson's target committee felt Kyoto had another highly significant attribute. It observed that the town had "the advantage of the people being more intelligent," and therefore better able to understand what the A-bomb meant. The city was taken off the list of conventional bombing targets and reserved for nuclear obliteration, until Secretary Stimson struck it from that list as well.[50]

Stimson had visited Kyoto at least three times in the 1920s. Charmed by its beauty, he appreciated its cultural and religious importance. One day he asked Assistant Secretary of War McCloy whether McCloy would consider him "a sentimental old man" if he removed Kyoto from the list of proposed targets. McCloy encouraged him to do it. Stimson told the director of the A-bomb project, General Leslie R. Groves, that he did not want Kyoto attacked. Groves disagreed, stressing the city's importance to the Japanese war economy. Stimson remained adamant. He called Chief of Staff Marshall into his office, and as they talked Stimson's reasons for not wanting Kyoto obliterated gradually emerged, including the argument that destroying the city would damage America's postwar "historical position." Groves told General Norstad to inform Hap Arnold that the secretary had not approved the A-bomb list, particularly Kyoto. Later Stimson explained to Arnold that as one of the world's holy cities, with outstanding religious significance, Kyoto must not be bombed without the secretary of war's permission.[51]

Though the Twentieth Air Force agreed formally not to attack the old capital, the controversy continued, and the secretary of war found it difficult to impose his wishes. General Arnold thought Kyoto should be destroyed. Officers in Twentieth Air Force Headquarters and at LeMay's base in the Marianas wanted to burn it out with conventional bombs. General Groves kept trying to put it back on the A-bomb target list, and Stimson's military advisors in the Manhattan Project let him know that his "pet city" was their first choice for nuclear attack. On July 21 Stimson went to see the president and explained his reasons for preserving Kyoto. After Truman told him he felt the same way, Stimson called Arnold in for another discussion and went over the political and economic reasons for leaving Kyoto alone, while the AAF chief argued for choosing targets that would most speedily destroy Japan. Afterwards, Arnold recorded in his diary that "Kyoto, the holy city, was again ruled out," but Stimson sensed that the battle had still not ended and went back once more to the president.[52]

This time Truman was particularly emphatic in agreeing with Stimson's rationale. The president and the secretary both felt that bitterness caused by such a "wanton act" (as Stimson called it) could seriously compromise the long-run objectives of American policy. It might make it impossible to reconcile the Japanese to the United States rather than the Soviet Union after the war, and could hinder the emergence of a postwar Japan that would be sympathetic to the United States in the event of Soviet aggression in Manchuria.[53]

That settled the dispute. Truman firmly backed the secretary of war and Kyoto was spared from destruction by firebombing or nuclear attack, though by the standards currently accepted by most of the military and civilian leaders responsible for bombing Japan it was eminently qualified for both.

Dropping the Atomic Bombs

The day of this meeting the president noted in his private journal that he had instructed the secretary of war to use the atomic bomb "so that military objectives and soldiers and sailors are the target and not women and children. . . . The target will be a purely military one and we will issue a warning statement asking the Japs to surrender and save lives." Several scientists in the atomic bomb project had informed the president or his aides that they too wished to delay full use of the bomb until the Japanese could be warned of its effects, perhaps by a demonstration. And during a meeting between the president and the Joint Chiefs of Staff, Assistant Secretary of War McCloy had also proposed a warning as part of an attempt to achieve a political settlement and avoiding an invasion of the main islands.[54]

The United States did issue a warning at the Potsdam conference on July 26, together with China and Great Britain. The three governments told the Japanese that the Allies did not intend to enslave them or destroy them as a nation or permanently occupy their islands, but threatened the Japanese with the utter destruction of their homeland if they continued to fight. The three governments did not specify the kind of power about to be unleashed, however, and omitted any specific reference to the fate of Emperor Hirohito, a very important matter to Japan.[55]

Several of Japan's military and civilian leaders had long realized that the Allies were going to win, and some had been trying, ineffectively, to terminate the war. They declined to make a direct approach to the Western governments and insisted instead on working through the Soviet Union, although the Soviets had an incentive to delay the end of the Pacific war until they could enter it themselves and secure a share of the spoils. But the Potsdam Declaration, even though it contained no explicit provision regarding the emperor, offered terms that most Japanese could live with; it could even be interpreted as allowing the imperial institution to survive in some form.

Japanese cabinet members understood that they must find a way to accept those terms. Yet they had to contend with a war faction within their ranks, and found it difficult to express, either to one another or to their enemies, a willingness to capitulate. Prime Minister Kantaro Suzuki announced that his government was responding to the Potsdam Declaration with a policy of *mokusatsu*, a word susceptible to a number of interpretations. He may have meant by it that the government was "withholding comment," perhaps to give further thought to the Allied demands or to await developments from peace feelers sent through the Soviets. It could also be understood as "not taking seriously" or "rejecting by ignoring." The United States took Suzuki's announcement as a rejection of the Potsdam Declaration. It proceeded with plans to break Japanese resistance using the most powerful means at its disposal.[56]

While these futile diplomatic efforts were taking place, the 509th Composite Group prepared to deliver the first nuclear bomb. General Carl Spaatz had now assumed command of American strategic bombing operations in the Pacific.[57] Like other AAF leaders, Spaatz did not believe nuclear weapons were required to end the war, since he felt conventional bombing could force the Japanese to surrender. Nevertheless, he prepared to carry out his instructions. But he arranged to have the record show that it was persons above him who were responsible. When he received verbal instructions to drop the A-bomb on a Japanese city, he insisted on having a written order. On the 15th of July the War Department sent him a directive signed by General Marshall and Secretary Stimson, which President Truman subsequently confirmed. Spaatz recalled a few years later that he had not wanted to warn the Japanese before delivering the first bomb because that would have endangered his flyers. But after the Hiroshima bomb exploded on August 6 he suggested, in a telephone conversation with Washington, that the air force drop the next one in a less populated area so it "would not be as devastating to the city and the people." He was told to go ahead and hit the targets already planned.[58] On August 9 the second bomb was dropped on Nagasaki.

When the Japanese agreed to surrender shortly afterward it was clear that Army Air Forces bombing had contributed immensely not only to the defeat of Japan, but also to its timing. The Soviet declaration of war on August 8, the sea blockade, and countless naval encounters and ground battles in the Pacific all played their incalculable parts, but the strategic air offensive brought home to the Japanese people the reality of American power and forced their leaders to choose between further hostilities and the prospect of unlimited physical destruction. Finally, the atomic bombs provided advocates of peace in the Japanese government an acceptable reason to end hostilities.

U.S. warplanes bombed Japan's sixty-six largest cities, destroying an average of 43 percent of built-up areas. They forced 8,500,000 people, about a fourth of the country's urban population, to leave their communities. They damaged or destroyed roughly 2,300,000 homes, left an estimated 330,000 to 900,000 civilians dead and 475,000 to 1,300,000 injured, and exposed thousands of people in two of Japan's cities to the long-term effects of radiation. While bombing did not wholly eliminate Japan's ability to make war—U.S. military experts estimated that the Japanese could have killed and wounded hundreds of thousands of Allied troops in an invasion of the main islands—the American air offensive severely reduced Japan's military capacity, largely by dislocating the Japanese economic system.[59]

To achieve these results the AAF had, as in Germany but to a far larger degree, altered the selective bombing doctrine it had developed before the war. The immense destructive power of conventional and nuclear bombers meant that the air force no longer had to choose the most vital targets. From the first months of 1945 to the end of hostilities it joined daylight precision bombing to area raids, conducting overall offensive against the Japanese economy and Japanese morale, doing to Japan what the RAF and the AAF had done together to the Germans.

When the atomic bomb explosions culminated the Pacific air offensive, planned so carefully by so many military and civilian specialists over so many years, American civilians and servicemen and other people throughout the world rejoiced, for a terrible war was ending. But debate had already started over the way the United States used air power to punish and defeat the empire of Japan.

—— 8

The Bombing of Japan: American Perceptions of the Moral Issue

When people cause events to occur that are as cataclysmic as the destruction of the Japanese cities, it is natural to wonder how they thought about the moral issues involved. Did the Americans responsible for the way Japan was bombed reflect on those issues? How did they justify what they did? During the war or afterward, did any of them question the ethics of the policies proposed or carried out? And how did their response to moral issues, or the absence of response, affect the course their country followed? Finding the answers to these questions is a challenge to the historian, who, in addition to grappling with the usual problems of faulty memory, gaps in the record, and rationalization, must disentangle matters of ethics from a complex of military and political considerations weighed by those who played leading parts in the air war against Japan: the Army Air Force generals, the leaders of the other military arms, civilian scientists, technical specialists, and consultants on strategic and economic issues, and the presidents and their highest civil advisors.

The Army Air Force Leaders

Taken at face value, the statements of some AAF commanders might lead to the conclusion that they felt no concern whatever about the morality of the nuclear and firebomb attacks on Japan. General Eaker's remark that he never thought there was any moral sentiment among leaders of the AAF applied to those who directed the attacks against Japanese urban centers, officers he knew well. General LeMay's comments seem to verify Eaker's view. When an Air Force cadet asked him how much moral considerations affected his decisions about bombing Japan, LeMay replied, "Killing Japanese didn't bother me at that time. It was getting the war over with that bothered me. So I wasn't worried particularly about how many people we killed in getting the job done. . . . All war is immoral, and if you let it bother you, you're not a good soldier." General Spaatz presented himself as equally indifferent to moral issues. He told an air force historian that he had "no attitude" toward the firebombing of Japanese cities. It was a fait accompli by the time he arrived in the Pacific, and he had "not too much feeling about it one way or another." Dropping the atomic bomb caused him, he said, "no difficulty."[1]

General Arnold appeared to view air warfare as a wholly amoral activity. Toward the end of May 1945, while AAF bombers were burning the cities of Japan, he sent Chief of Staff Marshall a statement about the potential effects on war of new developments in military technology. This statement, which Arnold called the Army Air Forces view, envisioned a future air war waged with guided missiles and enormous planes carrying fifty-ton bombs. Aircraft would disseminate nerve gases, lethal fogs, and agents that destroyed lungs and eyes and burned skin and flesh "as surely and painfully as flame." A heavy gas, currently under development, would flow into underground shelters where, igniting in explosive blasts of flame, it would remove city after city from the face of the earth. Bacteriological weapons would spread epidemics so rapidly "that self-preservation might become the sole, frantic concern of millions." Nuclear devices would threaten the extinction of humanity. In the official air force view of future war, violence would only be limited by man's ability to conceive destructive instruments and the fear of retaliation.[2]

The AAF chief's preoccupation with the technology of weapons, exemplified by his wish to send an atomic blast through the Kokura tunnel to see what the effects would be, suggest an indifference to the moral questions raised by nuclear warfare—for instance, whether the human cost might outweigh, or could even be measured against, the military value of the experiment. One of Arnold's field generals, Kenneth B. Wolfe, head of the B-29 project and commander of the first unit of Superfortresses that bombed targets in Japan, seemed to exhibit the same kind of technological amorality. When someone asked Wolfe after the war if he thought it had been necessary to drop the atomic bomb, he replied, "Well, . . . this is a controversial question, but I and many of my associates in the wartime Air Force, believe that it was the thing to do. If we had not dropped it and found out the capabilities of the bomb, we certainly would not have the hydrogen bomb today."[3]

Nevertheless, it would be a mistake to accept all this apparent lack of interest in the morality of air war and the claim that moral issues were irrelevant to their jobs as proof that the air leaders entirely ignored the ethical side of the war against Japan. If that were so, why, for example, did General Spaatz insist on written orders to drop the Hiroshima bomb and later state that he had wanted to explode the second bomb outside a populated area "so that the effects would not be as devastating to the city and the people"?[4] In fact, when one examines the actions of the leaders of the AAF and the statements they made during and after the war, one finds that they really did perceive a moral dimension to their activities and offered a variety of justifications for what was done to the Japanese.

To Eaker, Spaatz, and LeMay, the role civilians played in the Japanese war effort and the difficulty of hitting purely military targets in a totally mobilized society helped justify the fire raids. "It made a lot of sense," Eaker remarked, "to kill skilled workers by burning whole areas." He also observed, concerning civilian war workers generally, that he considered them just as much legitimate targets as the troops who used the weapons they produced. When a historian asked General Spaatz after the war if the fire raids on Japan violated the precept of precision bombing and were fundamentally area raids, Spaatz answered that he thought not. He explained how difficult it would have been for precision bombing to destroy machinery used to make war goods when the machines were scattered in people's homes throughout the cities.[5]

In his report on the March 10 Tokyo raid, LeMay declared that the object of the XXI Bomber Command's incendiary attacks "was *not* to bomb indiscriminately civilian populations." Several years later, he clarified what he had meant. His men, he said, had aimed at military targets. "No point in slaughtering civilians for the sake of slaughter." But Japanese war industry was dispersed through the residential districts, where civilians had become blended with the industrial "target mass." To understand this all you had to do "was visit one of these targets after we'd roasted it, and see the ruins of a multitude of tiny houses, with a drill press sticking up through the wreckage of every home." In Japan, the entire population, "even little bits of kids," helped manufacture airplanes and munitions. "We knew we were going to kill a lot of women and kids . . . ," he remarked. "Had to be done."[6] As far as the director of the XXI Bomber Command was concerned, methods like those employed in the March 10 Tokyo raid were not indiscriminate bombing. They were a military necessity.

To General LeMay, precedents from the history of warfare undermined the charge that the AAF had acted immorally in the Pacific war. Denying that the United States had crossed some moral boundary when it dropped the A-bombs, he argued that it was no more "wicked" to kill people with nuclear weapons than to break their heads with rocks. In his memoirs he noted how the Romans had dealt with Carthage, and reminded his readers of the way victorious armies in ancient times had slaughtered the inhabitants of fallen cities. Apropos of the atomic bombs he declared, "Nothing new about death, nothing new about deaths caused militarily. We scorched and boiled and baked to death more people in Tokyo on that night of March 9–10 than went up in vapor at Hiroshima and Nagasaki combined."[7]

LeMay and Spaatz both felt that the system of command absolved air force leaders from moral responsibility for the effects of nuclear bombing. "There was no transgression," LeMay declared, "no venturing into a field illicit and immoral. . . . Soldiers were ordered to do a job. They did it." Spaatz said he was untroubled by having to order the A-bomb dropped because people above him had ordered it. "The military man carries out the orders of his political bosses," he told an Air Force historian after the war, "so that didn't bother me at all."[8]

The idea of shortening the war appears repeatedly in statements by air force officers, sometimes as a moral conception. The implication was that if the war could be won more quickly, fewer people would suffer. LeMay remarked in his memoirs that if a nuclear weapon shortened the war by a single week, it probably saved more lives than it destroyed. General Hansell offered a similar justification for the A-bomb: it brought the war to an early end, saving the lives of Americans and Japanese who would otherwise have died in an Allied invasion of the main islands.[9]

Despite Hansell's remarks about saving Japanese lives, it is unlikely that most AAF generals gave much thought during the war to sparing Japanese civilians. Just the opposite: they wanted revenge against the Japanese nation for atrocities committed by its armed forces.

Air force leaders had begun to hear about Japanese military brutality long before the attack on Pearl Harbor. At the Air Corps Tactical School they had studied Japanese air raids against Chinese civilians and they learned, well before the American public did, about the Bataan Death March, in which hundreds of sick, exhausted American and Filipino prisoners captured on Luzon died on the way to a prison camp, some bayoneted by their Japanese captors or buried alive, others victims of starvation and disease. They knew how the Japanese had executed captured flyers who bombed Japan with General Doolittle in 1942, and about the brutal way the Japanese armed forces had treated other American prisoners.[10]

All this had a noticeable effect on the attitude of AAF leaders. General Spaatz recalled that "we" had an "urge," a "feeling" about bombing the Japanese that did not hold for the Germans, who had never bombed American territory. General Hansell believed that the brutality of Japan's armed forces persuaded Generals Eaker and LeMay that the people of Japan had forfeited the right to be treated like human beings. During the war, Hansell remembered, it was the "universal feeling" that the Japanese were "subhuman."[11]

Hap Arnold knew a great deal about Japanese atrocities. As a member of the Joint Chiefs of Staff he had argeed to withhold information about the Bataan Death March; the U.S. government feared that American public reaction would expose captured servicemen to additional punishment and deprivation. Arnold also knew about Japanese experiments with bacteriological warfare, and he may have heard of the laboratory in Manchuria where the Japanese army used Allied prisoners of war as human guinea pigs.[12]

In June 1945 General Arnold visited Manila, just after Japanese troops had ravaged it. In his diary for the 16th he wrote:

> Apparently the atrocities by the Japs have never been told in the U.S.—babies thrown up in the air and caught on bayonets—autopsies on living people—burning prisoners to death by sprinkling them with gasoline and throwing in a hand grenade to start a fire. If any tried to escape they were killed by machine guns as they came through the door. More and more of the stories which can apparently be substantiated.

He learned about a mass murder of Filipino boys, and that soldiers of a retreating Japanese division had raped women and young girls. In the section of Manila where he stayed there was "no feeling of sparing any Japs . . . men, women or children," but rather a desire to use "gas, fire, anything to exterminate the entire race." The accounts he had heard were not "pretty stories"; they explained "why the Japs can expect anything."[13]

In Arnold's mind these events were linked to thoughts about air strategy. The next item he recorded in his diary that day was the sketch of a plan to end the war through bombing, including B-29 attacks to "completely destroy Jap industries and major cities" and "plans for complete destruction of Japan proper" with B-29s from the Marianas and Okinawa, heavy bombers and tactical planes from Kyushu (after an Allied landing there), and carrier plan attacks against areas the AAF missed.

The atrocities in the Philippines did not cause Arnold to recommend the incineration of Japanese cities, a process already under way. As early as November 1944 he had intended to destroy the Japanese capital. But together with other evidence of Japanese brutality, these indications that the Japanese military forces had crossed a line between moral and immoral behavior justified to General Arnold the kind of warfare his air forces conducted.

The chief of the AAF considered the atomic bomb a proper instrument for retribution. When General Leslie R. Groves, the director of the Manhattan Project, told Arnold and General Marshall about the attack on Hiroshima, Marshall suggested that it would be a mistake to rejoice too much, since the explosion had undoubtedly caused a large number of Japanese casualties. Groves replied that he was not thinking as much about those casualties as about the men who had made the Bataan Death March. Afterwards, in the hallway outside Marshall's office, Arnold slapped Groves on the back and exclaimed, "I am glad you said that—it's just the way I feel."[14]

The air leaders felt the people of the United States had given them carte blanche to bomb the Japanese. General Spaatz remarked after the war that "we didn't hear any complaints from the American people about the mass bombing of Japan. As a matter of fact, I think they felt the more we did the better." General Eaker believed that 90 percent of Americans would have "killed every Japanese." Eaker's estimate is probably too high. Only 20 percent of those who responded to a survey in December 1944 said that ordinary Japanese citizens should be tortured, exterminated, or otherwise treated with great harshness. But the airmen were correct in believing that a great many of their countrymen shared their desire for revenge.[15]

The attack on Pearl Harbor had crystallized anti-Japanese feeling in the United States that had been gathering for half a century. Earlier it had led to restrictions on land ownership by Japanese in California, to special barriers to the immigration of Japanese workers, to attempts to segregate Japanese and Japanese-American schoolchildren, and finally, to the mass removal of people of Japanese ancestry to concentration centers away from the Pacific coast. During the war, hatred of the Japanese people was fed by accounts of enemy barbarism and by portrayal of the Japanese in American media as barely human creatures who were either comical, sinister, or grotesque. An advertisement in *Time*, for instance, drawn by the artist Artzybasheff for the Wickwire Spencer Steel Company, shows a Japanese man with buck teeth, thick glasses, squinting eyes, and a rat's tail. Even highly educated Americans sometimes lumped together all persons of Japanese ancestry with the particular organizations and individuals responsible for attacking Pearl Harbor and for later Japanese atrocities.[16] Anti-Japanese sentiment was quite different from the predominant American opinion about Germans, which acted as a brake against bombing civilians rather than an impetus to attack them.

The Scientists and Technical Specialists

General Eaker once said that "scientists are a lot like military men. They were challenged to a task and they went about it." There was plenty of evidence for that statement. Like military men, scientists were moved by patriotism, by the desire to defeat their country's enemies, and by the feeling that they were involved in a great common enterprise. "It was a good time," Robert Wilson of the Los Alamos laboratory recalled. "It was a good time in America. It was a good time to be an American. It was a time when the whole country was pulling together. . . ."[17]

If Eaker's remark is interpreted to mean that many scientists became so preoccupied with techniques of fighting the war that they did not ponder the ethics of their actions, it is certainly true. A number of scientists who developed the atomic bomb remarked afterward that they had gotten so deeply involved in their work that they lost sight of its moral implications. Frank Oppenheimer, brother of J. Robert Oppenheimer and a physicist at Los Alamos during the war, described the phenomenon. Like many participants in the Manhattan Project, he had wanted to build the bomb out of fear of what would happen if Hitler had one and the United States did not; then, when Hitler was defeated, he just went on with his work. "Amazing how the technology tools trap one," he told an interviewer, "They're so powerful. . . . When VE day came along, nobody slowed up one little bit. . . . We all kept working. And it wasn't because we understood the significance against Japan. It was because the machinery had caught us in its trap and we were anxious to get this thing to go." Only as he heard about what happened at Hiroshima, Oppenheimer recalled, did he start to sense the moral effects of his handiwork. His first reaction was "Thank God it wasn't a dud." Then he suddenly began to feel horror about the people the bomb had killed. He had talked before about having a demonstration in an unpopulated area, but until the announcement he hadn't really thought "off all those flattened people."[18]

Robert Wilson recalled a similar absence of moral reflection. Afterward, he said, he could not understand why he had not simply quit the Manhattan Project after Germany's defeat; but then the thought of leaving "simply was not in the air . . . at the time it just was not . . . part of our lives. Our life was directed to do just one thing. It was as though we had been programmed to do that, and we as automatons were doing it."* When the nuclear physicist Hans Bethe was asked in 1954 how the atomic scientists at Los Alamos had felt about moral or humane problems that others had discerned in their work, he said that he was unhappy to admit that he had not paid much attention to those problems during the war: "It seemed to us most important to contribute to victory in the way we could. Only when our labors were finally completed when the bomb dropped on Japan, only then or a little bit before then maybe, did we start thinking about the moral implications."[19]

Other scientists felt the fascination of discovering how things needed for war could be made to work. When an NDRC panel in Cambridge, Massachusetts, asked Jerzy Neyman of the University of California at Berkeley, a renowned theoretical statistician, to help determine the optimum destructive mix of incendiary and high-explosive bombs, Neyman replied, "You must be aware of the fact that the problem of IB-HE is very interesting to me and I would be delighted to continue the work on it for your Group." For some a sense of almost magical power suffused their activities and dominated their minds, excluding thoughts about the mundane consequences of their work. The physicist Freeman Dyson, who became

*Oppenheimer and Wilson's memories were faulty on this point, as will presently appear.

involved with the atomic bomb after the war, described how this sense affected him: "I have felt it myself, the glitter of nuclear weapons. It is irresistible if you come to them as a scientist. To feel it's there in your hands—to release this energy that fuels the stars, to let it do your bidding. To perform these miracles—to lift a million tons of rock into the sky."[20]

Important war scientists exhibited the kind of deference to higher authority that soldiers are expected to display, subordinating to the national interest any qualms they might have had about the work they were doing. Louis Fieser, leader of the Harvard group that perfected napalm, was told in 1941 to work on poison gases, particularly vesicants—chemical agents that burned and destroyed tissue. This did not please him, he wrote later: "Use of poison gas seemed to me inhumane." Besides, he doubted that vesicants would be used in the Second World War. But he "swallowed" his "personal feelings" and brought together a team to do the work. J. Robert Oppenheimer, who had directed the scientists at Los Alamos, stated after the war that he had had "terrible" moral scruples about killing or injuring tens of thousands of Japanese with atomic bombs. But when he was asked if he had not helped to pick the target, Oppenheimer replied, "I did my job which was the job I was supposed to do. I was not in a policymaking position at Los Alamos. I would have done anything that I was asked to do, including making the bombs in a different shape, if I had thought it was technically feasible."[21]

Professor J. Enrique Zanetti, the Columbia University chemistry professor who helped develop incendiary bombs, shared the opinion of some of the air force generals that morality was irrelevant to modern warfare. In words Douhet might have written, Zanetti declared that "Whether one is prepared to accept the long foreseen 'all-out' type of warfare, in which the destruction of civilian morale plays such an important part, or whether one condemns it as brutal, inhuman, and uncivilized matters little. 'All-out' warfare is here and must be faced. . . ." It was "elementary," the chemist believed, that bombers attacking the combustible areas of large cities should try to establish conflagrations.[22]

A number of Manhattan Project scientists thought about the moral and other consequences of dropping A-bombs on Japanese civilians and concluded that their government would be right to do it. After hearing arguments against dropping the bomb or for delaying its use until the Japanese had adequate warning, Secretary Stimson's scientific panel concluded it was best to demonstrate the

weapon in actual combat. They could see too many possibilities for
failure in a demonstration,* too great a likelihood that the bomb
would not shock the enemy into surrendering if anything were
done to lessen the surprise. They believed, as AAF leaders did, that
higher objectives justified introducing nuclear weapons in a way
certain to destroy large numbers of enemy civilians.[23]

One group of scientists who favored dropping the bomb wondered how, after developing a weapon that could save American
servicemen from death in battle, their government could fail to use
it. "Are not the men of the fighting forces part of the nation?" they
asked. "Are not they, who are risking their lives for the nation
entitled to the weapons which have been designed? In short, are we
to go on shedding American blood when we have available a means
to speedy victory? No! If we can save even a handful of American
lives, then let us use this weapon—now!" A similar justification
underlay Raymond Ewell's view that Japan's major cities should be
razed with incendiaries as soon as possible—it would shorten the
war and save the lives of thousands of Americans.[24]

Leading scientific administrators felt the same way. After the
war, Vannevar Bush recalled that he had thought of the atomic
bomb as an instrument to save both American and enemy lives. He
remembered the preparations under way for an invasion which then
had seemed impossible to stop, and his hopes that the A-bomb, by
bringing a quick end to the war, would preserve more lives than it
snuffed out. Arthur Compton believed it was a tragedy that nuclear
power first had to be used to destroy humans, but he also hoped it
would lead to a quicker end to the war, thus sparing human lives.[25]

To Compton and to some of the other atomic scientists it
seemed that if the bomb were used on an enemy city it might help
prevent a subsequent nuclear war. Edward Teller argued that the
crucial consideration was whether war itself would be done away
with. Five weeks before Hiroshima he told a colleague in the Manhattan Project that the things they were working on were "so
terrible that no amount of protesting or fiddling with politics will
save our souls." Yet because the nuclear weapon was so decisive,
attempts to restrict its use in a future war would fail. The only hope
was to persuade public opinion that another war would be fatal and
for this purpose, "actual combat use might even be the best
thing."[26]

---

*The Manhattan Project scientists apparently did not fear that a U-235 gun-type bomb
would fail. They dropped one on Hiroshima without a preliminary test. It was the plutonium variety, the kind dropped on Nagasaki, that they felt needed testing.

Robert S. Stone, director of the Health Division of the University of Chicago Metallurgical Laboratory* agreed with Teller's conclusion. Stone felt that whatever respect the Russians had for the United States would "not be increased" if they discovered the Americans had developed but not used such a valuable weapon. He thought the United States would be in a better position to secure an international agreement on suppressing the A-bomb if "its effectiveness has first been demonstrated."[27]

Some members of the scientific community appeared to feel that conventional incendiary bombing and the development of other means of large-scale killing had broken through whatever moral barrier might have protected enemy civilians. In a wartime letter which favored dropping the atomic bomb, Evan J. Young, a chemist at Oak Ridge, noted that incendiary raids had already inflicted a "fiendish hell" on Japan. Vannevar Bush recalled, a quarter century after Hiroshima, that the A-bomb promised at the time to be "far less terrible" than the fire raids on Tokyo, and he had also been aware of the dangers posed by biological warfare and of the potentialities of nerve gas, which could be "as terrible as the A-bomb."[28]

It is clear, then, that as General Eaker observed, a good many scientists did resemble military men. They performed the tasks their government needed done. They endorsed its policies. They justified their activities with arguments like those the generals used. They felt, as air leaders did, an essential rightness about the American cause and in a number of instances they subordinated personal moral qualms to higher goals. Yet there was another sense in which scientists resembled the men in uniform, a sense General Eaker may not have meant. Collectively, scientists were similar to AAF leaders in that they included people who, like Colonel Hughes and Generals Cabell and McDonald, wondered about the morality of the air war and sometimes dissented from the dominant viewpoint.

Particularly at the University of Chicago, groups of atomic scientists, impelled at least partly by moral considerations, tried to keep their country from dropping the atomic bomb on the Japanese without first affording them a chance to witness its effects. Leo Szilard, the physicist who had arranged to bring the idea of an atomic bomb to President Roosevelt's attention, drew up a petition

*This laboratory, sometimes refered to as the Met Lab, was organized at the University of Chicago in January 1942 to do research on the bomb material plutonium.

urging President Truman to weigh moral responsibilities in determining whether to use the bomb against Japan. Szilard personally
believed it would have been immoral to employ nuclear weapons
against the Japanese under any circumstances, but found few of his
colleagues willing to follow that line. However, a committee from
the Chicago Met Lab, chaired by James Franck, sent Secretary of
War Stimson a report phrased in more pragmatic terms. They
warned against dropping a nuclear bomb on a Japanese city without
prior notification and urged the country's highest political leaders
and its military authorities to consider very carefully how the
weapon should be used.[29]

The Franck committee doubted that the first, comparatively
small atomic bombs would break Japan's will to fight or destroy its
ability to resist, especially since incendiary attacks would have already turned its major cities into ashes. But if the United States
nevertheless unleashed this weapon of indiscriminate destruction.
it would sacrifice public support for America throughout the world
and deliver a shock to other nations—including the Soviet Union—
that might make it extremely difficult after the war to establish
international control over atomic weapons. Without that control,
the committee foresaw a nuclear arms race possibly culminating in
an atomic war that would devastate the United States.

Arthur Compton conveyed to Stimson's Interim Committee
the concerns of scientists working under his direction at the Met
Lab. He noted that the issue of how the first bomb would be
employed "introduces the question of mass slaughter really for the
first time in history" and suggested that unless a final decision had
already been made to exterminate the Japanese, consideration
should be given to the political consequences in Japan of using the
weapon. While he imagined, he said, that the entire question might
have already received the broad study it demanded, he "merely
[wanted] to mention it as one of the urgent problems that have
bothered our men because of its many ramifications and humanitarian implications." Later, forwarding the report of the Franck
committee to Stimson's office, he added two arguments in opposition to its recommendations: unless the bomb were used in World
War II the world would not have adequate warning of what a
future war could be like; and dropping the bomb might effect a net
saving in human lives.[30]

While the Met Lab workers were the only scientists who
attempted in a concerted manner to influence the way atomic
weapons would be used, the anticipated results of their work

troubled individuals in other parts of the Manhattan Project. Robert Wilson organized a meeting of Los Alamos scientists at which participants considered whether what they were doing was morally right. Frank Oppenheimer remembered several discussions about dropping the bomb on a place where it would not kill human beings. A civilian engineer, Oswald C. Brewster, who had worked for the Manhattan Project on a process for separating bomb material from uranium ore, was so alarmed about the likely result of the atomic bomb program that he urged the president to bring the project to a halt. Two weeks after the end of the war in Europe he sent President Truman a long letter recommending that A-bombs not be dropped on Japan without prior demonstration. As long as the threat of Germany existed, Brewster said, he had favored proceeding with the Manhattan Project as rapidly as possible. But with that threat removed, he wanted the United States to stop its nuclear weapon program before it eventuated in an arms race and a world-wide nuclear holocaust. "This thing must not be permitted on earth," Brewster wrote. "We must not be the most hated and feared people on earth, however good our intent may be." Secretary Stimson intercepted his letter and brought it to the attention of General Marshall as well as the president.[31]

Scientists and technicians who participated in conventional warfare projects like incendiary bombing appear—at least as far as the record indicates—to have felt less anxiety than men like Brewster and Szilard did about the moral consequences of their work. But that does not mean they never reflected on those consequences. NDRC division chief W. A. Noyes, Jr., of the University of Rochester Chemistry Department, who had headed the technical division of the Chemical Warfare Service, observed after the war that, like it or not, science had forced upon warfare irresistible changes with serious moral effects. He regretted that his own branch of science had contributed to making war more terrible. The days when civilian populations were little affected by war were gone forever, he said, and admitted that chemistry bore no little responsibility for this change. But since "progress in Science" could not be stopped and war changed back into a "game for gentlemen," he argued, the only remedy for the horror of modern scientific conflict was to abolish war itself.[32]

To James K. McElroy, who had helped perfect techniques of burning down the cities of both Germany and Japan, there seemed only one way to rationalize his participation "in the death of God knows how many people." This was to feel that, after all, the Germans started mass destruction and we just did it better. It was a combination of all the efforts of all the people, the air forces, the statisticians, engineers, the people dealing with radar and all the rest of us combined, to plan destruction such as this world will, I hope, never see again. I personally don't want to have to participate again in wartime planned destruction.[33]

McElroy wrote these words after the war. Whether he harbored similar thoughts while working to help defeat his country's enemies is unknown.

Other Advisors to the AAF

The transcripts of meetings of the Committee of Operations Analysts show highly intelligent, thoughtful men wholly immersed in technical deliberations and problem solving. Thus when Colonel John F. Turner asked what the effects of a successful urban area fire bomb attack would be—"Would it prevent 15% of industry from going on if they do not have machine tools, if people who worked in the factories are dead. What effect would it have on the other 85%?"—Commander William McGovern, the OSS Japan scholar, answered, "It would have a marked effect. You begin to get into trouble. It would have a great deal of effect on other areas. The administrative head is in Tokyo. Losing records or orders would have an effect on them." Lieutenant Charles Hitch added, "There will be some difficulties, administrative problems, priorities. . . ." Similarly, when Colonel Turner mentioned that the Incendiary Subcommittee had "considered an optimum result of complete chaos in six cities killing 584,000 people," the response was purely technical.[34]

Occasionally a brief outbreak of emotion occurred. After Colonel Burgess commented that the committee had been looking at the issues "from a mathematical precision point of view," and wondered how the Japanese would react psychologically to the fire raids ("Would bedlam be created?"), Commander McGovern spoke with considerable feeling about "raising hell" among the people of Tokyo after they had dribbled back to their homes. McGovern was the exception. Others were more dispassionate.[35]

Were the committee members so narrowly focused on technical problems that moral issues never crossed their minds? While time has dimmed considerably the recollection of leading participants who were asked about these meetings many years later, one of them, Guido R. Perera, suggested how he had regarded the moral issues of the air war against Japan.

An attorney in peacetime for a leading Boston law firm, Perera, in the rank of AAF colonel, served as secretary of the COA. He thought of himself as a realist. In his memoirs he refers to idealistic but impractical churchmen, teachers, and social theorists who believed that "war was the supreme immoral example of human aggressive tendencies" and that it might be eliminated by nonresistance, world government, or total disarmament. He considered most of the community of atomic physicists politically unsophisticated and "unduly sanguine that abstract concepts of good and evil could be readily applied to the solution of human problems." Perera recalled that the question of·area bombing Japanese cities had produced an intense dispute within the committee and that while he and most of the COA's members preferred to continue precision bombing, AAF Intelligence enthusiastically favored urban raids as a way of getting at the small scattered workshops.[36]

It has not been possible to determine if the parties to this dispute divided over the moral issue or whether their differences were exclusively practical. The transcripts of COA meetings examined for this study do not record any controversy with A-2 over the morality of incendiary bombing, and Perera does not recall if he or any other member of the committee mentioned moral objections or engaged in any "extended" debate, on or off the record, about ethical matters per se. He did remember finding "the thrust" of a report by a fire expert on the bombing of Japanese urban areas "distasteful in its consideration of resulting casualties."[37] However, some of Perera's actions and subsequent remarks provide clues to how he viewed the moral question in the 1940s.

Since he signed the COA report which recommended attacking urban areas as well as other targets, Perera obviously did not think it was wrong in principle to kill enemy civilians. Indeed, he stated after the war that their lives had to be weighed against the lives of Americans who would have died had enemy cities not been attacked. The crucial matter was the purpose of the raids and the likelihood that the method employed would achieve that purpose. In his memoirs he remarked that indiscriminate attack with long-range weapons against the enemy's heartland "with the primary objective of destroying his people" did not seem a reasonable way of using force. "A cynic might add," he wrote, "'it is worse than immoral because it is ineffective.'" Perera considered the AAF doctrine of selective bombing "sound both militarily and morally."

But the United States was at war "with a fanatic enemy whose record of brutality was notorious," and "if his cities were indeed honeycombed with small war making plants and were a vital source of his war making power, as A-2 postulated, there were logical grounds for attacking them."[38] Thus Perera agreed with the AAF commanders: the behavior of the Japanese armed forces and the need to strike at the sources of Japan's military power justified urban area raids. And he accepted, as they and some of the scientists did, the necessity of trading the deaths of Japanese civilians, who were inseparable from their country's war effort, for the lives of American servicemen.

The Views of Army and Navy Leaders

At the highest levels of the navy, there were doubts about whether the trade-off was either necessary or wise, and about the permissibility of certain methods of warfare the United States considered using against Japan. These matters troubled Admiral William D. Leahy, the president's chief of staff. After the war Leahy remarked that it had been morally wrong to introduce the atomic bomb. "In being the first to use it," he wrote, "we had adopted an ethical standard common to the barbarians of the Dark Ages. I was not taught to make war in that fashion, and wars cannot be won by destroying women and children."[39] Leahy also believed certain proposals for defeating Japan with chemicals and bacteria disseminated from the air were morally repugnant.

Early in 1944 General Marshall recommended to the Joint Chiefs that biological warfare techniques be readied for offensive use against Japan after the defeat of Germany. The War Department established a special program, headed by George Merck, to develop ways of producing and delivering biological weapons. Anthrax and botulism bombs were developed for mass production. Army Air Forces air staff, meanwhile, drew up what it called an "Air Plan for Retaliatory Chemical Warfare against the Japanese," but which, as General Kuter, the assistant chief of air staff for plans explained, was actually a plan for initiating offensive chemical warfare against the Japanese if a decision were made to do so. Air force staff officers started to develop a contingency plan for gas attack on Japanese cities.[40]

Leahy regretted the "barbarous necessities" of a war that had led the United States to prepare to use chemicals against other people, and he took up with President Roosevelt his moral and practical objections to the biological warfare project. In July 1944, while the president and his aides were sailing to Hawaii to confer with General MacArthur and Admiral Nimitz, there was a discussion in Roosevelt's cabin about bacteriological warfare. Leahy told the commander in chief, "Mr. President, this would violate every Christian ethic I have ever heard of and all of the known laws of war. It would be an attack on the noncombatant population of the enemy. The reaction can be foretold—if we use it, the enemy will use it." Leahy recorded that the president seemed noncommittal.[41]

Undersecretary of the Navy Ralph A. Bard disagreed, partly on moral grounds, with the way Secretary Stimson and his advisors proposed to use the atomic bomb against the Japanese. Bard served on Stimson's Interim Committee. When it recommended that the first A-bomb be dropped on a Japanese city without warning, Bard concurred. A few weeks later he changed his mind. On June 27 he sent a letter to the secretary of war suggesting that the United States find a way to communicate with the Japanese government. Perhaps two or three days before the attack the United States should tell the Japanese something of the nature of atomic power, notify them of what would happen if they did not give in, "make representations" about Russia's position, and offer whatever assurances the president might wish to give them concerning the emperor and the treatment of the Japanese nation after unconditional surrender. Bard felt the Japanese were searching for a way to capitulate, and in the last days of the war he wanted the United States to try his approach as a way of preserving its place in history "as a great humanitarian nation." The "fair play attitude of our people," he said, had also influenced him. Five days later he resigned as undersecretary; shortly afterward he went to President Truman as Truman was preparing to leave for the Potsdam conference and repeated what he had told the secretary of war.[42]

The questions Bard and Leahy raised about moral issues of air warfare should be viewed in a larger context. They are related not only to the persistent conflicts between the American armed services during the war, but also to an evolving view at the navy's top level of future relations between the United States and other countries. Months before the war ended Secretary of the Navy James V. Forrestal began to think of Japan as a potential counter to Soviet power in Asia.[43] Given this premise, it would be folly for the United States to invade Japan, at enormous cost to both countries, or to employ weapons of unprecedented violence against the Japanese people if the war could be ended satisfactorily in another way.

Bard felt the blockade of Japan made an invasion unnecessary, a view shared by Admiral Leahy and Admiral Ernest J. King, the navy members of the Joint Chiefs of Staff. To King, the army's insistence on a landing was another instance of its underestimation of sea power. Admiral Leahy thought it would not be worth the cost in American lives to invade the Japanese home islands; if the United States could not force the Japanese to surrender unconditionally without an invasion, that was all right too. He reasoned that the United States would still not have lost the war and that the Japanese, whether they surrendered unconditionally or not, would no longer pose a significant threat to his country.[44]

With this view General Marshall wholly disagreed. The army chief of staff intended to employ against Japan the method of U. S. Grant—relentless application of vast military power until the enemy surrendered unconditionally. Marshall did not believe conventional bombing would end the war. In his view an American army, perhaps using a dozen atomic bombs as tactical weapons, would have to invade the main Japanese islands and fight a culminating battle on the plain of Tokyo.

General Marshall thought this final battle would cost the lives of thousands of American troops. In the hope of forcing Japan to surrender while sparing these lives, he approved the order to drop an atomic bomb before the first of two planned invasions, the landing on Kyushu. Concerned about the way others would regard the morality of this act, he suggested that the first bomb be exploded on a purely military objective, like a large naval base. If this did not secure unconditional surrender, he felt the United States should notify the inhabitants of several manufacturing areas that it intended to destroy their cities (not telling them which ones) and quickly obliterate a certain number. "We must offset by such warning methods," he said, "the opprobrium which might follow from an ill-considered employment of such force." Two years later he defended the use of the A-bomb as a humane act on the grounds that it shortened the war and made it unnecessary to exterminate the Japanese.[45]

Secretary Stimson and the Moral Question

The secretary of war shared Marshall's uneasiness about the effects the bomb might have on the image of the United States, and he appears to have devoted considerable thought to the moral consequences of attacking enemy civilians. On March 5, 1945, he talked at length with his assistant, Harvey Bundy, about issues related to the atomic bomb and, as Stimson himself recorded, "went right down to the bottom facts of human nature, morals and governments." Hap Arnold remembered a meeting during the Potsdam conference at which Stimson discussed the effects of the A-bomb on Japan. "We talked about the killing of women and children," Arnold recalled, "the destruction of surrounding communities, the effect on other nations, and the psychological reaction of the Japanese themselves."[46] While neither man recorded Stimson's exact statements, and the secretary of war did not write down the contents of either conversation, one can reconstruct from several sources the outlines of his thinking about moral questions raised by the air war.

It is clear that he took those questions very seriously. In a memorandum prepared to acquaint President Truman with the implications of the atomic bomb, he wrote that "the world in its present state of moral advancement compared with its technical development would be eventually at the mercy of such a weapon. In other words, modern civilization might be completely destroyed. . . ." He believed that America's role in creating that weapon, as well as its leadership in the war, had "placed a certain moral responsibility upon us which we cannot shirk without very serious responsibility for any disaster to civilization which it would further."[47]

Stimson thought, as Leahy did, that some measures were too barbarous to employ, even in World War II—the destruction of Kyoto, for example. He was as concerned as General Marshall and Undersecretary Bard were about the way America's use of military power would affect its postwar standing. The world's greatest asset for peace in the coming decades, he told President Truman, was "the reputation of the United States for fair play and humanitarianism," and he indicated that the country's image would suffer badly if it did not try to spare, as far as possible, the enemy's civilian population. He explained to the president that he was anxious to confine AAF bombing to precision targets, partly because he "did not want to have the United States acquire the reputation of outdoing Hitler in atrocities."[48]

To Stimson the Japanese were diverse human beings, members of an advanced civilization. He told the president that it would be incorrect to think of the island empire as "a nation composed wholly of mad fanatics of an entirely different mentality from ours." Japan had lived a "reasonably responsible and respectable

international life" in the decade before 1931, when a fanatical
military group had seized control. Even in 1945 its people included a
number of "liberals." Among its inhabitants were extremely intelligent individuals who in a very short time had adopted much of
Western culture (an important consideration for Stimson).[49] He did
not regard the Japanese people as mere parts of a "target mass,"
objects for the AAF to eradicate.

Stimson's upbringing among artists and writers, his education
as a gentleman, and his experiences as a traveler in the Far East had
made him sensitive to Japanese high culture and led him to view the
destruction of Kyoto as more than a military problem. While it
cannot be proved that the practical arguments he offered for saving
it were simply rationalizations, it does seem possible that in this
instance the hardheaded, methodical lawyer really was, as he suggested to John J. McCloy, a sentimental old man.

Pressures from the American public and from the U.S. Army
to end quickly Japanese resistance affected Stimson. In a memorandum on basic objectives in the Pacific war, General Marshall warned
him to be careful not to give any impression "that we are growing
soft." Early in July, Stimson noted in his diary, "I have to meet and
overcome the zeal of the soldier. . . . I have to meet the feeling of
war passion and hysteria which seizes hold of a nation like ours in
the prosecution of a bitter war." Yet it would distort the secretary's
character to view him simply as a cultivated humanitarian who
somehow became involved in destroying people he respected or
who bowed to the will of zealots, for his own hardened, fatalistic
view of warfare affected the way he thought about what should be
done to Japan. Looking back, in 1947, over his service as secretary
of war he saw "too many stern and heartrending decisions to be
willing to pretend that war is anything else than what it is. The face
of war is the face of death: death is an inevitable part of every order
that a wartime leader gives."[50]

When Stimson proposed to restrain American air power, the
arguments he offered were chiefly practical. He hoped the air force
would stick to precision bombing in order to keep the Japanese from
uniting in resistance to the death, as well as to save some targets on
which to demonstrate the A-bomb. He wished to spare Kyoto to
retain America's reputation for humanitarianism as "an asset for
peace." His country would need allies in the western Pacific for the
emerging struggle with the Soviet Union, and Japan was more
likely to tie itself to the United States if the Americans preserved
Japan's most holy city.[51]

In pursuit of early, tangible results, the secretary did not shrink from employing a radical new weapon, which contained, as he knew, the germ of disaster for civilization. The possibility that withholding it might lead to better relations with the USSR, as some of the scientists proposed, and the chance that a nonmilitary demonstration might make Japan capitulate were far outweighed in his mind by the likelihood that dropping it on cities would produce victory without a costly invasion. Never doubting that nuclear bombs should be employed if they were ready before the war ended, believing it was no worse to kill a large number of Japanese civilians with a few atomic bombs that ended the war than to kill a much larger number in conventional bombing raids, Stimson spoke, as the Manhattan Project approached its culmination, of trying to get Japan to give up after it had been pounded sufficiently, perhaps with nuclear weapons. "This is a matter about which I feel very strongly," he declared, "and feel that the country will not be satisfied unless every effort is made to shorten the war."[52]

After the bomb had been tested at Alamogordo, New Mexico, General Eisenhower told Stimson he hoped the bomb would not have to be dropped. Eisenhower imagined that if the United States did not use it, other nations could be kept from learning that the problem of nuclear fission had been solved. The general did not want his country to take the lead in introducing so horrible and destructive a weapon, whose employment he considered unnecessary with Japan so close to surrender. Stimson, speaking tensely and anxiously, replied by talking of the numbers of Americans who might have to die before surrender occurred, victims of fanatical resistance by Japanese ground forces and of raids by suicide aircraft on a scale never before experienced.[53] He was justifying the expected deaths of Japanese in nuclear bombings by the prospect of saving American lives.

Following the war, he elaborated on this argument:

> My chief purpose was to end the war in victory with the least possible cost in the lives of the men in the armies which I had helped to raise. In the light of the alternatives which, on a fair estimate, were open to us I believe that no man, in our position and subject to our responsibilities, holding in his hands a weapon of such possibilities for accomplishing this purpose and saving those lives, could have failed to use it and afterwards looked his countrymen in the face.

To this he added the additional justification that the A-bomb prevented death and injury to the Japanese because it stopped the fire raids and the strangling blockade and ended "the ghastly specter of

a clash of great land armies." He hoped, as Arthur Compton and
Vannevar Bush and Edward Teller had hoped, that out of the
explosion of the atomic bombs would come a lesson for humankind,
that there must never be another war.[54]

At the same time, Stimson wanted a peace that would preserve
American interests and serve American ideals. If his chief purpose
in approving the use of the bomb was victory over Japan with the
least cost in American lives, his most important secondary objective
was to influence postwar relations between the United States and
the Soviet Union. On the eve of the Yalta conference General
Schlatter had seen U.S. bombing of eastern German cities as a
display of America's conventional military power to be used in
bargaining with the Russians. Stimson viewed the atomic bomb in a
similar way. Several weeks before the Potsdam conference and
before the first A-bomb was tested, he described the weapon as a
"master card" and remarked that it was a "terrible thing" to gamble
for such large diplomatic stakes without actually holding that card
in one's hand.[55] In this matter, as in other great events connected
with the air war against Japan, Stimson identified the interests of
the United States with the welfare of humanity and viewed the
practical and the moral issues as inseparable from one another.

The Presidents and the Air War

Since Franklin D. Roosevelt habitually kept his views on sensitive
matters to himself, it is difficult to determine exactly how he felt
about the moral issues of the air war. Still, Roosevelt did say and do
certain things that suggest how he regarded the moral aspects of
bombing. When he responded through his press secretary in 1944
to Vera Brittain's attack on Allied area raids, he depicted the central
issue of the air war in absolute terms, with civilization on one side
and the forces of death and destruction, represented by Japan and
Germany, on the other.[56] And in the same response he defended
the bombing offensive in Europe with the argument that it was
shortening the war. Presumably Roosevelt understood that the
letter in which he proposed the Strategic Bombing Survey implied
that air power would be used to terrorize civilians. He could hardly
have failed to appreciate, at some point, what an atomic bomb
would do to people on the ground.

Surviving fragments of information suggest a faint possibility
that the president might have hesitated before using the new

weapon on an urban center in a surprise attack. The economist Alexander Sachs recalled a conversation in which Roosevelt appeared to agree with Sachs's idea of demonstrating the bomb and warning Germany and Japan before using it against them. But Roosevelt often gave people who spoke with him the impression that he shared their views, even when he did not. The wording of an aide-mémoire that Roosevelt and Churchill initialed in September 1944 implies the possibility of not using the weapon, for the two leaders agreed that when a bomb was finally available, "it *might perhaps*, after mature consideration, be used against the Japanese." A few days later, at a meeting with Admiral Leahy, Vannevar Bush, and a British representative, Roosevelt raised the question, in a matter-of-fact way, of whether the bomb should actually be used against the Japanese or whether a demonstration should be staged in the United States to threaten the enemy.[57]

Others thought Roosevelt, had he lived, would undoubtedly have dropped the bomb on Japan. Stimson, who discussed the Manhattan Project with Roosevelt many times, was sure Roosevelt had never doubted that the bomb should be used. The president's personal secretary, Grace Tully, remembered him saying, ". . . I can't tell you what this [project] is, Grace, but if it works, and pray God it does, it will save many American lives."[58] Indeed, it is hard to imagine that a politician as unsentimental as Roosevelt was about important matters, as sensitive to public opinion, and as dedicated to destroying the regime that had launched the attack on Pearl Harbor would have declined to employ nuclear bombs to end the war.

If the concrete evidence of Roosevelt's views is scanty, there appears to be ample proof that his successor, Harry Truman, never questioned whether the weapon should be used. Two days after the Nagasaki bomb exploded, President Truman declared:

> Nobody is more disturbed over the use of Atomic bombs than I am but I was greatly disturbed over the unwarranted attack by the Japanese on Pearl Harbor and the murder of our prisoners of war. The only language they seem to understand is the one we have been using to bombard them. When you have to deal with a beast you have to treat him as a beast. It is most regrettable but nevertheless true.[59]

In his memoirs, Truman stated, "The final decision of where and when to use the atomic bomb was up to me. Let there be no mistake about it. I regarded the bomb as a military weapon and never had any doubt that it should be used." He told his sister Mary that on the trip coming home from the Potsdam conference, "I ordered the Atomic Bomb to be dropped on Hiroshima and Nagasaki. It was a terrible decision. But I made it. And I'd made it to save 250,000 boys from the United States and I'd make it again under similar circumstances. It stopped the Jap War."⁶⁰

These statements are consistent with the image Truman created of himself as a self-assured leader. Yet they conflict with other information in the record. There one sees a man not altogether sure about the ethics of obliterating enemy cities with nuclear weapons.

The new president began his term wondering if he had the ability to take Franklin Roosevelt's place. Almost immediately he had to make a series of very significant choices in which he was aided, but also limited, by a succession of earlier policies and by distinguished, even awe-inspiring officials, such as Stimson and Marshall. He also had to take command of American public opinion.

Truman's initial reflections on ending the war led him to give highest priority to minimizing U.S. losses. On June 14, 1945, he informed the Joint Chiefs of Staff that he wished as far as possible to preserve American lives. Saving money and ending hostilities quickly were comparatively unimportant. Three of the four members of the Joint Chiefs of Staff—Admiral Leahy, General Arnold, and Admiral King—believed at that time that the war could be ended through bombardment and blockade, securing victory in the way Truman wanted. Admiral Leahy held that the war would be a success if Japan surrendered on terms, a view with which Truman appeared to agree. But General Marshall thought otherwise, and Marshall dominated the American chiefs of staff. He pressed for an invasion so as to instill in the Japanese a feeling of utter helplessness, which he considered essential to their unconditional surrender. At a meeting with the Joint Chiefs in the White House on June 18, Truman agreed to authorize a landing on Kyushu and the planning for an invasion of Honshu several months later.⁶¹

The president was also concerned about the reactions of the American people. Americans wanted total victory. Yet they also wanted their fighting men home, early and safe. At the June 18 meeting, after suggesting that it might be better to resolve the war politically than to insist on unconditional surrender, and after stating that he had left the way open for Congress to modify the unconditional surrender doctrine, Truman added that he did not think he could change public views on the matter. Yet he himself had reinforced the public's insistence on unconditional surrender when, after taking over President Roosevelt's office, he had strongly reaffirmed that principle, linking it to a recitation of Japanese atrocities.[62]

Truman believed, as Stimson did, that ending the war with the atomic bomb could provide significant advantages in negotiating with the Russians. But that was only one of several considerations weighing upon his mind. The U.S. Army and public opinion influenced him to shift his priorities and narrowed his options to dropping the bomb, invading the main islands, with all the casualties that would entail, or, if the Japanese did not surrender after the bomb was dropped, to a combination of invasion and nuclear attacks. His choice, as General Groves perceived it, was basically not to interfere with existing plans. Groves compared the president to a boy on roller skates who could not prevent himself from moving toward the decision to drop the bomb. "Truman did not so much say 'yes' as not say 'no,'" Groves explained. "It would indeed have taken a lot of nerve to say 'no' at that time."[63]

The president showed signs of divided feelings about exploding nuclear weapons on enemy cities. During the Potsdam conference, the desolation he observed in Berlin led him to reflect on the long view of history. He imagined humanity as "only termites on a planet" who might bore in too far someday and bring about "a reckoning." Echoing what Stimson had said to him weeks before in their first long discussion of the atomic bomb, Truman remarked, "I fear that machines are ahead of morals by some centuries and when morals catch up perhaps there'll be no reason for any of it."[64]

Yet he also exulted in the power the bomb gave to the United States and to himself. The news, which reached him at Potsdam, that the Manhattan Project scientists had successfully detonated a nuclear device, exhilarated him. He wrote in his journal, in a passage about Stalin's demands, of having "dynamite" of his own which he was not exploding yet, and he noted that he felt the Japanese would collapse before the Soviet Union entered the war, folding up when "Manhattan" appeared over their homeland. Yet images of catastrophe also appeared in his journal, along with other indications that the bomb troubled him. "We have discovered the most terrible bomb in the history of the world," he wrote on July 25. "It may be the fire destruction prophesied in the Euphrates Valley Era, after Noah and his fabulous Ark. . . ."[65]

The president agreed that the first target would be one of the cities the Interim Committee had selected. But he seemed confused about what the target contained, and his attitude toward attacking civilians with nuclear weapons appeared to fluctuate. The committee had chosen target areas with workers' housing, yet Truman noted in his journal that he had told Secretary Stimson to use the bomb "so that military objectives and soldiers and sailors are the target and not women and children. Even if the Japs are savages, ruthless, merciless and fanatic," he wrote, "we as the leader of the world for the common welfare cannot drop this terrible bomb on the old capital [Kyoto] or the new [Tokyo]." At the same time he understood that the bomb would kill and injure great numbers of civilians, and he proposed to protect his country's reputation by issuing a warning which he felt certain the enemy would ignore:

> [Stimson] and I are in accord. The target will be a purely military one and we will issue a warning statement asking the Japs to surrender and save lives. I'm sure they will not do that, but we will have given them the chance. It is certainly a good thing for the world that Hitler's crowd or Stalin's did not discover this atomic bomb. It seems to be the most terrible thing ever discovered, but it can be made the most useful.[66]

After the second bomb obliterated most of Nagasaki, he sent Senator Richard Russell of Georgia a letter that reflected his conflicting emotions:

> I know that Japan is a terribly cruel and uncivilized nation in warfare but I can't bring myself to believe that, because they are beasts, we should ourselves act in the same manner. . . . I certainly regret the necessity of wiping out whole populations because of the "pigheadedness" of the leaders of a nation and . . . I am not going to do it unless it is absolutely necessary. . . . My object is to save as many American lives as possible but I also have a humane feeling for the women and children in Japan.[67]

At a cabinet meeting on August 10 Truman suspended further atomic attacks. His reason, Commerce Secretary Henry A. Wallace noted, was that the thought of wiping out another 100,000 people seemed too horrible. "He didn't like the idea of killing, as he said, 'all those kids.'"[68]

In the wartime views and postwar recollections of the individuals considered here certain ideas repeatedly appear about the morality of bombing Japanese cities and civilians. One of the most common was the notion that a higher goal justified those actions. Air force generals, advisors, scientists, and statesmen all invoked it, usually noting that they wished to avert the deaths of American servicemen. General Groves made this point as well as anyone when he wrote about the A-bomb that "we were trying to perfect a weapon that, however repugnant to us as human beings, could nevertheless save untold numbers of American lives."[69] Some of these men argued that the atomic bomb benefited the Japanese by sparing a great many additional people who would have been killed had the fighting continued. Others invoked once again the hope of World War I, that the present conflict could be a war to end all wars. By demonstrating the bomb on a Japanese city, the United States, they felt, might persuade humanity that war was too horrible to engage in again. Some believed the atomic bomb could secure a world in which their country would predominate over the Soviet Union, a goal that combined national interest with democratic idealism.

People who did not want to drop the atomic bomb, or at least did not want to do so without first letting the Japanese know exactly what awaited them, also invoked a higher aim to justify their position. They claimed that employing a nuclear weapon against an enemy population would destroy the reputation of the United States or incite an arms race that would lead to another, vastly more horrible war.

Americans who played leading parts in the Pacific air war presented other justifications for the incendiary and nuclear bombing of Japan. Some espoused the ethic of an eye for an eye. To Groves and Arnold, Hiroshima was proper retribution for acts of the Japanese armed forces. General Hansell recalled a widespread belief that the Japanese had placed themselves outside the human community by acts of barbarism and by flouting the customs of warfare. One officer suggested that the Japanese government itself had dissolved the moral code that protected civilians when it forced them to support their nation's armed forces. AAF leaders noted the involvement of Japanese women and children in the war effort and suggested that protections for civilians did not apply, since Japan's civilians were actually combatants. Secretary Stimson, General LeMay, and some of the scientists suggested that incendiary bombing had obliterated the barrier against mass air attacks on cities, making nuclear attack morally no worse than the Tokyo raid, or actually better, because it promised to end the killing quickly. Rarely did anyone contend, on the record, that certain means of warfare did harm out of proportion to any good they achieved, or that they were immoral in themselves.

Did the views of participants about the morality of the Pacific air war affect the way the war was waged? The answer is probably yes, though the amount of influence those views exerted is unknown. The concept of just retribution, the notion that the military and political objectives of the air war justified the means employed, the view that it was proper to exchange the lives of civilians connected with the Japanese war effort for the lives of American servicemen, and the hope that destroying cities with nuclear bombs might convince nations to abolish the institution of warfare all supported what was done. Along with technical and political considerations and the belief that American public opinion favored harsh treatment of Japanese civilians, these moral attitudes outweighed, in the minds of the men who made key decisions, the moral objections that a few people raised.

With one exception, moral constraints in the hearts and minds of those responsible for the American air war do not seem to have prevented them from employing any of the measures they contemplated using against Japan. That exception was the saving of Kyoto, where the personal values of the secretary of war, mixed with political considerations, preserved several hundred thousand people and spared one of the great cities of the world.

— 9

Reactions to the Moral Issue: Accounting for the Variations

It is clear that the American air war leaders, their civilian and military advisors, and the scientists and technicians who devised the means for destroying Axis targets reacted to the moral implications of their work in divergent ways. Particular individuals and groups were far more sensitive than others to the moral issues that arose from bombing. Within organizations where moral questions were discussed, points of view varied widely. How do we account for these variations?

Limits on Time and Knowledge

One consideration that affected whether people responded at all to moral issues was the factor of time. In agencies pressed by deadlines, as were most of those examined here, attempts to weigh the human effects of bombing would have interrupted vital work. This can be illustrated by imagining what might have happened if the Committee of Operations Analysts or its Incendiary Subcommittee had begun to explore the morality of setting fire to Japanese cities.

During the spring and summer of 1944, as the COA examined proposals for bombing Japan, American armed forces were seizing islands, constructing air bases, assembling men, planes, and equipment—preparing to carry out the decision of the Joint Chiefs of Staff to devastate Japan from the air. To assure that the raids would be as effective as possible, committee members had to evaluate large quantities of data, prepare reports, and perform other time-consuming tasks for which freedom from distraction was essential. If, in the midst of these deliberations, members had started raising questions about moral issues—asking, for instance, whether it was possible to obstruct the Japanese war effort without killing so many civilians—long discussion would have ensued. The actions contemplated touched on moral issues at many points and the members of the planning group, chosen partly for their intellects, were accustomed to viewing complex problems from several angles. Once the precedent was set, moral questions might have arisen again and again, interfering with the committee's analytical work and costing the air force valuable time.

Most of the atomic scientists also operated under strict time constraints which, combined with the need for secrecy, made it difficult to inquire into moral issues raised by nuclear weapons. At the beginning of the war, many of the scientists had been driven by the need to develop those weapons before the Nazis did. But after Germany surrendered, the directors of the Manhattan Project actually intensified pressure to prepare the weapon for use. Hoping to forestall breaches of security and to force inquisitive scientists to "stick to their knitting," rather than indulge in time-wasting inquiries designed to satisfy their curiosity and extend their knowledge, General Groves tried to limit everyone who worked on the project solely to information needed for a specific task. Groves's system of compartmentalization did not survive intact throughout the Manhattan Project. At Los Alamos and at the Chicago Metallurgical Laboratory scientists considered it essential to speak with one another about issues of common interest, and Groves allowed them to communicate. But compartments remained at the Hanford and Oak Ridge facilities, and the army tried to prevent scientists from different laboratories from discussing the A-bomb program with one another. Even at Los Alamos J. Robert Oppenheimer, the laboratory director, discouraged organized inquiry into nontechnical issues, such as the morality of building nuclear weapons.[1]

The laboratory directors and other top scientists who advised the secretary of war on nuclear policy were very much pressed for time and spent little of it discussing moral questions. On May 31, 1945, for less than an hour during lunch and during part of the session that afternoon, they considered possible alternatives to obliterating Japanese cities with nuclear bombs, including a demonstration to impress the Japanese. Several days later, when members of Stimson's scientific panel met to complete a report on the control of atomic weapons and other important questions involving nuclear research and development, they again took up the question of a demonstration. But it was only at the University of Chicago Metallurgical Laboratory, whose most important work ended well before the first A-bomb was tested, that scientists had ample time to explore the moral problems presented by nuclear weapons.[2]

Lack of information hindered scientists and others from exploring moral issues. Even the Chicago scientists lacked crucial knowledge needed to appraise proposals for bombing Japanese cities—for instance, intercepts of Japanese peace feelers or other data concerning the state of mind of Japan's rulers. The same was true for the scientific panel, one of whose members, J. Robert Oppenheimer, later observed that he and his colleagues had conducted their discussions without independent political and military data. "We didn't know beans about the military situation in Japan," he recalled. "We didn't know whether they could be caused to surrender by other means or whether the invasion was really inevitable. But in back of our minds was the notion that the invasion was inevitable because we had been told that." Oppenheimer trusted Secretary Stimson to think through the moral implications of using the atom bomb.[3]

There is no question that Stimson examined those implications and possessed information that the scientists and top military men knew little about. His firsthand knowledge of Japanese civilization and his understanding of the conflict developing between the United States and the USSR contributed to his decision to spare Kyoto. Nevertheless, he seems not to have known certain key facts about the conventional bombing of Germany and Japan, although knowledge of those facts was essential to weighing the ethics of what was done.

During the first half of 1945 Stimson appeared remarkably unaware of what the AAF was doing to enemy cities. The day Operation CLARION was launched he told a press conference, "Our policy never has been to inflict terror bombing on civilian populations." Yet this is exactly what advocates of CLARION-type operations, like the scientist David Griggs, intended. After the furor erupted over the Dresden bombing, Stimson asked the air force for photographic evidence that the American objectives there were, as usual, military in character. After being told that they were he dropped his inquiry. He appeared not to recognize that American participation in such operations as THUNDERCLAP and CLARION had broken down the AAF's distinction between military and nonmilitary targets.[4]

Stimson also seemed not to understand what the AAF was doing to Japanese cities. He accepted a pledge from Assistant Secretary Lovett that the air force would use only precision bombing against Japan—a promise completely at odds with long-standing plans to firebomb urban areas. He seemed surprised when the XXI Bomber Command violated this pledge with a raid on Tokyo. But the bombing that disturbed him was not the one that produced the holocaust of March 10 or any of the incendiary attacks of the following weeks. It was a raid on the Japanese capital the night of May 25–26.

At one point that spring, long after the attacks on Dresden and Berlin, weeks after General LeMay's bombers had incinerated large sections of the Honshu cities, Stimson informed President Truman that it was possible to hold the American air force in the Pacific "to the 'precision' bombing it has done so well in Europe." On the first of June, he recorded in his diary that General Arnold, after explaining the difficulty of hitting scattered Japanese industry without injuring civilians connected with war work, had said the AAF was "trying to keep it down as far as possible." These statements conflicted with actual AAF policy, which was, as one of its officers explained, to systematically bomb out the eight leading cities of Japan with the intention of not leaving one stone upon another.[5]

Stimson's distorted view of Army Air Forces activities raises a number of questions. Could he really have been so misinformed about terror bombing in Germany, particularly since he had described David Griggs's proposal for terrorizing the German people as "intriguing"? Why did he accept without an independent inquiry the AAF's claim that during the Dresden raid the targets, as usual, were military ones? Was it possible that the secretary of war knew less about the March 10 bombing of Tokyo than a reader of the *New York Times*? Why did he accept Arnold's statement about attempting to limit the impact of bombing on Japanese civilians? Was he signaling that he really did not wish to be told what the AAF was doing to enemy civilians? Or did the secretary, seventy-seven years old, ill with heart disease and often unable to put in a full day's work, find it too difficult, in the midst of so many concerns, to inquire thoroughly into all the actions of the AAF which seemed to raise disturbing moral questions?[6]

Key Individuals and Frames of Reference

Important as time and information constraints may have been, they did not invariably prevent the parties to the American war effort from looking into such questions. Even before they learned what the A-bomb did to Hiroshima, scientists at Los Alamos began to think about the moral and political consequences of their work. Moral issues were debated in USSTAF headquarters and other places where time constraints were very powerful. There must be other reasons why in some offices moral questions were ignored while in others they were examined, why in certain agencies the inquiry was fairly systematic and in others superficial, and why some of the people responsible for the air war discussed its moral consequences openly while others veiled their thoughts.

One obvious factor was the presence of certain key individuals who either raised moral questions or made it easier or more difficult for others to do so. Those who stimulated moral inquiry changed the framework of thought within which others were operating. They encouraged people who spent their time answering technical questions to wonder if other kinds of questions should be asked. Those who discouraged moral inquiry tried to persuade people who ventured outside a technical frame of reference that a higher goal required them to confine themselves to solving technical problems. Colonel Hughes exemplifies the first type of key individual, and so do Eugene Rabinowitz and Leo Szilard at the Chicago lab. General Groves and J. Robert Oppenheimer were leading figures who tried, for the duration of the Manhattan Project, to keep scientists thinking about how to build a bomb, not debating whether it ought to be built.[7]

Robert Wilson described how Oppenheimer convinced a group of Los Alamos scientists who were thinking about moral and social questions that the important thing was to finish the job. Wilson had organized a meeting to discuss the impact of the A-bomb on civilization. Oppenheimer tried to prevent him from holding it, but it took place anyway, with thirty or more people attending, including Oppenheimer, who, Wilson observed, "always added a tone to any meeting." The scientists considered whether they should continue their work, some wondering if what they were doing was morally wrong. Oppenheimer argued that letting the world know about the possibility of the atomic bomb was more desirable than keeping it secret and persuaded those present, in Wilson's words, that "we ought to go back in the laboratory and work as hard as we could to demonstrate a nuclear weapon . . . so that the United Nations would be set up in awareness of this horrible thing to come."[8]

The highest political and military leaders also helped establish the framework within which people concerned with the air war considered or ignored the morality of bombing policies. Although Secretary of War Stimson encouraged his scientific and other civilian advisors to consider alternatives to using the atomic bomb on Japanese cities, he conveyed the impression that he thought it should be used that way. So did President Roosevelt.[9] In AAF headquarters, Hap Arnold helped shape the manner in which his subordinates thought about terror raids. Arnold's assistant chief of air staff for plans, General Kuter, disliked shedding civilian blood in terror attacks, but he analyzed ways of employing terror raids because Arnold wanted the subject investigated. At USSTAF headquarters General Spaatz indirectly helped Colonel Hughes and others raise moral issues because his tolerance of their activities and his own ambivalence about killing and terrorizing German civilians suggested that it was all right to consider those questions. General Marshall helped establish the framework within which the moral and other questions about using the A-bomb were considered by persuading the president that the only alternative to dropping it was a bloody invasion of the Japanese main islands.

The Role of Psychological Factors

Marshall, Stimson, Spaatz, and Arnold and all the other top leaders of the U.S. war effort wished to defeat the Axis as efficiently and rapidly as possible, and the methods of air warfare they approved all were aimed at that objective. Yet none of these men, nor any of the other people who determined the course of the air war, acted simply on the basis of rational calculation. Like everyone involved in the conflict, from combat troops to heads of state, the people responsible for American air attacks felt the stress of warfare and developed mental protections against it. Training, indoctrination, and battle experiences hardened some of them to suffering and death, helped deaden them to the enemy's humanity, and enabled them to bury their emotions. The routines of their work and the physical detachment of conducting war from offices far from the target area made it less difficult to inflict pain that might have been agonizing to administer face to face, and enabled them to avoid the combat fatigue that develops in people who think too much about those they are killing. Some of them compartmentalized their feelings so that, absorbed in specialized tasks, they ignored the moral effects of their work or left to higher authority the responsibility for considering "humanitarian" issues. Meanwhile, evidence of enemy crimes strengthened their feelings that what they did was right and justified their support of harsh military actions.[10]

A form of mental inertia contributed to actions by the AAF that proved catastrophic to enemy civilians and cities. It took enormous psychic as well as physical investments to support theaterwide bombing campaigns and programs like the Manhattan Project. People who worried about the ethics of bombing would have needed extraordinary will and tremendous influence to stop or divert those efforts.

Psychological inertia may have helped keep the AAF from shifting its bombers from Japanese urban areas toward targets with greater military value. For example, when the USSBS directors provided General Norstad and the Joint Target Group with information that conflicted with a bombing program already under way over Japan, their suggestions seem to have had little effect on policy. They told Norstad and the JTG that, based on what they had just learned about the effects of the air war on Germany, transportation attacks merited a much higher priority than area bombing and area raids might actually improve enemy civilian morale. Yet the Twentieth Air Force continued to launch devastating area attacks, many of them aimed at breaking morale, though it also struck at particular strategic targets.[11]

It was not that the AAF planners failed to hear, did not understand, or even disagreed with what the Strategic Bombing Survey people told them. When General Anderson suggested that bombing increased morale, General Norstad understood what he was saying, for Norstad remarked that he was astonished by the evidence Anderson presented.[12] A more likely explanation for the Twentieth Air Force's continued emphasis on area bombing, despite testimony to its relative inefficiency, is that Norstad now had such vast resources at his disposal that he could expend them on both area and precision attacks. But the arguments against giving high priority to urban area bombing made little impact for other reasons. First, they conflicted with a program the Twentieth Air Force had spent so much time and effort developing, and with the hope of General Norstad and others in the Twentieth Air Force that morale bombing would cause Japan to capitulate. Second, they implied that the air force might be wasting lives and resources. And third, acceptance of arguments against area bombing would have required air force strategists to rethink an analysis that had taken months to develop and that had persuaded them long ago that urban areas ought to be bombed.[13]

The USSBS directors did not tell the Joint Target Group that attacks on Japanese cities would kill people needlessly, although their observations in Europe suggested that conclusion. The fact that they never raised this point, which must have been obvious to them, may be explained by the pressure, which existed in USSTAF headquarters and was present in military organizations at all levels, to be tough, or at least not to appear soft and idealistic. Scientists felt this pressure too, and so did other civilians who worked with military people and needed to retain their confidence. It caused members of the Franck committee to shape their arguments almost exclusively in practical military and political rather than ethical terms. "We were all deeply moved by moral considerations," Eugene Rabinowitch, one of the committee members, remembered, "but we did not think that in the necessarily a-moral climate in which wartime decisions have to be made these would be effective."[14]

Even top leaders experienced the pressure to appear hard and resolute. Stimson was afraid of being thought sentimental for proposing to save Kyoto. One reason he gave President Truman for not allowing the AAF to wipe out all Japanese cities with area raids was as unsentimental as can be imagined: ". . . I was a little fearful that before we could get ready the Air Force might have Japan so thoroughly bombed out that the new weapon would not have a fair background to show its strength." The president laughed at this, Stimson recorded, and said he understood.[15] Since Truman harbored ambivalent feelings about killing Japanese women and children, it appears that both he and the secretary were concerned about appearing properly realistic.

It was especially important that President Truman seem tough. He was trying to fill the place of a very determined predecessor, and people whose judgment he valued and depended on made it clear that they wanted him to be as unwavering as Franklin Roosevelt had been. Thus at the June 18 White House meeting with the Joint Chiefs of Staff, General Marshall, the prestigious army leader whom the new president venerated,[16] conveyed to Truman a barely disguised warning not to appear weak before the armed forces and the nation.

President Truman's early thoughts about ending the war had led him to give highest priority to limiting U.S. losses. In mid-June he had informed the Joint Chiefs of Staff that as far as possible he wished to economize on American lives and that saving money and ending hostilities quickly were comparatively unimportant. He even hinted during the June 18 meeting that if Congress and the people would let him, he was willing to abandon the unconditional surrender doctrine. General Marshall felt differently about these matters.

After discussing prospective U.S. casualties from the landing on Kyushu, first of the home islands to be invaded, Marshall declared,

> It is a grim fact that there is not an easy, bloodless way to victory in war and it is the thankless task of the leaders to maintain their firm outward front which holds the resolution of their subordinates. Any irresolution in the leaders may result in costly weakening and indecision in the subordinates. It was this basic difficulty with the Prime Minister [Churchill] which clouded and hampered all our preparations for the cross-channel operation now demonstrated as having been essential to victory in Europe.[17]

Since Marshall was not in the habit of making speeches to his fellow chiefs of staff, his remarks could only have been directed at the onetime artillery captain who now sat as commander in chief.

The pressure to seem tough before colleagues and followers is only one example of the way psychological forces operating within groups affected the American air war. The interactions of these forces were complicated and sometimes quite subtle. Yet we can imagine how those interactions influenced responses to moral issues if we draw on studies of group behavior in analogous situations.

The work of the social psychologist Irving L. Janis is especially helpful here. Janis used experimental evidence and historical data to analyze the behavior of American leaders in a series of crises, including the Korean War, the attempted invasion of Cuba in 1961, the 1962 Cuban missile crisis, and the escalation of the Vietnam War. He observed that in some of those cases, the leaders' reactions were affected by what he called *groupthink*, a collective pattern of psychological defense through avoidance. This phenomenon tended to appear in a cohesive organization which had to make vital decisions when the organization's actions posed threats of personal or social disapproval to the members. Arising from their mutual effort to preserve self-esteem by concurring with one another, groupthink helped group members minimize anxiety and guilt and sustained their morale through the crisis, inducing elation or, at times, an exhilarating sense of omnipotence—a kind of group "high"—as they struggled against a common enemy.[18]

People affected by groupthink suffered from faulty perception and became complacent, uncritical, and irrationally optimistic. Ignoring the views of outside experts or even of other group members who challenged assumptions on which their decisions rested, they discussed the enemy in slogans and ideological clichés. Dissenting members censored their own doubts, refusing to disturb the apparent consensus that helped the group feel its position was correct. If everyone else agreed so strongly on a position, would-be dissenters imagined, the group's position must be right. However, if a nonconformist did speak up, instead of listening carefully to what he said other participants tried to change his mind, and if that proved impossible they subtly isolated him. If he continued to challenge shared stereotypes, illusions, or commitments, the group applied direct pressure to silence him. Sometimes members acted as "mindguards," telling those who disagreed with the consensus to keep their ideas to themselves regardless of whether the ideas were valid. This helped preserve the organization's placid surface, protecting the leader and other participants from information that might have threatened their self-confidence.[19]

Janis thought that the more amiable a group and the greater its esprit de corps, the more likely it was that groupthink would replace critical thinking, but he did not consider its emergence inevitable even in highly cohesive organizations. There were ways of sustaining tendencies toward realistic thinking—for instance, by breaking a larger group into smaller segments, or by keeping the leader away from certain phases of discussion. These kinds of improvements enabled virtually the same individuals who led the United States into the Bay of Pigs fiasco to avoid groupthink the following year during the Cuban missile crisis.[20]

The groupthink hypothesis offers a way of understanding why some of the American air war leaders and planners ignored evidence that morale bombing wasted U.S. resources, and it helps explain why certain groups considered the moral consequences of bombing while others overlooked them. If decisions that threaten the self-esteem of a decision-making body induce its members to seek concurrence, groupthink symptoms would be likely to arise when a choice of action posed a moral dilemma, particularly if the most advantageous course required the decision makers to violate their own standards of humanitarian behavior. Under those circumstances, each member would depend increasingly on the organization to maintain his self-image as a decent human being and would strive to preserve the group's unity.[21]

Janis observed that while organizations exhibiting groupthink behavior spent little time discussing moral issues, they regarded their own position as morally upright. They tended to be extremely hardhearted toward the external opponent, favoring harsh solutions such as large-scale bombings, while refusing to admit the possibility that what they proposed conflicted with their personal values. Disinclined to raise ethical issues, they appeared to feel, as Janis put it, that this "fine group of ours, with its humanitarianism and its high-minded principles," was incapable of adopting an inhumane and immoral course of action. Meanwhile, they tended to stereotype and dehumanize the enemy, to view him as immoral, weak, and stupid, deserving of the punishment planned for him. By sharing these views of the opponent, the group minimized the chance that any member would challenge its policy "by raising moral and humanitarian considerations, which would stimulate bickering, recriminations and discord."[22]

Janis felt that a cohesive group would not inevitably favor harsh treatment. If its dominant faction preferred peaceable methods, he thought the rest of the members would tend to fall into line. Without groupthink, they could debate moral issues openly, though the debate might be extremely painful because the protections groupthink afforded to self-esteem would be missing. This is what happened in the Cuban missile crisis, when, according to Robert Kennedy, during the first five days of deliberations the American planning group spent more time on the question of how to resolve the crisis without compromising America's moral integrity than on any other single matter.[23]

Applying Janis's findings to the American air war, we would expect to discover that, regardless of whether the groups involved exhibited the full groupthink syndrome, their members were subject to the kinds of influence Janis describes. Even those people who never mentioned moral issues would have sensed, at some level of consciousness, that what they were doing posed a threat to their self-esteem. Group defense mechanisms would have shielded them against this threat, but because those mechanisms interfered with critical thinking, the very existence of a moral problem would have made it difficult to undertake a serious examination of that problem.

The Committee of Operations Analysts was the kind of organization Janis considered likely to accept harsh measures against the enemy while avoiding overt moral recriminations. It was a highly cohesive, self-assured, and strongly motivated social group convinced of the rightness of the American cause and, as Guido Perera observed, of the brutality and dangerousness of the country's enemies. As far as the record shows, none of its members nor any consultants from the outside raised ethical objections to its recommendations. While the COA was aware that hundreds of thousands of civilians would be killed in the incendiary test raid it endorsed and in the massive area raids it expected would follow, discussing casualties in human rather than abstract terms would have brought considerable tension to the surface and, if Janis is right, threatened the self-images of the committee's members. This may have been what Perera referred to when he recalled finding "distasteful" a fire expert's remarks about the casualties that would result from incendiary bombing.[24]

Similarly, if the directors of the Strategic Bombing Survey, at their meeting with Norstad and the Joint Target Group, had challenged the morality of area bombing on Japanese cities instead of merely questioning its efficacy, they would have aroused unpleasant feelings. The JTG might have proceeded to discuss the moral effects of firebombing Japanese cities, but the atmosphere in the room would have become very uncomfortable. In LeMay's headquarters an effort to call attention to the humanity of the people who lived and worked in the Japanese central cities would have produced tension, to say the least.

Nevertheless, certain cohesive groups with high morale and strong dedication to the war effort did look closely at the moral aspects of bombing: the Intelligence section of USSTAF and the Chicago Metallurgical Laboratory scientists. Special factors already noted, such as the presence of key figures like Szilard and Hughes and the reduced pressure of time at Chicago, helped make this possible. But group characteristics also encouraged discussion of moral questions. At Chicago it was the presence of several scientists, refugees from the Nazis' persecution of the Jews, who focused their hostility against Germans and were more likely to regard other people on whom the atomic bomb might be dropped as human beings rather than a depersonalized enemy. These scientists also came from a tradition that sanctified debate. (At Los Alamos, where several refugee scientists worked, the director of the laboratory damped efforts to debate the moral question.) In USSTAF headquarters, a cluster of people from OSS and the air force who respected Colonel Hughes and sympathized with his view of the moral question probably encouraged him to pursue that question, even if the overwhelming majority of people surrounding him were "realists"; the presence of just two dissenting persons within a group tends to reduce drastically the inclination to conform.[25]

The analysis presented here is obviously suggestive rather than definitive. We do not have any record of what was thought but not expressed or of what was spoken outside the conference room and never recorded. Though the psychological explanations are based on experimental evidence, on clinical observations, and on records of historical events, they remain partly hypothetical and constitute less than absolute proof of why people responsible for the way the United States conducted its air war acted as they did.[26] Still, it is clear that several elements interacted to produce the result. Pressures of time and the availability of information, the presence of key individuals and of persons sharing their points of view, the need to appear tough, and other individual and group psychological phenomena combined with rational appraisals of military and political circumstances to produce a wide range of reactions, including no reaction at all, to the moral issues that arose from American bombing.

10

Epilogue

To people familiar with the development of airpower it was clear at the end of World War II that the next great power conflict was likely to be very different from all others. Eugene Rabinowitch, a veteran of the Metallurgical Lab, recalled how "in the summer of 1945 some of us walked the streets of Chicago vividly imagining the sky suddenly lit by a giant fireball, the steel skeletons of skyscrapers bending into grotesque shapes and their masonry raining into the streets below, until a great cloud of dust rose and settled over the crumbling sky." In a report on a postwar atomic test General Curtis LeMay noted that "it is possible to depopulate vast areas of the earth's surface, leaving only vestigial remnants of man's material works."[1] Yet despite enormous qualitative changes in the potential of weapons, the thinking of American military leaders, scientists, and statesmen in the postwar years contained important vestiges of earlier views about air warfare and its moral consequences.

Early Atomic War Plans

After the victory over Japan, the American air force continued to develop the Douhetian strategy of mass destruction with which it had ended World War II. Weakness in ground forces virtually dictated this approach, for while the U.S. demobilized the Soviet Union maintained a much larger army. In the fall of 1946, when the U.S. Army, including the AAF, was dwindling toward a force of less than two million, General Norstad informed the president that the Russians had 93 divisions in Europe alone, that its satellites fielded

100 divisions, and that the USSR appeared able to mobilize ten and a half million troops in one month and fifteen million in 150 days. In Germany between one and two American divisions would soon confront 42 divisions of Soviet troops. The United States still retained a far stronger navy,[2] but to oppose a great land power like the Soviets, American leaders believed they would have to rely primarily on the air force and atomic bombs.

This really meant relying largely on bluff, for even before the Russians developed their own nuclear weapons it was doubtful that the United States could have destroyed the Soviet Union's will to make war or its capacity to fight. In the American arsenal at the end of 1945 there were two nuclear bombs. By July 1946 the number was up to nine. A year later it had reached thirteen. By July 1948, in the midst of a crisis over a Soviet blockade of Berlin, the U.S. had fifty unassembled nuclear weapons, which required more than two days' work apiece by thirty-nine men to prepare for use. These five-ton bombs had to be carried by specially modified B-29s, for which no fighter escort existed that could travel to all identified targets in the USSR. American intelligence did not even know where all the important Russian targets were.[3]

In 1949 a special Pentagon committee, headed by Air Force Lieutenant General Hubert R. Harmon, estimated what would happen if the United States dropped 133 bombs on 70 Soviet targets. It concluded that if every bomb detonated precisely on target (which was highly unlikely), the effect, though devastating, would not "destroy the roots of Communism" or bring about capitulation. At least in the short run, Russian will to fight would probably increase and Soviet armies would be able to advance rapidly into selected areas of Western Europe, the Far East, and the Middle East.[4]

U.S. military leaders proposed to deter, and if necessary conduct atomic war with, the Soviet Union by targeting America's small stock of A-bombs against large, heavily populated industrial centers. War plan BROILER, developed late that year, called for the delivery of thirty-four bombs against Soviet government centers, urban industrial areas, and selected petroleum targets, many of which were located in cities. In 1948 the first operational plan of the Strategic Air Command selected aiming points with the primary objective of annihilating population. Destruction of industrial targets would be incidental. Three years later General LeMay, now head of SAC, told Air Staff planners to "concentrate on industry itself which is located in urban areas," rather than try to hit hard-to-find isolated objectives. That way, even if bombers missed a specific target, a "bonus" would result from using the bomb.[5]

Though these early nuclear war plans were intended primarily to safeguard American interests without resorting to general war, the prospect of using A-bombs if deterrence failed greatly disturbed the man who would have to order them dropped. For a time President Truman hoped that atomic power would be controlled by an international agency, and that nuclear bombs would be outlawed. When he was briefed in the spring of 1948 on War Plan HALFMOON, which called for a nuclear air offensive against the Soviet Union, Truman ordered an alternate plan prepared based solely on conventional forces. During the 1948 Soviet blockade of Berlin he sent B-29s to Europe equipped for conventional, not nuclear, bombing. The president told Air Force Secretary W. Stuart Symington in July that he "didn't think we ought to use this thing unless we absolutely have to," that it was terrible to use a weapon so destructive. "You have got to understand," he explained, "that this isn't a military weapon. It is used to wipe out women and children and unarmed people, not for military uses. . . ."[6]

Eventually, however, Truman came back to the position he had taken in the summer of 1945: the United States had to rely on the bomb. On the 13th of September he said to Secretary of Defense James Forrestal that while he prayed that he would never have to use the A-bomb, no one need have any misgiving that he would not make the decision if it became necessary. In July 1949 he told a secret meeting on atomic policy that he had concluded there would never be international control of nuclear weapons and consequently that the United States must have the strongest atomic arsenal. After technical advances made it possible to produce large numbers of fission weapons and to make them more powerful, efficient, and versatile, Truman promoted an atomic armaments program designed to deter a foreseeable Soviet attack, to blunt a Soviet air assault and stop the Soviet armies, and to devastate the urban-industrial structure on which Soviet capacity for war depended.[7]

The Admirals Take Up the Moral Issue

Objections to contingency plans for nuclear attacks on Soviet cities had arisen, meanwhile, within the navy. An influential group of admirals criticized the air-atomic strategy, which threatened to diminish the navy's role in the American military system. One group of admirals used the history of air power in World War II to denounce strategic bombing as immoral, but the leading spokesmen for that point of view arrived at their position by a very indirect route.

In 1946 Chief of Naval Operations Admiral Chester W. Nimitz questioned whether the United States should use atomic bombs to offset Soviet offensives. Because it appeared to him that the A-bomb might be outlawed or not employed, he thought the United States should stop including it in war plans. By the end of the next year, however, lower-level navy leaders were challenging this view. Admiral Daniel V. Gallery, the assistant chief of naval operations for guided missiles, warned that if the navy assumed the next war would be fought like the last one, it would become obsolete. Gallery thought strategic bombing would decide the next war and that the atom bomb, aimed at enemy capitals and industrial centers, would be America's "Sunday Punch." He wanted to develop carrier-based nuclear bombers, and he urged the navy to start an aggressive campaign to prove it could deliver A-bombs more effectively than the air force could.[8]

Admiral Ralph A. Ofstie felt very much the same way. An air officer who had served as the navy's highest-level representative to the Strategic Bombing Survey, Ofstie thought that if war broke out with the Soviet Union, the United States should use a carrier striking force to launch nuclear and conventional attacks, first disrupting command structures and national organizations by hitting urban industrial concentrations and political control centers, then striking tactical targets. In a January 1948 memorandum, to which four other admirals added their concurrence, Ofstie recommended that the United States build new, highly mobile, high-performance aircraft instead of the very heavy bombers on which the U.S. Air Force relied. He declared that "the day of the great strategic bombing force suited only to aerial bombing is finished."[9]

These ideas obviously did not ingratiate their proponents with the air force, which was then contesting for a share of the Truman administration's greatly reduced defense budget, and at first they did not have official navy support either. But as the interservice struggle intensified during 1949, a growing consensus within the navy backed Admiral Ofstie's views. Ofstie took the position that the air force's entire strategic air warfare approach was defective, for it was essentially based "on the wholesale destruction of urban and industrial areas and the civil populace of the enemy rather than direct attack on his active military machine." He did not feel the navy should concentrate on preparing for strategic air war in peacetime. Still, if the appropriate authority directed it to assist in strategic air warfare, he said, the navy would naturally be ready to take part.[10]

Admiral Gallery now reversed himself completely. In communications to navy colleagues, he disputed the notion of destroying cities. Sounding much like Colonel Richard Hughes, Gallery claimed that planned nuclear air offensives against industrial concentrations would not only fail, in all likelihood, to achieve their military objectives, but their social and economic effects would damage American interests. "For a 'civilized society' like the United States," he said, "the broad purpose of a war cannot be simply destruction and annihilation of the enemy." At best, warfare was a means to force the enemy to cease resistance and comply with one's wishes, an "elementary" point which many American military planners were losing sight of. They had adopted "the Douhet concept of flattening the enemy's cities from the air," though that kind of war was "not as simple as the prophets of the ten day atomic blitz" seemed to think. In World War II strategic bombing equivalent to 500 atomic bombs had not made the Germans surrender, for they capitulated only when their armies were defeated. Now the destruction of Germany was costing America huge sums of money to undo. Moreover, "levelling large cities has a tendency to alienate the affections of the inhabitants and does not create an atmosphere of international good will after the war." Gallery concluded that the United States needed a better way of securing its objectives than destroying the enemy's cities one after another until he gives up.[11]

Later, in an article for the *Saturday Evening Post*, he elaborated on these ideas. The proponents of the "atomic blitz," he said, were sugarcoating war, promising easy victory without much fighting and perhaps lulling Americans into thinking war was not so bad. But the atomic bomb was "a weapon of indiscriminate destruction and mass slaughter," he argued, and strategic nuclear warfare was "war against the common people," not against enemy leaders. Admiral Gallery asked what the United States would do if, while American strategic bombers were desolating Russian cities, the Red Army occupied the rest of Europe. "Do we blitz Paris, Rome and Brussels?" he asked. Wars had to be fought for political objectives, yet the means employed in fighting them might deny those objectives to the victor. While he favored using the threat of atomic war and was even willing to drop the bomb "if we have to," he insisted the bomb had to be backed up by sea and ground forces.[12]

When Secretary of Defense Louis Johnson, in the spring of 1949, abruptly canceled a project to complete the USS *United States*, a supercarrier designed as a floating base for nuclear and conventional bombers, naval officers reacted vigorously, launching public attacks on air force strategy and on the new long-range air force bomber, the B-36.[13] Much of what the admirals had to say dealt with the ability of the B-36 to conduct its mission and with other technical matters, but some of the navy officers, including Admiral Ofstie and Admiral Arthur W. Radford, commander of the Pacific fleet, invoked the history of World War II strategic bombing to attack the military value and the morality of atomic warfare.

In an earlier phase of the dispute between the services, Admiral Radford had wanted the navy to build carriers large enough to launch heavy nuclear bombers against the Soviet Union. But in October 1949 he told the House Armed Services Committee, which was investigating the interservice controversy, that he did not believe in mass killing of noncombatants. While he felt strategic bombing had its place in war, he insisted that the B-36 was bound to kill people en masse, since it was incapable of hitting precise military targets under battle conditions and would inevitably be used against civilians in a war of annihilation. After considering the findings of the Strategic Bombing Survey, he had decided that the United States had to be smarter than in the last war if it wanted a "livable world." An atomic war of annihilation would be economically and politically senseless. If the American people were informed about all the factors involved, he warned, they would consider it morally reprehensible.[14]

Admiral Ofstie used both the British and the American strategic bombing surveys to criticize current policies. He recalled how, at the beginning of the Second World War, Allied bombers had not intended to make people or cities their chief targets but had eventually resorted to area raids because they were "incapable of precision attack." Strategic bombing was still "inherently inaccurate," and regardless of how its objectives were defined, it unavoidably included "mass slaughter of men, women, and children in the enemy country."

Ofstie contended that this kind of assault could not possibly achieve the results that advocates of strategic bombing promised. It would not significantly retard a Soviet advance into Western Europe, for the Red Army would begin the war fully mobilized and would be able to move into other countries, turning the areas they occupied into arsenals for their own use. Would the United States then "atomize" Western European cities where friendly people outnumbered the invaders by fifty or a hundred to one? Evidence from World War II proved that strategic bombing had undermined the physical structure of society, intensifying hunger, poverty, and disease, encouraging the enemies of "our kind of civilization." After another war, with the homes and cities of belligerent nations in ruins, a stable world economy might be impossible to maintain.

Strategic bombing, the admiral contended, with its ruthless, barbaric methods, threatened the moral standards of American society. The United States should not employ military techniques that robbed it of self-respect while adding virtually nothing to its security or the security of its allies. It must cease to follow an erroneous doctrine of atomic air war. "Must the Italian Douhet continue as our prophet," he asked, "because certain zealots grasped his false doctrines many years ago and refuse to relinquish this discredited theory in the face of vast costly experience? Must we translate the historical mistake of World War II into a permanent concept merely to avoid clouding the prestige of those who led us down the wrong road in the past?"[15]

The air force answered with a methodical rebuttal, prepared with the help of W. Barton Leach, the Harvard law professor who had served on the Committee of Operations Analysts. Its witnesses denied they had made the exaggerated claims for strategic air power which the admirals attributed to their service. They offered evidence supporting the view that American long-range aircraft could bomb with considerable precision, defended the B-36, and maintained that they had never intended to rely solely on the kind of long-range bombing Ofstie and his colleagues decried.[16]

Air Force Secretary Symington told the congressmen that as far as he knew, "this opinion that war is immoral is a fairly recent one for anybody in the Military Establishment," and he wondered how and why it came up. Symington had not thought that the morality of warfare was a problem for the military. It had seemed obvious to him that the president and the secretary of state were supposed to deal with it. Nevertheless, he offered his own opinion about the ethics of bombing civilians, which corresponded almost exactly with General Eaker's view:

> If this country's safety is at stake, for the life of me I can't see the difference in trying to stop the functioning of a man on a lathe building a bomber to attack the United States, and trying to stop a soldier. It would seem to me that in total war it is just as important to stop building a bomber being created to attack the United States, and the people who are building that bomber, as it would be to attack a railroad transportation line.

When a friendly congressman suggested that it could not always be wrong to bomb civilians, since the bombing of Hiroshima and Nagasaki had saved the lives of a great many American soldiers, Symington remarked, "If civilians are going to be killed, I would rather have them their civilians than our civilians."[17]

The chairman of the Joint Chiefs of Staff, General Omar Bradley, sharply criticized the admirals for devaluing the A-bomb and the Strategic Air Command. He told the committee that he favored outlawing atomic bombs through international control, but until that happened he was not going to minimize their effects or limit their use. As "a believer in humanity," Bradley said, he deplored the bomb's employment. As a soldier he respected the bomb. As an American citizen he felt the country should be prepared to use it to prevent war and, if attacked, to help win. The naval officers' "careless detraction" of its power had done American security no good and might have done collective security untold harm. For the good of the nation, he wished the admirals had never given their testimony.[18]

Commenting on the admirals' claim that strategic air warfare was immoral, Bradley distinguished between "wanton destruction of cities or people" and the incidental bombing of workers who lived near factories. Strategic bombing had contributed to victory in the past by damaging war-making potential and doing great injury to national morale. Though he agreed that methods used to win a war might lose the peace, the crucial point was not to lose the war. Besides, war itself was "immoral." A Communist dictatorship, lacking any kind of humanitarian outlook toward warfare, would sacrifice human life at the slightest provocation. If the United States responded to a Communist attack with its strategic air power, he thought the American people might consider that response militarily and morally justified.

These hearings may have brought the air force unpleasant publicity, but as far as the investigating committee was concerned, the admirals failed to make their case. Eventually the navy itself accepted the air-atomic strategy, receiving carrier planes that could carry new small atomic weapons and developing its own nuclear missile-firing submarines.[19]

To people in the air force, these developments showed that navy charges against the immorality of strategic bombing were just a tactic in the interservice struggle. The way Ofstie, Gallery, and Radford changed their views on atomic warfare when it seemed that their service would not be allowed its own nuclear air arm suggested that skepticism was warranted.[20] Still, navy testimony reflected more than simple pragmatism. The air admirals had worried for some time about the ability of long-range strategic bombers to penetrate modern anti-aircraft defenses and they had doubted the value of a pure bomber strategy. At the same time, they feared that their service might be reduced to an inferior role if strategic nuclear bombing became the heart of national defense and the navy had no strategic bombers. Consequently, they asked for the kind of equipment that would allow the navy the option of fighting an atomic war.[21]

Some navy spokesmen had always been troubled by the morality of area bombing. It is inconceivable, for example, that Ofstie, who had examined the results of the first atomic attacks and studied the effects of the postwar atom bomb test at Bikini Atoll, did not believe that nuclear bombing would be a horrifying event. During the hearings of 1949 the admirals found it expedient to express a view of nuclear warfare that they, like other officers, carried around in a particular compartment of their minds.

The Moral Issue in the Hydrogen Bomb Controversy

The dissenting admirals were by no means the only people who changed position on the issue of nuclear warfare. After World War II several atomic scientists, including some who had not challenged the use of nuclear weapons before Hiroshima, attempted to restrict those weapons' development and deployment.[22]

In the fall of 1949, after the Soviet Union set off its first nuclear device, a group of advisors to the Atomic Energy Commission, which ran the nation's atomic weapons program, considered whether the United States should stage a crash program to develop a thermonuclear "superbomb." This weapon, which developed most of its energy by fusing nuclei of hydrogen isotopes, was expected to produce explosions enormously more powerful than the ones that destroyed Hiroshima and Nagasaki.

Several scientists, including Ernest O. Lawrence and Edward Teller, wanted the United States to maintain its lead in nuclear weapons by producing the superbomb as rapidly as possible; however, all but one member of the AEC's General Advisory Committee, which consisted of eight scientists and science administrators and one businessman, strenuously opposed a crash program, partly on technical but mostly on moral grounds. The committee felt that large fusion weapons could not be used discriminately against military targets and carried "much further than the atomic bomb itself the policy of exterminating civilian populations." Six members, including J. Robert Oppenheimer, the committee chairman, and James B. Conant, wished to renounce the hydrogen bomb completely, calling it a potential weapon of genocide and an intolerable threat to the human race. They argued that its use would involve "a decision to slaughter a vast number of civilians," and warned that a few superbombs might cover the globe with an alarming amount of radiation. To these men, the extreme danger that fusion weapons posed to humanity wholly outweighed any military advantage that might arise from their development.* 23

While two other General Advisory Committee scientists, Enrico Fermi and Isadore Rabi, thought a decision on proceeding with the superbomb should depend on whether the Soviet Union agreed to renounce it, they regarded the fusion bomb with as much horror as any of their colleagues. It was clear, they said, that its use could not be justified "on any ethical ground which gives a human being a certain individuality and dignity even if he happens to be a resident of an enemy country." They were certain that if the United States employed a thermonuclear weapon it would damage its moral position in the world. Such an "inhuman application of force" could not possibly produce a desirable peace since the hatred it engendered would go on for generations. Postwar problems, including radioactivity that would make vast areas uninhabitable, would dwarf the difficulties America faced in the aftermath of World War II. Fermi and Rabi regarded the superbomb as "necessarily an evil thing considered in any light." They recommended that the president tell the American people and the world that "we think it wrong on fundamental ethical principles" to begin the development of such a weapon.25

The Joint Chiefs of Staff disagreed with all these views. They argued that it would be intolerable if the USSR developed a hydrogen bomb and the United States did not. Public renunciation of fusion bomb development, they said, might appear as the first step toward American abandonment of all nuclear weapons, leading to a dangerous realignment of world power. If the United States went ahead with the H-bomb program, rather than damaging its moral

*The businessman member of the committee, Hartley Rowe, a vice-president of the United Fruit Company, later elaborated on his reasons. "I don't like to see women and children killed wholesale," he declared, "because the male element of the human race are so stupid that they can't get out of war and keep out of war."24

position in the eyes of the world this would fulfill the expectations of friendly peoples who believed in the integrity and rectitude of the United States as a world leader and expected America to take whatever action was necessary to retain "moral and physical leadership." While moral arguments might be made against developing and testing a thermonuclear bomb, military considerations, including the need to maintain enough American military power to deter and win a war, outweighed such objections. Besides, they said, it was "folly to argue whether one weapon is more immoral than another. For in the larger sense, it is war itself which is immoral, and the stigma of such immorality must rest upon the nation which initiates hostilities."[26]

President Truman, who continued to be troubled by the idea of using nuclear weapons even while he believed them essential for American security, thought the arguments of the Joint Chiefs of Staff "made a lot of sense." In January 1950 he ordered the Atomic Energy Commission to proceed with the superbomb, a decision he viewed as merely another development in the American buildup of nuclear weapons.[27]

Preventive and Preemptive War

Besides intensifying U.S. efforts to develop thermonuclear weapons, the 1949 Russian atomic test led certain American officials to recommend "preventive" war against the Soviet Union before the Russians were able to destroy the United States. Some of them used this term interchangeably with "preemptive" war, which meant initiating an attack when an enemy seemed about to strike. Either concept entailed killing several million civilians.

While the ideas of preventive and preemptive war had long been part of strategic thought, they took on special significance in the United States at the end of World War II, as American military leaders recognized how vulnerable their country would soon be to a surprise air assault. "The next sneak attack," General Arnold wrote five days before the Hiroshima bomb was dropped, "may not come 2,000 miles from our shores. . . . It bodes fair to be sudden death out of a clear sky." Less than two months later, the Joint Chiefs of Staff declared that when it became evident that "the forces of aggression" were being arrayed against the United States, America could not afford, "through any misguided and perilous idea of avoiding an aggressive attitude, to permit the first blow to be struck against us." They felt the United States should press for diplomatic settlement while preparing to strike the enemy first, if necessary. The JCS Joint Intelligence Committee recommended in November 1945 that American warplanes hit Soviet cities not only if a Soviet assault seemed imminent, but if enemy scientific or industrial developments suggested the ability to launch an eventual attack against the United States or to defend against an American attack. The Joint Chiefs' evaluation board for the Bikini tests recommended in 1947 that Congress redefine "acts of aggression" to include the readying of atomic weapons against the United States and provide authority for a preemptive strike.[28]

Some officers doubted that either preventive or preemptive war could ever become American policy. General George A. Lincoln told a meeting of the Joint Staff planners on September 12, 1945, that even though it might be desirable to strike the first blow, it was "not politically feasible under our system to do so or to state that we will do so." The following April, General Earle E. Partridge, the assistant chief of air staff for operations, observed that national policy made it unlikely that the United States would attack another nation before being attacked itself.[29]

Nevertheless, after the Soviets' first nuclear explosion defense leaders gave a good deal of thought to the idea of preventive war. A consultant to the air force, the strategic analyst Bernard Brodie, recalled how he had heard an Air Force general advocate a preventive strike against the Soviet Union. When Brodie asked if that would not be immoral, the general answered that he had checked it out with his minister and the clergyman had said it would be all right.[30]

Defense officials estimated that by 1954 the Soviet Union would have 200 fission bombs, enough to deliver a devastating surprise attack on the United States and its European allies. Some of them wondered if it would not be prudent to attack the Russians before then, or to present them with an ultimatum while threatening a nuclear strike. In the spring of 1950 the National Security Council weighed the arguments for launching a surprise nuclear war against the Soviet Union and rejected them, partly because such an action would be "morally corrosive" and would lead many Americans and Western Europeans to doubt the United States was waging a just war. Nevertheless, since modern weapons gave the side that struck first such a large advantage, the NSC recommended that the United States prepare to launch a massive attack as soon as it was hit and, if possible, before a Soviet blow had landed.[31]

In the summer of 1950, after the outbreak of the Korean War, word began to reach the American public that some of their leaders favored preventive warfare. Hanson W. Baldwin, the *New York Times* military specialist, reported that Secretary of Defense Louis Johnson was "selling the . . . doctrine of preventive war in private conversations around Washington." On August 25, 1950, at a ceremony honoring the sesquicentennial of the Boston Naval Shipyard, Secretary of the Navy Francis P. Matthews declared that "we should boldly proclaim our undeniable objective to be a world at peace. To have peace we should be willing, and declare our intention to pay any price, even the price of instituting a war to compel cooperation for peace," though it cast the United States in "a character new to a true democracy—an initiator of a war of aggression." Americans, Matthews said, could not escape the role of "aggressors for peace."[32]

Air Force General Orvil Anderson, the onetime World War II commander, was probably the most vocal advocate in the U.S. military establishment of preventive war against the Soviet Union. Like many of his colleagues in the air force, Anderson believed that the evolution of warfare, driven by the power of science, had made cities and workers legitimate targets. He felt that when people weighed the morality of a strategic air attack against the Soviet Union they should keep in mind that during the First World War England and France had lost the "cream" of their young manhood in regular surface combat, while in the Second World War strategic air warfare had helped keep American troop losses relatively low. Anderson argued that the United States faced a fundamental moral question: "Which is the greater immorality—preventive war as a means to keep the U.S.S.R. from becoming a nuclear power; or, to allow a totalitarian dictatorial system to develop a means whereby the free world could be intimidated, blackmailed, and possibly destroyed."[33]

As commandant of the Air War College, General Anderson lectured on how a preventive war could be carried out. In what he later claimed was an off-the-record interview, he told a reporter that it was silly to talk of "preventive war" when the fighting had already begun. He called for "a little realism in America before it is too late," then declared, "Give me the order to do it and I can break up Russia's five A-bomb nests in a week! And when I went up to Christ, I think I could explain to Him why I wanted to do it—now—before it is too late. I think I could explain to Him that I had saved civilization." These remarks appeared on September 1, 1950, in the

Montgomery (Alabama) *Advertizer* and were reprinted throughout the United States.[34]

The Truman administration and top military leaders immediately repudiated these ideas and reprimanded those who publicly expressed them. The State Department, backed by the White House, denounced Secretary Matthews's statement. A few hours after General Anderson's remarks appeared, Air Force Chief of Staff Hoyt S. Vandenberg ordered him suspended from his Air War College post. The U.S. Air Force, Vandenberg declared, "first, last and always, is primarily an instrument for peace." At the highest levels of the American armed forces, the view that America should resolve its conflicts with Communist nations through preventive or preemptive war remained officially unacceptable.[35]

Nevertheless, even after the Anderson and Matthews incidents the same idea kept surfacing in secret national security discussions. At a March 1954 briefing on Strategic Air Command plans and capabilities for war, SAC leader General LeMay was asked how those plans fit with the stated policy of the United States that it would never strike the first blow. LeMay answered that he had heard this thought expressed many times and that it sounded fine. But considering who started the Revolutionary War, the War of 1812, the Indian Wars, and the Spanish-American War, it was "not in keeping with United States history." LeMay emphasized that he was not advocating a preventive war. He believed, however, that if the United States were pushed far enough into a corner, it would not hesitate to strike first.[36]

In any case, it was up to the president to order any kind of nuclear attack, and when the idea of preemptive war was suggested to President Truman he appeared to reject it. Atomic Energy Commissioner Thomas Murray asked Truman in January 1953 if he really meant to rule out a preemptive strike against Russian nuclear forces if a Soviet attack seemed imminent. He responded that the commissioner had misinterpreted how he felt about using the bomb. "It is far worse," he said, "than gas and biological warfare because it affects the civilian population and murders them by wholesale."[37]

President Eisenhower pondered the preventive war issue very seriously over a period of years, weighing not only the military aspects of the problem but its political and economic implications as well, including the possibility that even if there were no war, a continuing arms race would wreck America's economy and transform its system of government. During the summer of 1953 he discussed with Secretary of State John Foster Dulles the nation's growing vulnerability to Soviet attack. The country's only security, Eisenhower felt, was the enemy's belief that the United States could inflict more damage on him than he could do to the United States. But if the contest to maintain this superiority went on indefinitely, its cost "would either drive us to war—or into some form of dictatorial government. In such circumstances, we would be forced to consider whether or not our duty to future generations did not require us to initiate war at the most propitious moment we could designate."[38]

In May 1954 the president was briefed on a proposal of the Joint Chiefs of Staff Advance Study Group to consider "deliberately precipitating war with the USSR in the near future" before thermonuclear weapons became a "real menace." Army Chief of Staff Matthew Ridgway denounced this notion as "contrary to every principle upon which our Nation had been founded" and "abhorrent to the great mass of American people." The president did not commit himself at that time; however, a few months later he approved a policy paper that declared "the United States and its allies must reject the concept of preventive war or acts intended to provoke war."[39]

The subject came up again early in 1956 when the Soviet Union had several hundred nuclear bombs. A committee headed by retired air force general Harold L. George estimated the damage that would occur in the first stages of a U.S.-Soviet nuclear war. Eisenhower summarized its conclusions in his diary. If there were no warning until Soviet planes first appeared on American radar screens, he wrote, the United States would undergo a complete economic collapse. Members of the federal government would be wiped out. American casualties would be "enormous," with some 65 percent of the population requiring medical care and most people having no chance for treatment whatsoever. The United States, meanwhile, would inflict roughly three times greater damage on Russia, for which, in Eisenhower's words, "the picture of total destruction of the areas of lethal fallout, of serious fallout, and of at least some damage from fallout, was appalling." The Russians would be completely incapable of carrying on the war any longer, while for the United States "it would literally be a business of digging ourselves out of ashes, starting again." Even if the United States had a month's warning that Soviets were preparing to strike, the results would be essentially the same, since the United States could do little in that time to protect its people and its economy.

The only possible way to reduce American losses was for the United States to launch a surprise attack during the warning period. But this, the president wrote, would not only violate national tradition but would require rapid, completely secret action by Congress and immediate implementation. For these reasons, Eisenhower wrote, it appeared that the United States could never launch a preemptive war.[40]

Massive Retaliation and Counterforce

While the presidents may have ruled out an American-initiated attack on the Soviet Union, they also had to consider whether to employ nuclear weapons against Russia's allies. This became a serious practical problem in 1950, when Communist North Korean troops crossed into South Korea and the United Nations, led by the United States, decided to fight the invaders.

During the Korean War, and especially after the People's Republic of China entered the conflict, critics of the Truman administration wondered why the United States persisted in fighting a limited ground war and suffering continuing American casualties instead of bombing cities and supply routes in China or the Soviet Union. During a congressional inquiry into the conduct of the war, Senator Russell B. Long of Louisiana asked the army chief of staff, General J. Lawton Collins, why, if the United States was going to try to punish the Chinese for their aggression with the least possible losses of American life, it didn't simply burn down China's cities with firebombs. "That would not entail a great loss of American lives to do, would it?" Long asked.

Collins responded with a moral objection. "No sir," he said, "but it certainly would entail the loss of lives of many Chinamen. . . . From what little I do know of China, I am confident that the average peasant in China out in the hills probably doesn't even know that there is a war going on in the first place or what it is all about, and for us to simply go in and bomb Chinese cities . . . would be I think a dreadful mistake."[41]

Regardless of how Collins and the rest of the Joint Chiefs may have felt about the moral issue, practical considerations led them to warn against escalating the U.S. air offensive too far. The terrain in Korea was unsuitable for nuclear attacks against well-dug-in troops. America's allies did not want nuclear war. And it seemed to the Joint Chiefs that the Communists, who were themselves waging a limited war, would gain far more than would the United Nations from an escalation of the conflict. General Hoyt Vandenberg contended that the U.S. Air Force lacked the resources to bomb China successfully and also wage war against the Soviet Union, which the American government regarded as the main enemy. Vandenberg imagined that in a campaign over the countryside of Manchuria and the principal cities of China, aircraft losses would leave the United States "naked for years to come." General Bradley, chairman of the Joint Chiefs of Staff, testified to the Senate committee investigating the war that if the Russians entered the war they could easily gain air superiority in the Far East and with thirty-five army divisions and eighty-five submarines could force the United Nations to evacuate Korea. An Air Force intelligence officer informed the senators that if the Soviets attacked the United States with their own strategic bombers they might be able to land fifty atom bombs on American cities. Nevertheless, among the solutions the United States adopted at this time for its strategic problems was the threat to respond to further Communist advances with massive retaliation.[42]

In the case of Korea and China, American leaders meant this threat very seriously. Early in the Eisenhower administration, while peace negotiations with North Korea and the People's Republic of China were dragging on, the president discussed with the National Security Council the question of using atomic weapons to end the war. While he admitted that there were a few good tactical targets in Korea and recognized that the Western allies feared becoming a nuclear battleground, Eisenhower thought the weapons should be used if they could produce a substantial victory. Secretary Dulles argued that world opinion precluded their use in the Korean War. But Dulles agreed completely with the president's view that somehow or other the taboo surrounding the use of nuclear weapons would have to be destroyed. When the issue came up again, Eisenhower remarked that atomic weapons would cost much less to use in Korea than conventional arms, especially if the cost of transporting conventional ammunition from the United States to the front line was counted. When the Joint Chiefs indicated that taking a stronger approach to the war would involve action beyond Korea's boundaries and would mean using the atomic bomb, the president responded that his only real worry was over the possibility that the Soviets would intervene, for the nuclear blow would fall so swiftly and with such force on the Chinese that their "intervention" would be eliminated.[43]

In October 1953 Eisenhower's idea of relying on nuclear weapons to defend American interests at a bearable cost became official U.S. policy for the entire globe. Henceforth, U.S. planners were to assume that only small brushfire wars and border incidents would be fought with conventional weapons. There would be no more conflicts of the Korean kind and no conventional general wars. The secretary of state announced in January 1954 an administration policy of massive retaliation against Communist attacks. This meant, in the case of Europe, that the United States would use tactical nuclear weapons to hold the line and give first priority to the Strategic Air Command.[44]

At a 1954 briefing for representatives of all services the Strategic Air Command explained what massive retaliation would mean in practice. According to Captain William B. Moore, who was present as a navy representative, the SAC "Optimum Plan" was to hit the USSR with about 600 to 750 bombs. "No aspect of the morals or long-range effect of such attacks [was] discussed," Moore recalled, "and no questions on it were asked." His final impression was that "virtually all of Russia would be nothing but a smoking, radiating ruin at the end of two hours."[45]

As massive thermonuclear retaliation emerged as the central element of America's security system, it came under attack from several directions. Dulles's announcement caused angry reactions, particularly from Democrats, and he was forced to show that he had not intended to say that the United States would begin World War III because of a minor Communist action in an insignificant place. The army, whose forces would be considerably reduced under the Eisenhower program, protested through General Ridgway, its chief of staff. Ridgway urged the Joint Chiefs to see to it that the Strategic Air Command used its striking power in accordance with a national policy "which seeks to attain national objectives without indiscriminate mass destruction of human life." Even President Eisenhower perceived fundamental defects in the doctrine. He asked the Joint Chiefs, "If we batter Soviet cities to pieces by bombing, what solution do we have to take control of the situation . . . so as to achieve the objective for which we went to war?" In April 1956 he told the Joint Chiefs that he thought there might be no winners in a thermonuclear war, though "we don't want to lose any worse than we have to."[46]

Despite the fact that the Eisenhower policy made SAC the spearhead of American military power, massive retaliation doctrine was questioned in the Air Force itself. During the early 1950s an

Air War College instructor, Colonel Raymond S. Sleeper, challenged some of the Douhetian ideas that underlay Air Force strategy. Sleeper had become convinced that the objective of air power was not to destroy enemy civilians or enemy cities (if that could be avoided) or to produce panic or destroy morale. Rather it was to change the temper of the enemy, inducing the opposing government to behave in a way acceptable to the United States. Colonel Sleeper felt that the limited air war methods the British had used in Iraq and Aden might be applied to the Cold War. With a staff of civilian professionals from the Air University and students from the Air Command and Staff College, Sleeper investigated RAF techniques that the United States might have used to affect events from 1930 through 1945.[47]

Project Control, as Colonel Sleeper's inquiry was called, had no chance at that time of overthrowing the strategy of massive retaliation. But another approach that also promised less damage to cities and civilian populations began to win acceptance in the air force. This was the counterforce doctrine, designed to disarm the enemy with accurate nuclear strikes aimed at weapons rather than urban industrial targets. Bernard Brodie and other civilian theorists had been urging consideration of a "no cities" strategy since the early 1950s. At the end of the decade, as the United States developed the ability to photograph small Soviet military installations and as the navy was preparing to deploy its Polaris missile-firing submarines, which could destroy large targets like enemy cities almost as effectively as SAC, the counterforce idea took hold strongly among airmen.

Simulation of a "no cities" counterforce war on the air force's Air Battle Model Computer indicated that counterforce strategy would save numerous American and Soviet lives. Its proponents saw it as a flexible deterrent which offered more security to America's allies than did the massive retaliation doctrine's implied promise that to preserve Western Europe from a Communist attack, the United States would allow itself to be blown up in a thermonuclear exchange. One air force advocate of counterforce observed that obliterating cities really could not help win a war and was therefore "irrational and politically and morally unjustifiable."[48]

Yet to critics there were gaping defects in counterforce strategy. It required the United States to build enough missiles and warplanes to saturate enemy defenses, to harden its own launching sites against enemy counterforce attacks, perhaps with an antimissile and anti-aircraft system, and to provide fallout shelters for American civilians—exactly the steps a nuclear power would take if it intended to launch a first strike. In fact, the air force chief of staff, General Thomas D. White, wanted the United States to be able to deliver a first strike. He stated that a nation which lacked the capacity to take the initiative and knock out the enemy's military power was "hopeless . . . politically, diplomatically, and militarily." But the navy argued that preparations for counterforce would cause the enemy to develop more offensive weapons and possibly launch a preemptive strike of its own. Thus instead of deterring World War III, counterforce would cause it.[49]

President Eisenhower concluded that a purely counterforce strategy would not work. "All we really have that is meaningful," he told his advisors, "is a deterrent." Unable to envision anything in a general war beyond a first disastrous nuclear exchange, he came increasingly to favor, for want of anything better, a strategy that targeted Soviet cities. In 1960 he accepted an air force target list that included, along with 218 military and government control centers, over a thousand objectives located primarily in 131 urban areas.[50]

Limited War and Its Air Force Critics

Nevertheless, at the beginning of the Kennedy administration the air force continued to recommend that the United States develop forces needed to launch a disarming first strike. Secretary of Defense Robert S. McNamara rejected its recommendation on the grounds that surviving Soviet forces, including missile-launching submarines, could inflict an estimated fifty million direct fatalities in the United States, a level McNamara told the president he did not consider "acceptable."* [51]

The Kennedy administration tried to push up the threshold at which an exchange of nuclear weapons was likely to occur. Adopting an approach that army leaders had been advocating for years, it prepared to employ controlled gradations of warfare ranging up-

---

*In 1975 the Department of Defense produced a much more favorable estimate. It concluded that in a purely counterforce attack by the Soviet Union, no more than some twenty-two million Americans might lose their lives. Still, this was over eighteen times the estimated number of German and Japanese civilians killed by American and British bombs in the Second World War.[52]

ward from small unit counterguerrilla action through limited conventional tactics, large-scale conventional encounters, and battles with small nuclear weapons. If the enemy launched a strike at the United States there would be enough protected large strategic weapons to survive the attack, cripple the enemy's armed forces, and then, if necessary, obliterate the enemy's cities.[53]

This strategy promised to be even more expensive than massive retaliation, for it required a large increase in conventional as well as nuclear forces. Some of its ideas were difficult to grasp, like the notion that in the midst of a war, even a nuclear war, countries would pause at certain thresholds and negotiate before escalating to a higher level. It was linked to the theory of mutually assured destruction (MAD), which held that nations would refrain from using their most powerful weapons for fear that they would be obliterated themselves. Among the reasons why the United States conducted the Vietnam War in an area the Joint Chiefs of Staff had described as devoid of decisive military objectives was to illustrate these concepts—demonstrating not only that the United States could deliver carefully graduated blows but also, since it was willing to spill so much blood for an area of minor significance, that it might be mad enough to use thermonuclear weapons if the Communists attacked a really vital place.[54]

Americans found limited war as frustrating and repugnant in Vietnam as it had been in Korea. As the war continued year after year, some of them condemned the U.S. government for bombing Vietnamese civilians. These protests became much larger and more vehement than any American complaints during World War II about AAF bombing of Axis cities. Others wondered why their government did not unleash the full power of the air force. Among those who criticized the restrictions on American air power in Vietnam, or the very concept of graduated attack, were Generals Eaker, Twining, and LeMay, each of whom had succeeded in World War II by hitting the enemy with all available destructive power.

During the Johnson administration General Eaker advised the president to issue an ultimatum to North Vietnam and then, if it did not give in, to mine the harbor at Haiphong and break the dams on the Red River, putting North Vietnam's rice fields and many of its principal cities under ten feet of water. If the enemy continued to resist, Eaker would have given Hanoi "the Berlin treatment," then progressively destroyed its war-making potential and all its rail transportation, cutting off weapons and supplies from China and the Soviet Union.[55]

In 1954, when the French were struggling against the Communist-led Viet Minh, General LeMay had said that he would not choose to fight a war in Indochina because the "squabble" there could be settled politically, perhaps by offering the people independence. But after the United States had become an open belligerent, he was willing to bomb North Vietnam "until we have destroyed every work of man" if that was what it took to win. Like Eaker, he would have wiped out every factory in the area, mined Haiphong harbor, eliminated North Vietnam's power system and transportation facilities, and, if necessary, blown up dikes that made it possible to grow rice in North Vietnam. "This is one of the most heavily populated areas in the world," he wrote, noting that without the dikes, severe flooding would occur in the monsoon season. Yet he also said that the civilian population should be spared and that the United States ought to warn the civilians before attacking. He did not rule out the use of nuclear weapons but doubted they would be necessary. He felt that if the United States took the steps he proposed, North Vietnam's allies, China and the Soviet Union, would not intervene.[56]

The problem, as LeMay saw it, was that the U.S. government had fought the Vietnam War with the wrong attitude. It should not have entered a counterguerrilla conflict which might turn into a general war unless it was fully prepared to wage general warfare. "Whenever we commit our young men to mortal combat," LeMay insisted, "we should be equally prepared to commit our leaders, our cities, our families, and *civilians*—our own or the enemy's. Modern war is that serious."[57]

While the Johnson administration was trying to secure its objectives in Vietnam through controlled escalation, General Twining repudiated limited warfare altogether in favor of a strategy based on the threat of general nuclear conflict. Twining thought Orvil Anderson's views on preventive war had not received a fair hearing in the military establishment or the State Department. He wanted the United States to develop ballistic missiles with destructive power greater than one hundred megatons. These would be harder to defend against than existing weapons because even if they exploded miles above the earth, their effects would still be devastating. He disliked the notion of announcing that the United States might try to contain nuclear war below the threshold of an all-out holocaust and he disapproved of what defense experts called a damage-limiting strategy, which sought to apply American power without "unnecessary destruction of civilian lives and property." To

Twining these measures did not make military sense because they would telegraph to the enemy that he could take large risks without having to pay "the full price for his aggression."[58]

After they retired, Twining, Eaker, and LeMay spoke openly about the morality of bombing. At a 1978 Air Force Academy symposium General Eaker declared "how much better it would have been, if necessary, to destroy North Vietnam than to lose our first war. That would have saved us 50,000 American dead, 250,000 Allied dead, and, subsequently, the greatest genocide in this century. Already the Hanoi butchers have murdered or starved to death more than three million men, women, and children in South Vietnam, Laos, and Cambodia."[59]

General LeMay argued that it was "politically immoral" to use less force than necessary to achieve a military objective when adequate force was available. This was because more young American men were killed, wounded, or made prisoners of war than would have been necessary if more than enough force were used. It was also immoral because a protracted war caused more losses overall than a quick decisive conflict. Sometimes it was "more humane and moral to perform drastic surgery in order to save a victim from cancer. The same reasoning can often apply to the waging of war."[60]

LeMay's argument implied that the welfare of American servicemen carried a value so high that it justified enormous danger to civilians. General Twining left no doubt about his own view of this matter. Writing about the scientists who had opposed the H-bomb in 1949, he said that their objections stemmed from

> an instinctive moral objection to strategic bombing and the subjugation of civilian populations to the hazards of war. In such judgment, the morality of war might involve only putting teen-agers and young adults into uniform, calling them soldiers, and allowing them to be blown to bits or eviscerated by a bayonet in some remote part of the world. But it might be considered immoral to bring the war into the front yard and back yard of everyone.[61]

General Twining presented the argument, which the Joint Chiefs had offered on behalf of the H-bomb program, that weapons were not immoral in themselves. The basic immorality, he said, "lies in the causes of war and not in the instruments of war."[62]

Yet it continued to be true that the World War II generals did not think in a uniform way about the moral questions of war. In the era of the hydrogen bomb General Spaatz maintained that certain weapons were inherently immoral. When an Air Force historian asked him if he saw any moral distinction between firebomb raids and atomic bombing, he answered that there was "a terrific distinction" between a bomb of Hiroshima size and fusion bombs of five, ten, twenty and fifty megatons. "I think it is indecent," he stated, "and there is no excuse for it." This did not mean, he added, that a nation possessing these weapons would not use them rather than lose a war.[63]

Reflections of World War II

Despite the vast qualitative changes in warfare that had occurred since Spaatz commanded the United States Strategic Air Forces, within the American military system there were numerous links between wartime and postwar views of bombing and its moral effects. Both the principle of selective bombing with which the AAF had entered the war and its practice of area bombing at the end had their counterparts in postwar strategy. Massive retaliation was area bombing vastly multiplied. Counterforce relied on precision air attack techniques, and some of its advocates presented it as conventional precision bombing had been presented, as a relatively humane form of warfare.[64] General Eaker's prescription for giving North Vietnamese cities the "Berlin treatment" directly mirrored World War II experience. LeMay's strategy of aiming warheads against military targets in urban areas so as to achieve a "bonus" effect on the population resembled, in an involuted way, the method he applied against Tokyo and other Japanese cities—set residential districts on fire both to destroy workshops and eliminate workers and to secure the added advantage of a conflagration which spreads to major war factories and produces chaos. His policy of warning Japanese residents to flee the cities before his airmen made their living area uninhabitable parallels the policy he favored for Vietnam.

In the postwar decades, as in World War II, fear of what might happen if the American public became aroused against U.S. bombing methods affected the thinking of American leaders. This concern helped shape navy strategy for undermining the B-36 program. It affected the reaction of the Truman administration and the air force to press reports that General Anderson and Secretary Matthews favored preventive war. It contributed to restrictions the

Johnson administration imposed on U.S. air power during the Vietnam War. In October 1966 Secretary of Defense McNamara sent President Johnson a gloomy memorandum which observed that while the United States could bomb North Vietnam sufficiently to make a radical impact on its political, economic and social structure, the effect required "would not be stomached . . . by our own people."[65]

The analytical reasoning that underlay much American thought in the postwar years about nuclear strategy resembles the efforts of the Committee of Operations Analysts and other World War II agencies to devise efficient ways of destroying the Axis war machine. Yet both the analysts for the AAF and the people who developed plans for nuclear conflict based their proposals partly on surmise. Bernard Brodie complained in 1950 that the United States had no calculated target strategy, that its planners did not know where Soviet electric power facilities were or how much electricity the Russians could do without. Planners simply expected the USSR to collapse when struck by the American "Sunday Punch." This situation recalls the problems facing the COA when, with scanty information, it tried to determine what it would take to break Japanese resistance.

There were close parallels between wartime and postwar attempts to estimate the effects of bombing on civilian morale. An analysis by Pentagon consultants in 1955 of the impact of nuclear bombing on Soviet morale resembles Professor Allport's effort to judge the psychological consequences of bombing Axis civilians. A Defense Department committee asked Dr. Max Millikan of MIT to gauge the probable effects on Russian will to fight of a nuclear attack that caused seventy-seven million Russian casualties, sixty million of them fatal. Millikan consulted with eight outstanding social and political scientists and psychologists. They concluded that no basis existed on which to assess quantitatively how the attack described would affect Russian willingness to continue a war. However, they assumed the results would be "calamitous."[66]

Among postwar civilian strategic thinkers and weapons designers there tended to be, as in World War II, mental detachment from the objects of attack and unwillingness or inability to focus on moral questions. Professor Brodie noted that his fellow strategic analysts normally regarded moral considerations as "tiresome impediments to the flow of one's thought." He attributed their attitude to a need to secure the confidence of the military people they worked with, to the fact that very few people were equipped both emotionally and intellectually to deal with moral issues, and to the tendency of nuclear weapons to arouse "special anxieties." In one famous case, failure to share this way of feeling became cause for suspecting disloyalty. When J. Robert Oppenheimer's security clearance was removed in 1954, one of the charges against him was that he had "strongly opposed the development of the hydrogen bomb . . . on moral grounds."[67]

For some American military people (and for some civilians as well) an absolutist view of warfare persisted from era to era. In World War II AAF leaders and civilians they worked with felt they were defending civilization from barbaric, ruthless enemies. When the Soviet Union replaced the Axis powers as America's adversary, officers such as Orvil Anderson saw what was happening as a virtual reenactment of 1941–45, another crusade against evil enemies, with air power again the chief safeguard of civilized life. General Anderson and his air force colleagues were prepared to fight the new enemy, like the old one, with everything they had.

The memory of World War II seems to have led some air force leaders to feel that all-out annihilation war was the sole tradition of America's armed forces. General Twining wrote during the Vietnam conflict that he had "never heard of limited war before 1950," which meant that he had overlooked the War of 1812, the war with Mexico, and the Spanish-American War, as well as the U.S. interventions in Third World areas before World War II for which official service doctrine prescribed securing objectives with the minimum necessary force.[68]

Accompanying the inclination to wage the kind of total war that had worked in World War II was a sense of omnipotence. Thoughts of obliterating all works of man in an enemy country or drowning it under ten feet of water, of turning the largest country in the world into a "smoking, radiating ruin," reflect a feeling of power that some Americans began to experience at the end of the Second World War when, after years of costly struggle, Allied warplanes finally secured command of the air and could attack German towns at will, burn down Japanese urban areas, and destroy an entire city with a nuclear bomb. Afterwards Soviet military power, the difficulties Americans encountered when they fought Communist armed forces, and, above all, the development by other countries of nuclear weapons made it illogical to believe in unchallenged U.S. supremacy. Yet for some World War II leaders, such as

Generals Eaker, LeMay and Twining, a sense of unassailable power endured. The problem, as they saw it, was America's hesitancy to employ military resources to their limit.

Yet just as in World War II, in the military establishment and among civilians connected with it there was no simple uniformity of feeling about the use of air power. Orvil Anderson's ideas about staging a preventive nuclear war evoked dissent within his service. Several officers, including some in the air force, raised the question that Colonel Hughes and others had posed in World War II: how to prevent the means of war from destroying the ends for which the war is fought. While the Strategic Air Command was preparing to turn the Soviet Union, if necessary, into a "smoking, radiating ruin," Air Force officers connected with Project Control were looking for alternatives to an all-out thermonuclear war. If a Twining or a LeMay wrote as if American military power were irresistible, the Joint Chiefs of Staff and the presidents repeatedly indicated that despite a vast strategic weapons arsenal, U.S. power had its limits.

People responsible for developing and employing American air power during the Cold War continued to be, like their World War II counterparts, divided among one another and sometimes within themselves about the moral issues of air attack. Though Truman saw to it that the numbers of American nuclear weapons and their destructive power were greatly increased, and though he indicated he would be willing to order them used if necessary, he continued to feel, as he had at the end of the war, that there was something terrible about employing them. In World War II Eisenhower had said he hoped his country would never have to drop the atom bomb on any enemy because he did not want America to introduce into war something so horrible and destructive. Yet during the Korean War he wanted to abolish the taboo against its use. At times President Eisenhower appeared to regard the bomb as just a more efficient weapon which the United States ought to employ to save itself from bankruptcy. On other occasions he thought of nuclear war as a pointless disaster which might nevertheless take place.

These divisions and contradictions also appeared at lower levels of the U.S. military system. The Joint Chiefs of Staff maintained that weapons in themselves could not be immoral. Yet General Spaatz saw a moral distinction between hydrogen bombs and lesser instruments of destruction. The air admirals were prepared to play their part in nuclear war, but following in the tradition of Admiral Leahy, they asserted that strategic nuclear bombing was militarily self-defeating and morally wrong. While the majority of scientists on the General Advisory Committee considered the H-bomb an immoral weapon posing dangers to mankind that outweighed any military advantage it could possibly secure, other scientists firmly disagreed. Bernard Brodie noted an absence of moral consciousness among his fellow strategic analysts. Yet he was a member of that group, and his writings offer ample evidence that he considered moral questions crucially important.[69]

Some observers noted in the history of air power in World War II and afterward not just parallels and vestiges but signs of a revolution—in weapons, in military techniques, and in the moral outlook of those who used the means of war. This was how Atomic Energy Commission chairman David E. Lilienthal and General LeMay saw what had happened. In 1947 Lilienthal noted in his diary that while men had fought earlier wars with rules and boundaries, as in a game, the ethical limitations on warfare began to dissolve when the Italians bombed Ethiopian villages, Germans obliterated part of Rotterdam, and V-2s were fired to kill anyone they landed on.

> Then we burned Tokyo, not just military targets, but set out to wipe out the place, indiscriminately. The atomic bomb is the last word in this direction. All ethical limitations of warfare are gone, not because the *means* of destruction are more cruel or painful or otherwise hideous in their effect upon combatants, but because there are no individual combatants. The fences are gone. And it was we, the civilized, who have pushed standardless conduct to its ultimate.[70]

Twenty-one years later General LeMay noted how moral compunctions against city bombing had disintegrated in World War II as retaliation and re-retaliation led the Allies to all-out strategic air warfare whose ultimate expression was the raids on Hamburg and Tokyo and the atomic bomb attacks. Strategic bombing had proved "phenomenally successful" as a war-winning tactic, LeMay remarked. But "the break with tradition in which war had been waged primarily against combatants, and the moral revulsion caused by indiscriminate killing in city bombings, caused much controversy following the war over the advisability of continuing the strategic bombing role." Ultimately, however, when the independent strategic air force was established, "realism prevailed . . ."[71]

During the Second World War, while the changes described by LeMay and Lilienthal were taking place, some Americans who participated in the air war accepted them, some fought against them, some ignored them, and some, like Henry Stimson, did all three. The American people as a whole took slight and sporadic notice of the moral revolution in warfare. It is now clear, however, that to continue to disregard such changes, letting technology do what it can, or to accept them without careful thought, is extremely dangerous. If people are to limit what war can do to them, they will need to contemplate what their predecessors did to one another and how and why they did it.

Notes

Abbreviations Used in the Notes

ACPS *Report*	*Report of the American Commission for the Protection and Salvage of Artistic and Historic Monuments in War Areas.* Washington, D.C., 1946.
AFSHRC	Albert F. Simpson Historical Research Center, Maxwell Air Force Base, Alabama.
ARP Tokyo	United States Strategic Bombing Survey. *Field Report Covering Air Raid Protection and Allied Subjects.* N.p., March 1947.
C&C	*The Army Air Forces in World War II.* Edited by Wesley F. Craven and James L. Cate. 7 vols. Chicago, 1948–58.
CCS	Combined Chiefs of Staff [Anglo-American].
COA History	[Guido R. Perera,] "History, Organization and Operations of the Committee of Operations Analysts" (microfilm). File 168.7042, 1936–1960, AFSHRC.
COHC	Columbia Oral History Collections, Butler Library, Columbia University, New York City.
COS	Chiefs of Staff [British].
FDR Library	Franklin D. Roosevelt Library, Hyde Park, New York.
JCS	Joint Chiefs of Staff [American].
LC	Library of Congress, Washington, D.C.
Maxwell AFB	Maxwell Air Force Base, Alabama.
NA	National Archives, Washington, D.C.
OSRD	Office of Scientific Research and Development.
RG	Record Group, National Archives.
USSBS	United States Strategic Bombing Survey.

A directory of all collections of papers used in this book appears in the Essay on Sources following the Notes.

Preface

1. [Bruce C. Hopper], "Jeeping the Targets in the Country That Was," (April 20, 1945 entry), box 5, Frederick L. Anderson Papers, Hoover Institution, Stanford, California.

Chapter 1. *Leaders of the American Air War*

1. Robert Dallek, *Franklin D. Roosevelt and American Foreign Policy, 1932–1945* (New York, 1979), pp. vii, 6.

2. Ibid., p. 439.

3. Ibid., p. 9; Roosevelt quoted in Anne Armstrong, *Unconditional Surrender: The Impact of the Casablanca Policy upon World War II* (New Brunswick, 1961), p. 17.

4. Elting E. Morison, *Turmoil and Tradition: A Study of the Life and Times of Henry L. Stimson* (New York, 1964), pp. 5–7, 28, 31, 33, 38–39, 393–94.

5. Ibid., pp. 13, 70.

6. Ibid., pp. 15–16, 190, 232, 308; Otis Cary, "The Sparing of Kyoto, Mr. Stimson's 'Pet City,'" *Japan Quarterly* 22 (Oct.–Dec. 1975): 342.

7. Morison, *Turmoil*, pp. 48, 113, 117, 248, 388–89, 463.

8. Ibid., pp. 13, 32, 144, 184, 188, 189, 193, 195.

9. Forrest C. Pogue, *George C. Marshall: Education of a General, 1880–1939* (New York, 1963), p. 323; idem, *George C. Marshall: Ordeal and Hope, 1939–1942* (New York, 1966), p. 23.

10. Pogue, *Ordeal*, p. 72; Dallek, *Roosevelt*, p. 370.

11. Pogue, *George C. Marshall: Organizer of Victory, 1943–1945* (New York, 1973), pp. ix, xi, 3.

12. The officers are Frederick L. Anderson, Henry H. Arnold, Lewis H. Brereton, Charles P. Cabell, James H. Doolittle, Ira C. Eaker, Muir S. Fairchild, Harold L. George, Barney McK. Giles, Haywood S. Hansell, Jr., George C. Kenney, Laurence S. Kuter, Curtis E. LeMay, Lauris Norstad, Thomas S. Power, Elwood R. Quesada, Carl A. Spaatz, Nathan F. Twining, Hoyt S. Vandenberg, Kenneth N. Walker, Thomas D. White, and Donald Wilson. (Since these men went through various promotions during the period treated in this chapter, their ranks are omitted here.)

13. Biographical dictionaries for the survey of air force leaders are Flint O. Du Pre, ed., *U.S. Air Force Biographical Dictionary* (New York, 1965); *Who's Who in America* (Chicago, various dates); *Who Was Who in American History—The Military* (Chicago, 1975); and *Webster's American Military Biographies* (Springfield, Mass., 1978) (hereafter cited as *Webster's*.)

14. Du Pre, *Dictionary*, pp. 244, 258; "General Nathan F. Twining USAF, Chairman-Designate Joint Chiefs of Staff," *Airman* 1 (Aug. 1957): 16; Lowell Thomas and Edward Jablonski, *Doolittle: A Biography* (Garden City, N.Y., 1976), pp. 1–2; Curtis E. LeMay with MacKinlay Kantor, *Mission with LeMay: My Story* (Garden City, N.Y., 1965), p. 13; interview with Carl A. Spaatz, January 1959, H. H. Arnold Project, Columbia University Oral History Collections (hereafter cited as COHC); "Anderson, Frederick L.," *Current Biography 1944*, p. 11; H. H. Arnold, *Global Mission* (New York, 1949), p. 5; Haywood S. Hansell, Jr., *The Air Plan That Defeated Hitler* (Atlanta, 1972), p. 311; "Giles, Barney McKinney," *Current Biography 1944*, p. 233.

15. Thomas, *Doolittle*, p. 50; Hansell, *Air Plan*, p. 311; Du Pre, *Dictionary*, pp. 61, 220.

16. Thomas, *Doolittle*, pp. 3, 12, 19, 24–25, 28–30, 39–41, 77, 83–87, 125.

17. Ibid., pp. 24, 68–73, 94–103, 107–109, 134–35, 150; *Webster's*, pp. 105–6; Du Pre, *Dictionary*, p. 59.

18. Hansell, *Air Plan*, pp. 310–11.

19. *Webster's*, p. 111; Du Pre, *Dictionary*, pp. 61-62.

20. Raymond R. Flugel, "United States Air Power Doctrine: A Study of the Influence of William Mitchell and Giulio Douhet at the Air Corps Tactical School, 1921-1935" (Ph.D. diss., University of Oklahoma, 1965), pp. 57-58; Arnold, *Global Mission*, pp. 142-44; Alfred F. Hurley, *Billy Mitchell, Crusader for Air Power* (Bloomington, Ind., 1975), pp. 100-101, 103-5.

21. *Webster's*, p. 111; Du Pre, *Dictionary*, pp. 61-62; interviews with Ira C. Eaker, 1959 and 1960, pp. 4-6, 14, 17, Arnold Project, COHC; Ira C. Eaker, "Air Chiefs Patrick and Fechet," *Aerospace Historian* 20 (Summer, June 1973): 59; DeWitt Copp, *A Few Great Captains* (Garden City, N.Y., 1980), p. 73.

22. Spaatz interview, pp. 1-3, Arnold Project, COHC; Du Pre, *Dictionary*, pp. 219-20; Alfred Goldberg, "General Carl A. Spaatz," in *The War Lords: Military Commanders of the Twentieth Century*, ed. Michael Carver (Boston, 1976), p. 569; Herman S. Wolk, *Planning and Organizing the Postwar Air Force, 1943-1947* (Washington, D.C., 1984), p. 207.

23. Copp, *Captains*, p. 152; Ira C. Eaker, "Memories of Six Air Chiefs, Part II: Westover, Arnold, Spaatz," *Aerospace Historian* 20 (Winter, Dec. 1973): 194-95; Goldberg, "Spaatz," p. 568.

24. W. W. Rostow, *Pre-Invasion Bombing Strategy: General Eisenhower's Decision of March 25, 1944* (Austin, 1981), pp. 44-45, 54-56, 65; Spaatz interview with Alfred Goldberg, May 19, 1965, copy in Albert F. Simpson Historical Research Center (hereafter AFSHRC), Maxwell Air Force Base, Ala.

25. Doolittle interview, p. 53, Air Force Academy Project, COHC.

26. Arnold, *Global Mission*, pp. 7-8; *Webster's*, pp. 14-15; Thomas M. Coffey, *Hap: The Story of the U.S. Air Force and the Man Who Built It, General Henry H. "Hap" Arnold* (New York, 1982), pp. 14-15, 19. Eaker says that Spaatz was Arnold's only lieutenant, in the sense used by Douglas Southall Freeman in *Lee's Lieutenants: A Study in Command* (New York, 1942-44). Eaker, "Memories of Six Air Chiefs, Part II," p. 195.

27. Interview with Lovett, 1959, pp. 14-20, Arnold Project, COHC: interview with Charles P. Cabell, p. 5, ibid.

28. Coffey, *Hap*, pp. 105, 265, 305-306, 312, 319, 343, 358; Arnold, *Global Mission*, p. 6.

29. Arnold, *Global Mission*, pp. 195-96; Jonathan F. Fanton, "Robert A. Lovett: The War Years" (Ph.D. diss., Yale University, 1978), p. 12.

30. Laurence S. Kuter, "The General vs. the Establishment: General H. H. Arnold and the Air Staff," *Aerospace Historian* 22 (Winter 1974): 185-87.

31. N. F. Parrish, "Hap Arnold and the Historians," ibid. 20 (Fall, Sept. 1973): 113-15; Arnold, *Global Mission*, pp. 139, 532-33; *The Army Air Forces in World War II*, ed. Wesley F. Craven and James L. Cate (7 vols., Chicago, 1948-58) (hereafter C&C), 6: 234-36; Arnold journal, July 13, 1945, box 272, H. H. Arnold Papers, Library of Congress (hereafter LC). Arnold's son Bruce married Barbara Douglas in 1944. Coffey, *Hap*, p. 353.

32. Eaker, "Memories of Six Air Chiefs, Part II," p. 191; interview with Eaker, 1959, p. 1, Arnold Project, COHC; Doolittle interview, p. 53, Air Force Academy Project, ibid.

33. Coffey, *Hap*, pp. 62-63, 67.

34. Eaker interview, 1961, pp. 183-84, Arnold Project, COHC; Coffey, *Hap*, pp. 85, 87.

35. Thomas, *Doolittle*, pp. 52–54.

36. Eaker interview with Alfred Goldberg and Charles Hildreth, May 22, 1962, p. 4, AFSHRC; LeMay, *Mission*, pp. 381, 382–83, 384.

37. LeMay, *Mission*, pp. 167–68, 170.

Chapter 2. American Air War Doctrine and the Bombing of Civilians

1. Clausewitz, *On War*, translation of first chapter by Peter Paret in Paret, *Clausewitz and the State* (New York, 1976), pp. 383–85; Douhet, *The Command of the Air*, trans. Dino Ferrari (New York, 1942), pp. 5–8; quote is from p. 196. The Ferrari translation includes the original work, *The Command of the Air*, published in 1921 (Ferrari translation pp. 3–92); an addition made by Douhet in 1926 (Ferrari translation pp. 93–141); *The Probable Aspects of the War of the Future*, originally published as a monograph in 1928 (Ferrari translation pp. 145–207); a recapitulation that appeared in *Rivista Aeronautica* in November 1929 (Ferrari translation pp. 211–92); and "The War of 19——," which appeared in the same journal in 1930, shortly after Douhet's death (Ferrari translation, pp. 295–394.)

2. Mahan, *The Influence of Sea Power upon History, 1660–1783* (New York, 1957), p. 75n; idem, "The United States Looking Outward," *Atlantic Monthly* 66 (Dec. 1890): 823; Douhet, *Command*, p. 32.

3. Douhet, *Command*, pp. 22–23, 57. Douhet believed that the collapse of morale at home had caused Germany to surrender in 1918 while its armed forces were still capable of fighting: ibid., p. 126.

4. Ibid., p. 58.

5. This was neither the first nor the last appearance of the argument that introducing more deadly weapons into warfare might be a humanitarian act. In 1889 Lord Wolseley, the commander in chief of the British army, argued that advances in military technology tended to make nations hesitate before going to war, to reduce percentages of losses, and to shorten the lengths of campaigns, thus minimizing the suffering of inhabitants: Donald C. Watt, "Restraints on War in the Air Before 1945," in *Restraints on War: Studies in the Limitation of Armed Conflict*, ed. Michael Howard (Oxford, 1979), pp. 60–61. A similar argument was used at the end of World War II to justify dropping atomic bombs on Japanese cities.

6. Douhet, *Command*, pp. 181, 185, 195.

7. Ibid., pp. 194–95.

8. Ibid., pp. 181–82. He referred here to a prediction that poison gas would be used widely in the next war.

9. Arnold, *Global Mission*, pp. 131–32; Flugel, "Air Power Doctrine," pp. 94–5.

10. Flugal, "Air Power Doctrine," pp. 200–201, 201n; [Thomas H. Greer et al.,] *The Development of Air Doctrine in the Army Air Corps, 1917–1941*, USAF Historical Studies no. 89 (Maxwell AFB, Ala., 1955), pp. 50–51; Robert F. Futrell, *Ideas, Concepts, Doctrine: A History of Basic Thinking in the United States Air Force, 1907–1964*, 2 vols. (Maxwell AFB, Ala., 1971), 1: 38–39, 63; 2: 815–816n.

11. Spaatz interview, USAF Academy Oral History Project, Sept. 27, 1968; copy in file K239.0512-583, AFSHRC. Hansell, *Air Plan*, p. 4; ACTS lecture "Strategic Offense and Strategic Defense," April 3, 1939, file 248.2019 A-6, 1937–1938, AFSHRC. Original date of this lecture is March 30, 1938; original listed instructor is H. S. Hansell—both crossed out.

12. Flugel, "Air Power Doctrine," pp. 189–90, 192–93. Compare Douhet, *Command*, pp. 22–23, with ACTS text "Air Warfare," March 1, 1936, p. 15, file 248.101-1, AFSHRC, on effects of bombing on civilian and military morale.

13. Interview with Ira C. Eaker, March 1974, p. 14, Air Force Academy Project, COHC; Russell F. Weigley, *The American Way of War: A History of United States Military Strategy and Policy* (New York, 1973), pp. 210–12. For the influence of Clausewitz and Liddell Hart, see Hansell, *Air Plan*, pp. 10, 38–40, and Hansell interview with Bruce C. Hopper, Oct. 5, 1943, box 135, Carl Spaatz Papers, LC.

14. Hansell, "American Airpower in World War II," ch. 2, p. 12, ms. in file K112.3-2 May 1968, AFSHRC.

15. Hurley, *Mitchell*, pp. 145–46; Futrell, *Ideas*, p. 38; Burke Davis, *The Billy Mitchell Affair* (New York, 1967), pp. 173–74, 178–79; Flugel, "Air Power Doctrine," p. 142.

16. Greer, *Development*, p. 17; Hurley, *Mitchell*, pp. 81–82; Futrell, *Ideas*, p. 35; Flugel, "Air Power Doctrine," pp. 61, 129–30, 134, 145; William Mitchell, *Winged Defense: The Development and Possibilities of Modern Air Power—Economic and Military* (New York, 1925), pp. 126–27.

17. Weigley, *American Way*, pp. 233, 515.

18. Wilson quoted in Harvey A. De Weerd, *President Wilson Fights His War: The American Military Experience in World War I* (New York, 1968), xx; Baker to Peyton C. March, Nov. 4, 1918, quoted in Hurley, *Mitchell*, p. 37; War Department, *Report of the Secretary of War to the President, Nov. 11, 1919* (Washington, 1919), p. 68.

19. Douhet, *Command*, p. 182.

20. William Mitchell, *Memoirs of World War I: "From Start to Finish of Our Greatest War"* (repr. Westport, Conn., 1975), pp. 3–5.

21. Flugel, "Air Power Doctrine," pp. 184–85.

22. ACTS, "The Air Force," ch. 5, "Objectives," p. 69, file 248.101, Apr. 1930, AFSHRC.

23. Ibid., p. 70.

24. Douhet, *Command*, p. 20; Weigley, *American Way*, p. 237.

25. ACTS texts "Air Force," part I, "The Character and Strategy of Air Power," file 248.101-1, 1 Dec. 1935; "Air Force: Air Warfare—The Aim in War," file 248.101-1, 1 Feb. 1938; ACTS lectures "Air Force: The Aim in War," Mar. 28, 1939, file 248.2019A-2; M. S. Fairchild (instructor), "Air Force: National Economic Structure," June 1, 1940, file 248.2021 A-7, 1939–40, all in AFSHRC; Joe G. Taylor, "They Taught Tactics," *Aerospace Historian* 13 (Summer 1966): 67–72. Hansell mentions a 1930 Royal Air Force contribution to the theory of bombing for economic dislocation in *Air Plan*, p. 46.

26. C&C 6: 204–5; Weigley, *American Way*, p. 337.

27. H. H. Arnold and Ira C. Eaker, *Winged Warfare* (New York, 1941), p. 134. At least one of the authors originally felt that it would never be possible to break a nation's will by bombing human beings: see ms. typescript of this book, chapter on tactics, p. 34, container 46, Ira C. Eaker Papers, LC. For the effects of financial pressures on aircraft procurement see Franklin D. Roosevelt for Secretary of War, Jan. 15, 1936, Secretary of War Secret File, National Archives (hereafter NA). For the impact of pacifism and anti-militarism on the U.S. Army between the world wars see Ronald Schaffer, "The War Department's Defense of ROTC, 1920–1940," *Wisconsin Magazine of History* 53 (Winter 1969–70): 108–20; and idem, "General Stanley D. Embick: Military Dissenter," *Military Affairs* 37 (Oct. 1973): 89–95.

28. Arnold, *Global Mission*, p. 227. Like much of Arnold's memoirs, this section was based on a daily journal.

29. Taylor, "Tactics," p. 68; Fairchild, "National Economic Structure," see n. 25 above.

30. ACTS "Air Force," Dec. 1, 1935, "Air Force: Air Warfare," March 1, 1936, ACTS lecture, "The Aim in War," Mar. 28, 1939, see n. 25 above; ACTS problem, "Air Force: Air Operations Against National Structures," Apr. 11, 1939, p. 14, file 248.2020 A-25, AFSHRC.

31. In 1932 the War Plans Division of the War Department General Staff observed that "where the objectives [of an air attack] are located in populous areas it is impossible to make such attacks without danger to considerable numbers of the civilian population." Brig. Gen. Joseph P. Tracy, asst. chief of staff, WPD for the Chief of Staff, June 16, 1932, Adjutant General's file 388.3 (1-2-26) sec. 3, NA.

32. Fairchild, "National Economic Structure," see n. 25 above. (Emphasis in original.)

33. Dallek, *Roosevelt*, p. 195; *New York Times*, Dec. 3, 1939.

34. Hansell, *Air Plan*, pp. 65, 69, 70, 80, 85.

35. AWPD-1, tab 1, pp. 1, 7; tab 2, p. 5, file 145.82-1, Aug. 1941, AFSHRC.

Chapter 3. American Air Operations in Europe:
Occupied Countries and Axis Satellites

1. David Irving, *The Rise and Fall of the Luftwaffe: The Life of Luftwaffe Marshal Erhard Milch* (London, 1973), pp. 46, 101; Hugh Thomas, *The Spanish Civil War*, pp. 624–27; George H. Quester, *Deterrence before Hiroshima: The Airpower Background of Modern Strategy* (New York, 1966), pp. 114–16.

2. Martin Middlebrook, *The Battle of Hamburg: Allied Bomber Forces against a German City in 1943* (New York, 1980), pp. 23–24; Max Hastings, *Bomber Command* (New York, 1979), pp. 128–29; Charles Webster and Noble Frankland, *The Strategic Air Offensive against Germany, 1939–1945* (London, 1961), 1: 174–75, 178–82; 4: 144, 205.

3. Thomas M. Coffey, *Decision over Schweinfurt: The U.S. Eighth Air Force Battle for Daylight Bombing* (New York, 1977), pp. 103–5, 157–58, 167; Frederick L. Anderson to George Stratemeyer, July 21, 1943, file 312.1-E, box 194, RG 18, NA.

4. Interview of Spaatz by Noel F. Parrish and Alfred Goldberg, Feb. 21, 1962, AFSHRC; Eaker interview by Goldberg and Charles Hildreth, Mar. 22, 1962, ibid.; Eaker to author, Jan. 11, 1979.

5. Spaatz interview, Arnold Project, COHC, p. 51.

6. Perry McCoy Smith, *The Air Force Plans for Peace, 1943–1945* (Baltimore, 1970), p. 15; Arnold to Eaker, June 29, 1943, container 16, Eaker Papers.

7. Eaker, "The Case for Day Bombing," file 520.547c, Jan. 43, AFSHRC.

8. Hastings, *Bomber Command*, pp. 184–85; Arnold, *Global Mission*, p. 397.

9. C&C 2: 269–71, 3: 238–39; United States Strategic Bombing Survey (hereafter USSBS), Military Analysis Division, "Daylight Bombing Accuracy of the 8th, 9th, and 15th Air Forces," file 137.306.6, 24 Aug. 1945, AFSHRC; F. L. Anderson to Commanding General, Eighth Air Force, May 1, 1944, box 84, Spaatz Papers; Eaker to Commanding General, VIII Bomber Command, July 28,

1943, container 18, Eaker Papers; "Report by Intelligence Operations Section, Supreme Headquarters . . . Giving Details of the Results Achieved, Casualties Inflicted and the Reaction of the French People," Apr. 25, 1944, box 203, Spaatz Papers; Carl Kaysen to Charles P. Cabell, May 4, 1944, par. 9, ibid.; "Report by the Intelligence Operations Section, Supreme Headquarters, on the Bombing of Railway Targets in France and Belgium . . . ," May 5, 1944, ibid.

10. Message from American GHQ broadcast in the "America Calling Europe" transmission, Oct. 6, 1942, box 215, Spaatz Papers.

11. James B. Gordon to Commanding Generals, VIII Air Force Service Command, VIII Bomber Command, VIII Fighter Command, and VIII Air Support Command, Nov. 6, 1942 with enclosed copy of Air Ministry Bombardment Policy of Oct. 29, 1942, box 84, Spaatz Papers; Ira Eaker to N. H. Bottomley, Apr. 9, 1943, container 19, Eaker Papers; C. Portal to Eaker, Apr. 21, 1943, box 41, Arnold Papers; Eaker to Commanding General, VIII Bomber Command, June 28, 1943, container 18, Eaker Papers.

12. Robert A. Lovett for General [George E.] Stratemeyer, Mar. 10, 1943, box 114, Arnold Papers; Lovett to Eaker, Mar. 23, 1943, file 373.11 (1) General Eaker (VIII AF), Record Group (hereafter RG) 107, NA.

13. Eaker to General [Frank M.] Andrews, Apr. 22, 1943, container 18, Eaker Papers; Eaker to Charles Portal, Apr. 22, 1943, ibid.; Andrews to H. H. Arnold, Apr. 28, 1943, box 41, Arnold Papers.

14. W. W. Rostow, *Pre-Invasion Bombing Strategy: General Eisenhower's Decision of March 25, 1944* (Austin, 1981), pp. 4, 14.

15. Spaatz to Dear Henry, June 18, 1943, box 111, Spaatz Papers.

16. Rostow, *Bombing Strategy*, pp. 41, 43; Hansell, *Air Plan*, pp. 234–35.

17. Rostow, *Bombing Strategy*, p. 45; Hastings, *Bomber Command*, p. 276.

18. Rostow, *Bombing Strategy*, p. 51; Henry D. Lytton, "Bombing Policy in the Rome and Pre-Normandy Invasion Aerial Campaigns of World War II: Bridge-Bombing Strategy Vindicated—and Railyard Bombing Strategy Invalidated," *Military Affairs* 47 (April 1983): 54; C&C 3: 79.

19. C&C 3: 79; Winston S. Churchill, *The Second World War*, vol. 5, *Closing the Ring* (Boston, 1951), pp. 527–30.

20. C&C 3: 174–75; Rostow, *Bombing Strategy*, pp. 55, 56, 148; Hansell, *Air Plan*, p. 235.

21. Spaatz to Eisenhower, Apr. 22, 1944, file 168.7026-6, AFSHRC.

22. Rostow, *Bombing Strategy*, pp. 42, 45.

23. Lytton, "Bombing Policy," p. 55.

24. Kent R. Greenfield, *American Strategy in World War II: A Reconsideration* (Baltimore, 1963), ch. 3.

25. C&C 2: 103, 534; Raleigh Trevelyan, *Rome '44: The Battle for the Eternal City* (New York, 1982), p. 36; Martin Blumenson, *Salerno to Cassino* (Washington, D.C., 1969), p. 146.

26. Spaatz to Dear Henry, June 18, 1943, box 11, Spaatz Papers; Spaatz Diary (personal), June 14, 1943, ibid.

27. William D. Leahy for the Joint Chiefs of Staff, June 10, 1943, file CCS 373.11 Rome (6-10-43), sec. 1, RG 218, NA; Leahy for the President, June 11, 1943, ibid.; Leahy for the Joint Chiefs of Staff, June 14, 1943, ibid.

28. CCS 261, "Bombing of Rome. Memorandum by Representatives of the British Chiefs of Staff," June 22, 1943, file ABC 384.3 Rome (6-10-43), RG 319,

NA; notes on CCS 99th meeting, June 25, 1943, ibid.; quotation from CCS 99th meeting supplemental minutes, June 25, 1943, file CCS 373.11 Rome (6-10-43), sec. 1, RG 218, NA; Arnold's handwritten comment on Deane for General Marshall, Admiral King, General Arnold, July 3, 1943, box 39, Arnold Papers.

29. Minutes, Trident conference, May 1943, file 119.151-2, May 1943, AFSHRC; Eisenhower for Combined Chiefs of Staff, June 30, 1943, file CCS 373.11 Rome (6-10-43), sec. 1, RG 218, NA.

30. Combined Chiefs of Staff to CG FORTUNE ALGIERS, June 15, 1943, file CCS 373.11 Rome (6-10-43), sec. 1, RG 218, NA; H. D. Kehm for the Secretariat, Joint Chiefs of Staff, June 28, 1943, ibid.; ALGIERS to WAR, July 8, 1943, file ABC 384.3 Rome (6-22-43), RG 319, NA; President to the Prime, July 9, 1943, Leahy File #14, RG 218, NA; Combined Chiefs of Staff for Eisenhower, June 19, 1943, container 33, Map Room file 303, Bombing of Rome, Franklin D. Roosevelt Library (hereafter FDR Library).

31. Headquarters, North African Strategic Air Force (NASAF), Operations Summaries etc., July 1943, Operations of 19 July 1943, file 615.3061-1, July 1943, AFSHRC; Northwest African Photo Reconnaissance Wing, Detailed Interpretation Report no. D.73, n.d., file 615.55-1, 19 July 1943, ibid.

32. Trevelyan, *Rome*, p. 11; Henry Newton, "Report on the Bombing of the Basilica of San Lorenzo," Aug. 19, 1944, file CAD 000.4 (3-25-43) (1) sec. 4, RG 319, NA; Rome: Precision Bombing Problem Was What to Hit Also What Not to Hit," *Impact* 1: 42–45, file 142.036, Apr.–Dec. 1943, AFSHRC.

33. Albert N. Garland and Howard McG. Smyth, *Sicily and the Surrender of Italy* (Washington, D.C., 1965), pp. 243, 266, 268; ALGIERS to BOSCO no. 1682, Aug. 15, 1943, Leahy file #14, RG 218, NA.

34. Garland and Smyth, *Sicily*, pp. 278–79; Spaatz Diary (personal), Aug. 4, 1943, box 11, Spaatz Papers. For the decision not to agree to open city status, see JCS minutes, Nov. 15, 1943, file CCS 373.11 Rome (6-10-43), sec. 1, RG 218, NA. The U.S. Joint Chiefs were amenable to a partial demilitarization of Rome; the British chiefs were not. "Notes for Informal Consideration of the Chief of Staff," May 23, 1944, "Arrangements for the Safety of Rome," file ABC 384.4 Rome (Aug. 14, 43), sec. 1-A, RG 319, NA; Carter and Mueller, *Combat Chronology*, p. 920.

35. Arnold Journals, 1944 June 8–21 Trip to England, June 18 entry, box 272, Arnold Papers.

36. Blumenson, *Salerno*, pp. 69, 182; Ernest R. May, *"Lessons" of the Past: The Use and Misuse of History in American Foreign Policy* (New York, 1973), p. 128.

37. *Report of the American Commission for the Protection and Salvage of Artistic and Historic Monuments in War Areas* (Washington, D.C., 1946) (hereafter ACPS *Report*), pp. 1, 47; William Bell Dinsmoor to Henry L. Stimson, Mar. 15, 1943, file 130 G-5 SHAEF, Arts, Monuments, Fine Arts & Archives, RG 331, NA.

38. McCloy to author, Oct. 28, 1977; Secretary of War to Dinsmoor, May 22, 1943, file CAD 000.4 (3-25-43) (1), RG 165, NA; Hull to Mr. President, June 21, 1943, Official File 5372, FDR Library; Roosevelt to My dear Chief Justice, Apr. 24, 1943, ibid.

39. ACPS *Report*, pp. 3–4. The words "Far East" were substituted in the title for "Europe" the following April.

40. William B. Dinsmoor, "Summary for the Month of July 1943," Committee of the American Council of Learned Societies on Protection of Cultural Treasures in War Areas, file CAD 000.4 (3-25-43) (1), RG 165, NA; M. W. Moss

to C. L. Kades, Oct. 27, 1943, ibid.; Henry C. Newton for General Hilldring, Apr. 6, 1944, file CAD 000.4 (3-25-43) (ser 2), RG 18, NA.

41. Moss to Kades, Oct. 27, 1943, RG 165, NA; John J. McCloy to David E. Finley, Oct. 9, 1943, McCloy folder, box 15, RG 239, NA; ACPS *Report*, p. 20; History Second Bombardment Group, Mar. 1944, file GP-2-H Mar. 44, AFSHRC; Doolittle to Commanding Generals, 5th, 42nd, 47th wings et al., Oct. 14, 1943, file 652.355, Aug.-Nov. 1943, ibid.; Doolittle to CG 5th Depienne, Nov. 11, 1943, ibid.; Mediterranean Allied Photo Reconnaissance Command, "The Ancient Monuments of Italy," Feb. 1944, file 622.610-2, folder 1, 1944, ibid.

42. Lauris Norstad, preface to "The Ancient Monuments of Italy." Feb. 23, 1944. See n. 41 above. For Frascati and Orvieto, see Frederick Hartt, *Florentine Art under Fire* (Princeton, 1949), p. 8, and C&C 2: 517.

43. Eisenhower to all commanders, Dec. 29, 1943, file 622.610-2, folder 2, 1944-45, AFSHRC.

44. John J. McCloy for Eisenhower, Dec. 13, 1943, Pre-Presidential file, Eisenhower Library; brief of Spaatz to Arnold, July 3, 1944, Air AG, Arnold's briefs of messages, RG 18, NA; report on conversation with Herbert Matthews, Apr. 24, 1944, in "Newton, Col. Henry C." folder, box 16, RG 239, NA; David Tutaev, *The Consul of Florence* (London, 1966), p. 220.

45. Blumenson, *Salerno*, pp. 403-8, 413; C&C 3: 362-63; Henry C. Newton, "Report on the Bombing of the Abbazia di Montecassino," Aug. 20, 1944, with Newton to the Director, Civil Affairs Division, War Department, Aug. 26, 1943, file CAD 000.4 (3-25-43) (1) sec. 4, Aug. 26, 1944, RG 391, NA. David Hapgood and David Richardson, *Monte Cassino* (New York, 1984), pp. 3, 234, 239.

46. Trevelyan, *Rome*, pp. 129-30; Harold L. Bond, *Return to Cassino: A Memoir of the Fight for Rome* (Garden City, N.Y., 1964), p. 113.

47. Blumenson, *Salerno*, pp. 401-7.

48. Ibid., pp. 403, 409, 413; Bond, *Return*, p. 114.

49. Giles to Eaker, Apr. 25, 1944, box 105, Arnold Papers; Journals, 1944 June 8-21 Trip to England, June 18 entry, box 272, ibid.

50. Blumenson, *Salerno*, pp. 413-16; Hapgood and Richardson, *Monte Cassino*, p. 214 (the Germans and the Allies also hit the building with artillery fire on other occasions, p. 240).

51. Doolittle to CG 5th Depienne, Nov. 11, 1943, file 652.355, Aug.-Nov. '43, AFSHRC; Tutaev, *Consul*, pp. 133-34; Eaker to Twining, Mar. 12, 1944, and attached message, Twining to Eaker, container 23, Eaker Papers.

52. Eaker to Arnold, Mar. 24, 1944, container 23, Eaker Papers.

53. Entry for April 2, 1945, Arnold Journal, Mar. 31-May 8, 1945, box 272, Arnold Papers.

54. For a discussion of Allied damage to cultural monuments and artifacts through ignorance, carelessness, or vandalism, see Herbert Matthews's conversation cited in n. 44 above and Gerald K. Haines, "'Who Gives a Damn About Medieval Walls,'" *Prologue* 8 (Summer 1976): 97-106. For German vandalism and official German attempts to prevent it, see Hartt, *Florentine Art*, pp. 19-21, 61, 76.

55. Marshall L. Miller, *Bulgaria during the Second World War* (Stanford, 1975), p. 52.

56. D. Dalziel to E. P. Curtis, Oct. 24, 1943, box 13, Spaatz Papers.

57. Joint Chiefs of Staff, JCS 537, "Bombing of Sofia. Memorandum from the Joint Staff Planners" (with enclosures), Oct. 22, 1943, file CCS 373.11 Bulga-

ria (10-20-43), RG 218, NA; Combined Chiefs of Staff to Eisenhower, Oct. 23, 1943, ibid.

58. Miller, *Bulgaria*, p. 166.

59. HQ NAAF A-5, "Bombing Attacks on Sofia and Immediate High Priority Targets for Heavy Bombers," Dec. 3, 1943, file 622.317-1, 1943–1944, AFSHRC.

60. Miller, *Bulgaria*, p. 167; War Cabinet Joint Intelligence Sub-Committee, "Effect of Allied Bombing of Balkans on Balkan Situation," Jan. 29, 1944, JIC (44) 37 (0) Final, "Misc. Messages, Corresp. Photos etc." folder, Papers of Lauris Norstad, in Modern Military Records Division, NA.

61. War Cabinet Joint Intelligence Sub-Committee, "Effect of Allied Bombing." See n. 60 above; Miller, *Bulgaria*, p. 168.

62. Carter and Mueller, *Combat Chronology*, pp. 308–9; Lauris Norstad to [Laurence S.] Kuter, Apr. 9, 1944, "Personal Gen. Norstad" folder, box 7, Norstad Papers.

63. Eaker to Lovett, Sept. 18, 1944, container 23, Lovett file, Eaker Papers; Carter and Mueller, *Combat Chronology*, p. 336.

64. Norstad [by command of General Eaker], "Bombing Directive," Feb. 27, 1944, box 215, Spaatz Papers.

65. Eaker to Lovett, Apr. 17, 1944, file 373.11 (2) SCCI (2) General Eaker AFRICAN 1944, item #61, RG 107, NA; memorandum for Brigadier Redman from Forrest B. Royal, Feb. 12, 1944, file CCS 092 Bulgaria (8-2-43), sec. 1, RG 18, NA; Minutes, JCS 154th Meeting, Mar. 21, 1944, file CCS 092 Bulgaria (8-2-43), sec. 2, ibid.

66. "Script for Teletype Conference," Mar. 24, 1944, Spaatz for Arnold, F. L. Anderson Diary, box 316, Spaatz Papers; Anderson to L. S. Kuter, Feb. 3, 1944, box 276, Arnold Papers. For the attitude of Enemy Operations Unit analysts in the U.S. embassy, see C. P. Kindleberger to P. H. Coombs, Apr. 22, 1944, file 622.323-7, Jan.–Nov. 1944, AFSHRC.

67. Joint Staff Planners, "Bombing of Bulgaria" (JPS 410/1), Mar. 14, 1944, file CCS 092 Bulgaria (8-2-43), sec. 1, RG 18, NA.

68. Cable from Istanbul, Apr. 26, 1944, and from Washington, May 1, 1944, with Kindleberger to Bill and Phil, May 6, 1944, MAAF folder, OSS, RG 226, NA.

69. Winant to the President, Apr. 23, 1944, file CCS 373.11 (5-12-44), RG 218, NA.

70. Cordell Hull to Admiral Leahy, July 11, 1944, ibid.; Memorandum by the United States Chiefs of Staff, "Integration of Political Considerations with Military Decisions in Bombing Europe" (CCS 626), July 20, 1944, file ABC 384.5 (May 25, 45), RG 319, NA; Fifteenth Air Force Missions to Budapest, Nov. 27, 1944, file 670.4231, Nov. 1943–Oct. 1944, AFSHRC.

Chapter 4. The Bombing of Germany: Early Operations

1. H. H. Arnold to All Air Force Commanders in Combat Zones, June 10, 1943 (marked "as rewritten by Gen. Arnold"), bombing folder, box 41, Arnold Papers.

2. H. H. Arnold for Dr. Von Karman, Nov. 7, 1944, box 40, ibid.

3. T. H. Hanley, Jr., to AFABI, Colonel [Edgar P.] Sorenson, Nov. 25, 1942, file SAS400.112, box 117, ibid.; Sorenson to AFCAS [Chief of Air Staff], Dec. 6, 1942, ibid; B. W. Chidlaw to AFCAS attn: Gen. Hanley, Jan. 29, 1943, ibid.

4. Arnold to Assistant Chief of Staff, Matériel, Maintenance & Distribution, April 26, 1943, box 38, Arnold Papers; T. J. Hanley to Assistant Chief of Air Staff, Personnel et al., April 30, 1943, box 114, ibid.

5. Eaker to author, Jan. 11, 1979; Eaker interview with Alfred Goldberg and Charles Hildreth, May 22, 1962, USAF Oral History Collection, AFSHRC.

6. LeMay, *Mission*, pp. 383, 425.

7. Kuter interview with Hugh M. Ahmann and Tom Sturm, Sept. 30–Oct. 3, 1974, p. 375, USAF Oral History Collection, AFSHRC; Solly Zuckerman, *From Apes to Warlords* (New York, 1978), p. 352.

8. Carter and Mueller, *Combat Chronology*, p. 88.

9. Martin Middlebrook, *The Battle of Hamburg: Allied Bomber Forces against a German City in 1943* (New York, 1981), pp. 95, 194–96, 328.

10. Ira C. Eaker to Robert A. Lovett, Dec. 15, 1943, quoted in Hugh Odishaw, "Radar Bombing in the Eighth Air Force," p. 43, box 80, Spaatz Papers.

11. Coffey, *Schweinfurt*, pp. 241–42, 245, 250.

12. Ibid., pp. 1, 3, 21, 260; C&C 2: 685.

13. Lay to Commanding Officer, 100th Bombardment Group (H), Aug. 25, 1943, file 373.11(1), section 2, RG 107, NA. Lay coauthored the screenplays of *Twelve O'Clock High*, a postwar film about the AAF, and *Strategic Air Command*.

14. Coffey, *Schweinfurt*, pp. 1, 76, 259, 262–63, 268.

15. Eaker to Robert A. Lovett, Aug. 9, 1943, container 15, Eaker Papers; Anderson to Eaker, Aug. 13, 1943, box 143, Spaatz Papers.

16. Minutes of Combat Wing and Group Commanders meeting, Oct. 21, 1943, Curtis E. LeMay Papers, LC.

17. Tactical Mission Report signed by General F. L. Anderson, Oct. 10, 1943, file 2b (65), box 55, USSBS, RG 243, NA. While the report states that the First and Third Bomb Divisions were "assigned to attack the center of the City of Münster," the official *Combat Chronology* records for October 20 "236 HBs attack railroads and waterways in and around Münster": Carter and Mueller, *Combat Chronology*, p. 200.

18. Barney M. Giles to J. H. Doolittle, Jan. 26, 1945, box 18, James H. Doolittle Papers, LC; Lovett to Eaker, Mar. 23, 1943, file 373.11(1), General Eaker [VIII AF] [Item 63], RG 107, NA. See also "Report on Bombing Accuracy, Eighth Air Force, 1 September 1944 to 31 December 1944," included in Odishaw, "Radar Bombing," Spaatz Papers.

19. Eaker to Barney M. Giles, Dec. 13, 1943, container 17, Eaker Papers; Eaker to Artemus Gates, Dec. 16, 1943, box 324, Spaatz Papers.

20. Berliner for Colonel Loutzenheiser, Oct. 11, 1943, container 17, Eaker Papers. For Berliner's career, see *Who Was Who In American History—The Military*, p. 44.

21. Combined Chiefs of Staff Air Plan for the Defeat of Germany: Memo from Commanding General, AAF, Nov. 1, 1943, box 39, Arnold Papers.

22. Telephone conversation between Frederick L. Anderson and Orvil A. Anderson, Feb. 29, 1944, F. L. Anderson Official Journal, box 316, Spaatz Papers; F. L. Anderson Diary, Mar. 6, 1944, ibid. By "seeing" a city, Anderson probably meant locating it on a radar screen. The radar of that period could distinguish only cities located on obvious landmarks, such as river bends.

23. Transcript of telephone conversation between Anderson and Doolittle, Mar. 9, 1944, ibid.; interview with Cabell by Bruce C. Hopper and Charles A. Foster, July 9, 1944, p. 16, box 135, ibid.

24. Office of the Director of Intelligence, HQ Eighth Air Force, "Target Priorities of the Eighth Air Force," May 15, 1945, p. 52, box 326, ibid.; Spaatz to Commanding General, HQ MAAF, May 16, 1944, in folder "Misc. messages, corresp., photos, etc., "Norstad Papers [located in Modern Military Branch, Military Archives Division, NA].

25. Vera Brittain, "Massacre by Bombing," *Fellowship* 10 (March 1944): 50–64; Early letter, ibid. (April 1944), p. 79; *New York Times*, Mar. 6, 1944. See, for example, "Area Bombing," *Commonweal* 39 (Mar. 17, 1944): 531–32, "Massacre by Bombing" (editorial) *Catholic World* 159 (May 1944): 97–104, and articles in *Newsweek* 23 (March 20, 1944): 86ff., and *The Nation* 158 (Mar. 18, 1944): 323.

26. *New York Times*, Mar. 11, 1944; Spaatz Daily Journal (Personal), June 9, 1944, box 15, Spaatz Papers; Memorandum from R. D. Hughes, July, 5, 1944, file 519.4511-14, Feb.–Aug. 1944, AFSHRC.

27. Lovett to Welsh, June 30, 1943, RG 107, NA; Jonathan F. Fanton, "Robert A. Lovett: The War Years" (Ph.D. diss., Yale University, 1978), p. 145.

28. Arnold to J. H. Doolittle, Nov. 26, 1942, file 131, box 19, Doolittle Papers; Arnold to Eaker, June 29, 1943, container 16, Eaker Papers; Arnold to Eaker, Nov. 26, 1944, container 22, ibid.; Perry McCoy Smith, *The Air Force Plans for Peace, 1943–1945* (Baltimore, 1970), p. 15.

29. Jerome S. Bruner, *Mandate from the People* (New York, 1944), pp. 126–27, 142; *Public Opinion Quarterly* 8 (Summer 1944): 296, 448–49; Richard W. Steele, "American Popular Opinion and the War Against Germany: The Issue of Negotiated Peace, 1942," *Journal of American History* 65 (Dec. 1978): 704–23; Eaker interview with Goldberg and Hildreth, May 22, 1962, AFSHRC; Laurence S. Kuter to Frederick L. Anderson (draft), file 145.161-7 Apr. 44–May 45, Misc. Corresp. Anderson and Kuter, ibid.

30. F. L. Anderson to Cols. [Charles G.] Williamson, [Richard D.] Hughes, [Charles P.] Cabell, [Joseph J.] Nazarro; Lt. Cols. [Frank P.] Bender and [William J.] Wrigglesworth, Feb. 12, 1944, file 519.4511-14, Feb.–Aug. 1944, AFSHRC; Carl Spaatz to Commanding General, Mar. 4, 1944, file 519.1612, 1943–44, ibid.

31. Plan for Completion of the Combined Bomber Offensive, supplement part I of "Prospect for Ending War by Air Attack Against German Morale," Mar. 5, 1945, file 519.318-1, ibid.

32. Enemy Objectives Unit, Economic Warfare Division, American Embassy, report, Feb. 29, 1944, ibid.; OSS Research and Analysis Branch, RA no. 1456, "The Social and Political Effects of Air Raids on the German People: A Preliminary Survey," June 9, 1944, file 187.2-52, AFSHRC; Assistant Chief of Air Staff, Plans to Assistant Chief of Air Staff, Intelligence, May 25, 1944, file 118.04A-8, 14 June 1944, ibid.; Assistant Chief of Air Staff, Intelligence to Assistant Chief of Air Staff, Plans, June 12, 1944, ibid.

33. C&C 3: 284; minutes, British Chiefs of Staff (hereafter COS), 219th meeting, item 6, July 3, 1944; Secretary COS committee to the Prime Minister, July 5, 1944, annex to COS (44) 222nd meeting, all in box 277, Arnold Papers. The RAF chief of air staff also doubted that reprisals made sense.

34. Spaatz to Commanding General, Eighth Air Force, June 9, 1944, file 519.1612, 1943–44, AFSHRC.

35. John P. Harris to George C. McDonald, June 27, 1944, file 519.322-1, Sept. 1944, ibid.

36. Drafts of "Operations in Germany with Particular Political and Psycho-

logical Significance," n.d., in file 519.4511-14, Feb.–Aug. 1944, ibid., and in THUN-
DERCLAP folder, box 153, Spaatz Papers.

37. Information about Hughes from Rostow, *Bombing Strategy*, pp. 17–18,
141–43; Hughes typescript memoir (pages supplied by Guy D. Hughes), pp. 16,
24, and unnumbered page; Guy D. Hughes to author, Feb. 7, 1981; interview of
Col. R. D. Hughes by Bruce C. Hopper, Sept. 15, 1943, box 135, Spaatz Papers;
and Hughes to F. L. Anderson, Oct. 6, 1944, box 143, ibid.

38. Rostow, *Bombing Strategy*, p. 142.

39. Memorandum by R. D. Hughes, July 5, 1944, file 519.4511-14, Feb.–Aug.
1944, AFSHRC.

40. Weicker to George C. McDonald, July 6, 1944, ibid.

41. Pincus to Bill, Phil and Russ, July 15, 1944, EOU file, MAAF folder, OSS
Records; EOU, "The Use of the Heavy Bomber Force from the Present to V-Day,"
July 21, 1944, file 519.3171-7, AFSHRC; undated memo from Col. Taylor to Col.
Williamson, file 519.4511-14, Feb.–Aug. 1944, ibid.; draft memo, F. L. Anderson
to Arthur Tedder, July 8, 1944, ibid.

42. Cabell to Deputy Commanding General, Operations, June 26, 1944,
THUNDERCLAP folder, box 153, Spaatz Papers.

43. F. L. Anderson to Director, Plans, July 11, 1944, on carrier sheet, file
519.4511-14, Feb.–Aug. 1944, AFSHRC; Hughes to C. P. Cabell, July 17, 1944, file
519.161-7, 1944–45 Misc. Corresp., ibid.

44. D. E[isenhower]. to Chief of Staff [copy], n.d., on minutes of COS 221st
meeting (0), July 5, 1944, box 277, Arnold Papers; Diary (Personal), July 21, 1944,
box 15, Spaatz Papers; F. L. Anderson to Director of Operations, July 21, 1944,
box 84, ibid.

Chapter 5. The Bombing of Germany: Transition to Douhetian Warfare

1. COS (44) 650 (0) (Revise), "Air Attack on Civilian Morale: Memorandum
by the Chief of Air Staff," Aug. 1, 1944, THUNDERCLAP folder, box 153, Spaatz
Papers.

2. L. S. Kuter for General Arnold, written Aug. 9, 1944, ibid.; Kuter to
Frederick L. Anderson, Aug. 15, 1944, ibid.; draft of Kuter to Frederick L. Anderson written Aug. 8, 1944, file 145.161-7, Apr. 44–May 44 misc. corres. Anderson
and Kuter, AFSHRC.

3. Kuter to Anderson draft written Aug. 8, 1944, cited in note 2 above.

4. Kuter to Anderson, Sept. 5, 1944, endorsement on Charles G. Williamson
for General Kuter, Sept. 4, 1944, THUNDERCLAP folder, box 153, Spaatz Papers.

5. Kuter to Anderson, Aug. 15, 1944, ibid.

6. COS (44) 650 (0) (Revise), "Air Attack on Civilian Morale: Memorandum
by the Chief of Air Staff," Aug. 1, 1944, ibid.; D.B. Ops., "Operation 'Thunderclap' (Attack on German Civilian Morale)," Aug. 2, 1944, ibid.

7. Cabell to Hughes, Sept. 8, 1944, in file 168.7026-9, Apr. 1944–5 Jan. 1945,
AFSHRC; [C. Spaatz] to Dear Hap, Aug. 27, 1944, box 15, Spaatz Papers.

8. Spaatz to Eisenhower, Aug. 24, 1944, with endorsement D.D.E. to Spaatz,
Aug. 28, 1944, Spaatz personal file, Sept. 9, 1944, box 18, ibid.

9. Minutes, 176th meeting of U.S. Joint Chiefs of Staff (hereafter JCS), Sept.

14, 1944, box 179, Combined Chiefs of Staff (hereafter CCS) decimal file, RG 218, NA; Robert A. McClure to A. R. Maxwell, Sept. 16, 1944, THUNDERCLAP folder, box 153, Spaatz Papers; C&C 3: 639.

10. Jack Roberts to Advisory Council, Army Air Forces, Jan. 24, 1945, box 288, Arnold Papers; Edward L. Bowles for General Giles, Oct. 3, 1944, file SAS 400.112, box 117, ibid.; Memorandum by the Commanding General, Army Air Forces, "Employment of War Weary U.S. Bombers Against Large Industrial Areas in Germany, Nov. 4, 1944, JCS 1150, file ABC 384.5 Germany (13 May 44), sec. 2, RG 319, NA; USSTAF ADV to USSTAF Ninth AF, Nov. 21, 1944, Aphrodite General file, box 193, Spaatz Papers; Minutes, JCS 190th meeting, Feb. 9, 1945, file CCS 373.11 Germany (11-4-44), RG 218, NA.

11. Arnold to Dear Tooey, Nov. 23, 1944, box 16, Spaatz Papers; Spaatz to Arnold, Dec. 10, 1944, ibid.

12. Spaatz to Arnold, Oct. 3, 1944, HURRICANE I & II file, Oct. 3 [1944], box 150, ibid.

13. Jack Roberts to Advisory Council, Army Air Forces, Jan. 24, 1945, box 288, Arnold Papers; John J. McCloy for the Chief of Staff, Mar. 16, 1945, ibid.; memo G[eorge] A. L[incoln] for the Assistant Secretary, War Department General Staff, Mar. 23, 1945, file ABC 384.5 Germany (13 May 44), sec. 2, RG 319, NA.

14. E. E. Partridge to Commanding General, Eighth Air Force, Jan. 20, 1945, file 527.431A, Jan. 1945, Aphrodite, AFSHRC. William D. Leahy to the President, Feb. 8, 1945, box 288, Arnold Papers; Draft memorandum, Roosevelt to the Prime Minister, with Leahy to Roosevelt, Mar. 26, 1945, file CCS 373.11 Germany (11-4-44), RG 218, NA [WOZ for Gen. McFarland, Mar. 30, 1945, ibid., says Roosevelt sent this memo Mar. 29]; Barney M. Giles for Carl A. Spaatz, Apr. 27, 1945, file 519.9701-15, '44-'45 Gen. Corresp., AFSHRC. On instructions from USSTAF, four robots were expended against industrial targets in German cities: L. S. Kuter to Charles Portal, Feb. 2, 1945, box 278, Arnold Papers.

15. Charles G. Williamson for F. L. Anderson, Sept. 12, 1944, box 18, Spaatz Papers.

16. Target Section, USSTAF, "Suggested Plans for Attack on German Transportation Systems," Sept. 14, 1944, file 519.322-1, Sept. 1944, AFSHRC.

17. Barnett to W. A. Salant and P. H. Coombs, Sept. 15, 1944, file 622.323-7, Jan.-Nov. 1944, ibid.; Anderson for Spaatz, Sept. 27, 1944, HURRICANE I & II file, box 150, Spaatz Papers.

18. F. L. Anderson to commanding generals, 8th, 15th, 9th Army Air Forces, Oct. 13, 1944, file 622.422-2, Oct. 1944-Mar. 1945, AFSHRC.

19. C&C 3: 639-40; Spaatz to Curtis, Oct. 1 [1944], HURRICANE I & II file, box 150, Spaatz Papers; Minutes, meeting of Combined Planning Staffs to discuss . . . Operation Hurricane, Oct. 1, 1944, AFSHO microfilm 109, AFSHRC.

20. R. D. Hughes to F. L. Anderson, Oct. 6, 1944, folder "Operational Planning I," box 143, Spaatz Papers.

21. Roosevelt quoted in Dallek, *Roosevelt*, pp. 472-73.

22. Franklin D. Roosevelt to The Secretary of War, Sept. 9, 1944 [copy], box 277, Arnold Papers.

23. David MacIsaac, *Strategic Bombing in World War II: The Story of the United States Strategic Bombing Survey* (New York, 1976), p. 48.

24. Excerpts from D. T. Griggs to E. L. Bowles, Oct. 17, 1944, with Bowles to Stimson, Nov. 21, 1944, box 2, Bowles files, formerly TS files, RG 107, NA

[A mimeographed copy of the complete Griggs letter is in box 5, Elwood R. Quesada Papers, LC]; Odishaw, "Radar Bombing," pp. 24–25, box 80, Spaatz Papers. Bowles was a leading MIT radar scientist. James P. Baxter III, *Scientists against Time* (Boston, 1948), p. 33.

25. E. L. Bowles to Mr. Secretary [Stimson], Nov. 21, 1944, Bowles file, box 2, formerly TS files, RG 107, NA; E. Blair Garland for General Quesada, Jan. 2, 1945, Quesada Papers; Henry L. Stimson Ms. Diary (Microfilm from Yale University Sterling Library), Nov. 19, 1944.

26. Copy of form letter from Gordon W. Allport, Nov. 27, 1944, USSBS file 64 b t (1), RG 243, NA; Franklin Fearing, "Civilian Reaction to Strategic Bombing in Germany and Japan: An A Priori Analysis," n.d., ibid.

27. Meier to Allport, Nov. 30, 1944, ibid.

28. [Gundlach] to Allport, Dec. 2, 1944 and English to Gordon [Allport], Dec. 1, 1944, ibid.

29. Fifteenth Air Force copy of Operation CLARION plan, Dec. 17, 1944, file 670.430-3, Feb. 1945, AFSHRC.

30. J. H. Doolittle to Commanding General, United States Strategic Air Forces in Europe, Dec. 27, 1944, file 519.430A, Dec. 44–Mar. 45, ibid.; Twining to Ira C. Eaker, Jan. 4, 1945, ibid.

31. Copy of "General Plan for Maximum Effort Attack against Transportation Objectives," Dec. 17, 1944, in file 168.7026-9. Apr. 1944-5 Jan. 1945, ibid.

32. Eaker to Spaatz , Jan. 1, 1945, box 20, Spaatz Papers.

33. Eaker to author, Jan. 11, 1979.

34. Memo, E. Blair Garland for General Quesada, Jan. 2, 1945, box 5, Quesada Papers.

35. Griggs for Lovett, Jan. 6, 1945, file 471.6 (1) Buzz Bomb (Item 113), RG 107, NA.

36. Lovett for Arnold, Jan. 9, 1945, box 20, Spaatz Papers.

37. Anderson to Director of Operations, Jan. 18, 1945, file 519.430A, Dec. 1944–Feb. 1945, AFSHRC; Anderson to Spaatz, Feb. 2, 1945, box 20, Spaatz Papers; Melden E. Smith, Jr., "The Bombing of Dresden Reconsidered: A Study in Wartime Decision Making" (Ph.D. diss., Boston University, 1971), p. 229.

38. Spaatz to Doolittle, Eaker, Twining, Vandenberg, Saville, Feb. 21, 1945, file 520.3233-40, AFSHRC; Anderson (signed Spaatz) to Arnold, Feb. 22, 1945, in file 519.430A, Dec. 1944–Feb. 1945, ibid.; Eaker to USSTAF, MAIN IN 19233, Feb. 23, 1945, and Twining to USSTAF, MAIN IN 19141, Feb. 23, 1945, CLARION folder, box 70, Spaatz Papers. Message numbers are listed to distinguish messages sent the same day, to indicate their sequence, and to identify messages where only one party is listed.

39. Frederick L. Anderson to Orvil A. Anderson, Mar. 2, 1945, Anderson Diary, Frederick L. Anderson Papers, Hoover Institution.

40. Webster and Frankland, *Strategic Air Offensive* 3: 101–4; Kuter to Giles, Cricket 38, Feb. 1, 1944, box 288, Arnold Papers.

41. Kuter to Giles, Cricket 35, Feb. 1, 1945, Frederick L. Anderson Diary, Anderson Papers; Anderson to Spaatz, Feb. 1, 1945, box 288, Arnold Papers.

42. D.B. Ops., "Operation 'Thunderclap' (Attack on German Civilian Morale)," see n. 6 above; Report by the Joint Intelligence Sub-Committee, "Strategic Bombing in Relation to the Present Russian Offensive," JIC (45) 31 (0) (Revised Final), Jan. 25, 1945, box 288, Arnold Papers; David M. Schlatter Daily Diary, Jan. 28, 1945, file 168.7052-5, 44/10/21–45/07/11, AFSHRC.

43. Doolittle to Spaatz CS93JD, Jan. 30, 1945, file 520.422, Sept. 44–Feb. 45, AFSHRC.

44. Spaatz to Doolittle, JD104CS, Jan. 30, 1945, ibid.; minutes of staff meeting, Feb. 2, 1945, box 20, Spaatz Papers; C&C 3: 725–26; minutes of Combined Strategic Targets Committee, Feb. 2, 1945, file 505.43-6, AFSHRC; Spaatz to Deane, Feb. 4, 1945, Anderson Diary, Anderson Papers; USAAF HQ Eighth AF History, vol. 1, p. 69, file 520.01, Feb. 1945, AFSHRC.

45. USAAF HQ Eighth AF History, vol. 1, pp. 30–31, file 520.01, Feb. 1945, AFSHRC; Smith, "Dresden," pp. 14, 32, 64, 269; F. L. Anderson to Commanding General, Army Air Forces, Mar. 29, 1945, file 519.1611, 1945 Official File Gen. Anderson D. Ops, AFSHRC; David Irving, *The Destruction of Dresden* (New York, 1965), pp. 190–91, 201, 205–6; Forrest C. Pogue, *George C. Marshall: Organizer of Victory, 1943–1945* (New York, 1973), p. 545.

46. Kuter to Spaatz, Feb. 13, 1945, IN Cables 1 Feb. 1945 to 15 Feb. 1945, RG 165, NA; Kuter to Giles, Cricket 38, Feb. 1, 1945, box 288, Arnold Papers.

47. Giles to Eaker for Kuter, WAR 37181, Feb. 14, 1945, CM-OUT messages, 30383–45313, Feb. 1–28, 1945, RG 165, NA; to Spaatz, signed Giles, Feb. 17, 1945, "Bombing Policies" folder, box 84, Spaatz Papers; Kuter to Giles, Cricket 35, Feb. 1, 1945, Anderson Diary, Anderson Papers.

48. Arnold to Spaatz, Feb. 18, 1945, box 288, Arnold Papers; Spaatz to Arnold, Feb. 18, 1945, Anderson Diary, Anderson Papers.

49. Howard Cowan, "Allies Decide on New Policy of Terror Raids," *St. Louis Post-Dispatch*, Feb. 18, 1945; F. L. Anderson to Spaatz, UA 64471, Feb. 19, 1945, box 20, Spaatz Papers.

50. F. L. Anderson to L. S. Kuter, Feb. 27, 1945, file 519.1611, 1945 Official File Gen. Anderson D. Ops, AFSHRC.

51. Rex Smith (signed Arnold) to Spaatz, Feb. 18, 1945, WAR 39722, box 20, Spaatz Papers; Spaatz handwritten note to Dear Fred on reverse of Anderson for Spaatz, Feb. 19, 1945, tab 15 in Correspondence on News Release, Anderson Papers.

52. Anderson (signed Spaatz) to Arnold, UA64484, Feb. 19, 1945, CM-INs Jan.–Feb. 1945 TS, RG 165, NA.

53. Spaatz to Arnold, UA64462, Feb. 18, 1945, ibid. A note on Anderson for Spaatz, Feb. 19, 1945, box 20, Spaatz Papers, identifies Anderson as the author of this memo.

54. "Air Terror Ruled Out by Stimson," *New York Herald Tribune*, Paris ed., Feb. 23, 1945, in Correspondence on News Release, Anderson Papers; Pogue, *Marshall: Organizer*, pp. 545–46.

55. Smith, "Dresden," pp. 78–81, 232–36, 251–53, 256, 263; Webster and Frankland, *Strategic Air Offensive* 3: 112–13.

56. George C. McDonald to Fred L. Anderson, Feb. 21, 1945, Anderson Diary, Anderson Papers.

57. Schlatter Daily Diary, 44/10/21–45/07/11, file 168.7052-5, AFSHRC.

58. Giles for Arnold, Mar. 7, 1945, Diaries Florida, 22 Jan.–21 Mar. 1945, box 223, Arnold Papers.

59. Interview with Cabell by Bruce C. Hopper and Charles A. Foster, July 9, 1944, p. 16, box 135, Spaatz Papers.

60. R. D. Hughes memorandum, July 5, 1944, file 519.4511-14, Feb.–Aug. 1944, AFSHRC.

61. Anderson to George E. Stratemeyer, July 21, 1943, file 312.1-E, box 194, RG 18, NA.

62. Eaker to author, Jan. 11, 1979.

Chapter 6. The Bombing of Japan: Preparing for the Fire Raids

1. Flugel, "Air Power Doctrine," p. 142; Course AIR FORCE: *Air Operations Against National Structures*, April 11, 1939, lecture, pp. 7, 13, 14, file 248.2020A-25, AFSHRC.

2. Leo P. Brophy and George J. B. Fisher, *The Chemical Warfare Service: Organizing for War* (Washington, D.C., 1959), pp. 45–46; Louis F. Fieser, *The Scientific Method: A Personal Account of Unusual Projects in War and in Peace* (New York, 1964), pp. 9, 25–32, 45; Baxter, *Scientists against Time*, p. 451; E. P. Stevenson, "Incendiary Bombs," in *Chemistry: A History of the Chemistry Components of the National Defense Research Committee, 1940–1946*, ed. W. A. Noyes, Jr. (Boston, 1948), pp. 388–91, 402–3.

3. [R. P. Russell,] "Memorandum on Incendiary Bomb Requirements," Sept. 15, 1942, with covering note by V. Bush, Director's Special Subject Correspondence file: Bombs, Incendiaries, Office of Scientific Research and Development (hereafter OSRD) files, RG 227, NA; MacIsaac, *Strategic Bombing*, pp. 55, 189.

4. Horatio Bond, "Applying Fire Experience to the Air War," in *Fire and the Air War*, ed. Horatio Bond (Reprint: Manhattan, Kansas, 1974), p. 188.

5. Bond, *Fire and the Air War*, p. viii; Bond, *Some Notes on Incendiary Attack*, Mar. 4, 1943, with Bond to Hughes, Apr. 3, 1943, and Hughes to Chem. Of., May 26, 1943, all in file 519.531-7, 1943, AFSHRC; John W. Mountcastle, "Trial by Fire: U.S. Incendiary Weapons, 1918–1945," (Ph.D. diss., Duke University, 1979), pp. 141–42, 145–46.

6. USSBS, *The Effects of Strategic Bombing on Japan's War Economy* (Washington, D.C., 1946), Appendix A, p. 78; S. Janow to Fowler Hamilton, Feb. 24, 1943, in box 2, R&A ETO General Corresp. OSS files, RG 226, NA. For Seymour Janow, see *Who's Who in America, 1972–1973*, p. 1581.

7. Guido R. Perera, *Leaves from My Life* (2 vols. Boston, 1974), 2: 59.

8. R. H. Ewell to R. P. Russell and E. P. Stevenson, Apr. 17, 1943, folder 2, FE Urban Areas, file 118.04-2, 1944, AFSHRC. For Raymond Ewell, see *Who's Who in America, 1978–1979*, p. 949.

9. Perera, *Leaves* 2: 64, 78, 96; Vannevar Bush to HQ AAF, attn: Brig. Gen. Byron E. Gates, Oct. 16, 1943, folder 2 FE Urban Areas, file 118.04-2, 1944, AFSHRC.

10. [Guido R. Perera,] "History, Organization and Operations of the Committee of Operations Analysts" (hereafter COA History) (microfilm), pp. 3–7a, file 168.7042, 1936–1960, AFSHRC; Perera, *Leaves* 2: 60, 71–3, 107; MacIsaac, *Strategic Bombing*, pp. 24–25; list of COA members in COA Memorandum for General Arnold, Nov. 11, 1943, file ABC 384.5 Japan (9 Nov. 43) sec. 1-A, NA.

11. [Perera,] COA History, p. 63; Byron Gates to Vannevar Bush, Oct. 17, 1943, folder 1, Urban Areas Current Study, file 118.04-2, 1944, AFSHRC; COA Memorandum for General Arnold, Nov. 11, 1943, cited in n. 10 above.

12. COA Memorandum for General Arnold, Nov. 11, 1943, cited in n. 10

above; COA, *Report on the Far East*, file 118.04 D (Draft), 11 Nov. 1943, AFSHRC; "Urban Industrial Areas" (n.d.), COA History, frames 787, 789.

13. Louis Morton, *Strategy and Command: The First Two Years* (Washington, D.C., 1962), p. 627; COA History, pp. 94, 98, frames 809, 812, 816–19, appended memo, Byron Gates to Assistant Chief of Air Staff, Intelligence, Feb. 17, 1944; Perera for Col. Lindsay, Aug. 29, 1944, folder 1, Urban Areas Current Study, file 118.04-2, 1944, AFSHRC.

14. Perera for Col. Lindsay, Aug. 29, 1944, cited in n. 13 above; minutes of Incendiary Subcommittee, Sept. 4, 1944, COA History, frame 690; H. S. Hansell, Jr., "Establishment of Operations Analysis Sections in Twentieth Air Force and Component Commands," July 26, 1944, XX AF Memoranda (Unnumbered), file 760.187-3, May 1944–June 1945, AFSHRC. The Twentieth Air Force reported to the U.S. Joint Chiefs of Staff and was commanded for the Joint Chiefs by General Arnold.

15. Unsigned memo to Fowler Hamilton, Feb. 16, 1943, in Seymour Janow folder, BEW, OSS, RG 226, NA; R. H. Ewell, "Recommendations regarding Incendiary Attack of Certain Cities Yawata, Tobata, Wakamatsu, Kokura, Nagasaki, Sasebo, Aug. 9, 1944," folder 11, Plans for Incendiary Attacks II, Office of C. G. Numerical, box 101, RG 18, NA; Charles Hitch to R. L. Stearns, Sept. 8, 1944, ibid. For a detailed analysis of these questions, see H. E. Landsberg, "Report on Discussions on and Demonstration of M69 Aimable Incendiary Cluster at Bayway Refinery, Standard Oil Company of New Jersey on 14 November 1944," ibid.

16. Notes on JPS 158th meeting, July 5, 1944, file ABC 384.5 Japan (9 Nov. 43) sec 1B, RG 319, NA.

17. Minutes of COA meeting, Sept. 13, 1944, p. 17, file 118.151-16, AFSHRC.

18. Minutes of COA meeting, Sept. 27, 1944, pp. 38–39, 43, file 118.151-18, ibid.

19. E. P. Stevenson, "Incendiary Bombs" in Noyes, *Chemistry*, pp. 392, 397; Chief of Air Staff to Assistant Chief of Air Staff, Operations, Commitments, & Requirements, Feb. 18, 1944, box 117, Arnold Papers; Mervin E. Gross for Chief of Air Staff, May 5, 1944, ibid.

20. L. S. Kuter and Joe L. Loutzenheiser to Commanding General, Twentieth Air Force, Apr. 24, 1944, folder 11, box 101, Office of CG Numerical, RG 18.

21. OSS R&A 2262, "Japanese Small-scale Factories in Relation to Air Bombardment," June 30, 1944, in COA History, frames 726–33; R&A 2220.1, "Concentration of Employment and Value of Production in Selected Japanese Cities by Industry," June 30, 1944, frames 734-37, ibid.

22. (Op-16-VA), "Japanese Earthquake and Fire of September 1, 1923" (n.d.), ibid., frames 655–62; (OP-16-VA) "The Economic Effect of Attacks in Force on German Urban Areas"(n.d.), folder 1, file 118.04-2, 1944, AFSHRC; minutes of COA meeting, Sept. 13, 1944, p. 18, file 118.151-6, AFSHRC. The report on Germany concluded that if German experience was any guide, incendiary raids would probably not destroy many priority targets, but might possibly be "successful" against Japan (quotation marks in the original) if destruction of nonindustrial targets and the breakdown of relief and housing indirectly reduced war production by "demoralizing" it.

23. "Economic Effects of Successful Area Attacks on Six Japanese Cities," COA History, frames 675-77, 690, 694; minutes of COA meeting, Sept. 13, 1944,

pp. 16–17, 20; minutes of COA meeting, Sept. 14, 1944, p. 25, file 118.151-17, AFSHRC; minutes of COA meeting, Sept. 27, 1944, pp. 138–39, file 118.151-18, ibid.

24. Minutes, COA meeting, Sept. 14, 1944, p. 39, file 118.151-17, AFSHRC; minutes, COA meeting, Sept. 27, 1944, p. 45, file 118.151-18, ibid.

25. Minutes, COA meeting, Sept. 27, 1944, pp. 39–40, file 118.151-18, AFSHRC.

26. Ibid., pp. 42–43.

27. Ibid., p. 44.

28. Ibid., p. 68.

29. Hamilton for Perera, Aug. 29, 1944, folder 1, Urban Areas Current Study, file 118.04-2, 1944, AFSHRC.

30. *Who's Who in America* 24: 1575; minutes, COA meeting, Sept. 27, 1944, pp. 68–75.

31. COA meeting, Sept. 27, 1944, p. 45, file 118.151-18, AFSHRC; C&C 5: 111–12.

32. R. H. Ewell, "Recommendations Regarding Incendiary Attack of Certain Kyushu Cities . . . , Aug. 9, 1944," folder 11, box 101, Office of CG Numerical, RG 18, NA.

33. Charles Hitch to Robert L. Stearns, Sept. 8, 1944, ibid.; minutes of COA meeting, Sept. 14, 1944, pp. 18–19, file 118.151-17, AFSHRC; Report of Committee of Operations Analysts, Oct. 10, 1944, p. 50, file 118.04 D-1, 10 Oct. 1944, ibid.

34. Ewell to Bush, Oct. 12, 1944, file 373.2, Reports of Operations General, RG 18, NA.

35. Bush to Arnold, Oct. 13, 1944, ibid.

36. Arnold to Norstad, Oct. 14, 1944, file 373.2, 20th AF HQ Decimal file 1944–1945, RG 18, NA; Robert L. Stearns to HQ 20th AF, attn: Col. C. E. Combs, Oct. 27, 1944, folder 11, box 101, Office of CG Numerical, ibid.; Combs for Norstad, Nov. 4, 1944, ibid.; C&C 5: 564–65.

37. James P. Hodges, to Deputy Assistant Chief of Air Staff, Intelligence for Targets, Dec. 6, 1944, file 142.6601-1, 1944, AFSHRC; "Guide to Intelligence Requirements in the War Against Japan" (Joint Target Group, Washington, D.C.), in F. L. Anderson Diary, Dec. 31, 1944, Hoover Institution; typescript, n.d., file 1 d(1) Doc(h), USSBS, RG 243, NA; Unsigned letter wtih Attride to Pincus, Oct. 19, 1944, London Joint Target Group Correspondence, OSS, RG 226, NA: Perera, *Leaves* 2: 114.

38. W. J. Crozier to Chief of Staff, Twentieth Air Force, Dec. 13, 1944, file 760.310-7, AFSHRC.

39. Norstad for Arnold, Nov. 29, 1944, file 373.2 Operations Reports, Aviation, RG 18, NA; minutes of COA meeting, Sept. 27, 1944, p. 75, file 118.151-18, AFSHRC.

40. Major Bower for Col. Posey, Jan. 16, 1945, folder 11, box 101, Office of CG Numerical, RG 18, NA; C&C 5: 611.

41. Hansell to Norstad, Dec. 2, 1944, box 1, HQ 20th AF Decimal file 1944–1945, RG 18, NA; Hansell to Arnold, Dec. 16, 1944 and Jan. 14, 1944, file 201, Hansell, Haywood S., Jr., RG 18, NA; Robert Nathans, "Making the Fires that Beat Japan," in Bond, *Fire and the Air War*, pp. 136, 138–42.

42. C&C 5: 466–67.

43. Philip G. Bower for Col. Posey, Jan. 30, 1945, folder 18, box 101, Office of CG Numerical, RG 18, NA; John A. Samford to HQ Twentieth Air Force attn: Brig. Gen. L. Norstad, Feb. 10, 1945, folder 11, ibid.; C&C 5: 569–70, 572.

44. Robert Guillain, *I Saw Tokyo Burning: An Eyewitness Narrative from Pearl Harbor to Hiroshima*, trans. William Byron (Garden City, N.Y., 1981), pp. 180–81; Gordon Daniels, "The Great Tokyo Air Raid, 9–10 March 1945" in *Modern Japan: Aspects of History, Literature and Society*, ed. W. G. Beasley (Berkeley, 1975), p. 117.

45. LeMay, *Mission*, pp. 347–48; idem, Report of Operations 10 March 1945 (LeMay to Commanding General Twentieth Air force, Apr. 15, 1945), folder Meetinghouse 2, Mission 40, Tokyo Urban Area, RG 18, NA.

46. C&C 5: 99, H. S. Hansell, Jr., to H. H. Arnold, Dec. 16, 1944, file 201, Hansell, Haywood S., Jr., RG 18, NA; St. Clair McKelway, "A Reporter with the B-29s: III. The Cigar, the Three Wings, and the Low-Level Attacks," *New Yorker* 21 (June 23, 1945): 30–31.

Chapter 7. The Bombing of Japan: From Tokyo to Nagasaki

1. McKelway, "Reporter," pp. 36–37, 39; Bruce Rae, "300 B-29's Fire 15 Square Miles of Tokyo," *New York Times*, Mar. 10, 1945, pp. 1, 6; LeMay, Report of Operations 10 March 1945, folder Meetinghouse 2, Mission 40, Tokyo Urban Area file, RG 18, NA; Target Information Sheet, Mission 40, Tokyo, Meetinghouse 2 (10 Mar. 45), RG 165, NA; C&C 5: 8; LeMay, *Mission*, p. 348.

2. McKelway, "Reporter," pp. 30–31.

3. United States Strategic Bombing Survey, *Field Report Covering Air Raid Protection and Allied Subjects, Tokyo* (n.p., March 1947) (hereafter cited as *ARP Tokyo*), pp. 12, 22, 25, 29, 33.

4. Guillain, *Tokyo Burning*, pp. 174–75; Thomas R. H. Havens, *Valley of Darkness: The Japanese People and World War Two* (New York, 1978), pp. 156–57, 159–60; Masuo Kato, *The Lost War: A Japanese Reporter's Inside Story* (New York, 1946), p. 202.

5. Guillain, *Tokyo Burning*, p. 173; Target Information Sheet, Mission 40; Daniels, "Tokyo Air Raid," p. 124.

6. Lars Tillitse, "When Bombs Rained on Us in Tokyo," *Saturday Evening Post* 218 (Jan. 12, 1946): 34, 82; *ARP Tokyo*, pp. 138–40; Guillain, *Tokyo Burning*, pp. 118, 174–75.

7. Havens, *Valley*, pp. 161–63; Daniels, "Tokyo Air Raid," p. 123.

8. Daniels, "Tokyo Air Raid," p. 124; *ARP Tokyo*, pp. 14, 16; LeMay, Report of Operations 10 March 1945.

9. Target Information Sheet, Mission 40.

10. LeMay, Report of Operations 10 March 1945; James K. McElroy, "Incendiary Warfare on Germany" in *Fire and the Air War*, ed. Bond, p. 75.

11. LeMay, Report of Operations 10 March 1945; HQ 20th AF, "Special Report on the Incendiary Attacks against Japanese Urban Industrial Areas," Dec. 13, 1945, file 760.551, 1944–45, AFSHRC (hereafter "Special Report," Dec. 13, 1945); Guillain, *Tokyo Burning*, p. 184.

12. Thomas S. Power, *Design for Survival* (New York, 1964), p. 28.

13. Daniels, "Tokyo Air Raid," pp. 125–26; LeMay, Report of Operations 10 March 1945; idem, *Mission*, p. 352; Rae, "300 B-29's Fire 15 Square Miles," p. 6;

Robert Nathans, "Making the Fires that Beat Japan" in Bond, *Fire and the Air War*, pp. 145–46.

14. Warren Moscow, "Center of Tokyo Devastated by Fire Bombs," *New York Times*, Mar. 11, 1945, p. 13; LeMay, *Mission*, p. 353.

15. Moscow, "Center of Tokyo," p. 1; LeMay, Report of Operations 10 March 1945; *ARP Tokyo*, p. 3.

16. Tillitse, "Bombs Rained," p. 82; USSBS, *The Effects of Strategic Bombing On Japanese Morale* (n.p., 1947) (hereafter cited as USSBS, *Japanese Morale*), p. 35; Guillain, *Tokyo Burning*, p. 183.

17. Guillain, *Tokyo Burning*, pp. 181–82; "Special Report," Dec. 13, 1945; Harold H. Martin, "Black Snow and Leaping Tigers," *Harper's Magazine* 192 (Feb. 1946): 151–53. For other examples of Japanese admiration of the beauty and technological perfection of the Superfortress, see Masataka Kosaka, *100 Million Japanese: The Postwar Experience* (Palo Alto, Ca., 1972), p. 27; USSBS, *Japanese Morale*, p. 33n.; and Kato, *Lost War*, p. 207. Mrs. Mamoru Iga, who witnessed the burning of Kobe, recalled the esthetic beauty of that spectacle: conversation with author, July 18, 1983.

18. Guillain, *Tokyo Burning*, p. 181; Daniels, "Tokyo Air Raid," p. 125; Forrest J. Sanborn, "Fire Protection Lessons of the Japanese Attacks" in Bond, *Fire and the Air War*, p. 181.

19. LeMay, Report of Operations 10 March 1945; *ARP Tokyo*, p. 33; Orville J. Emory, "Japanese Fire Departments under Air Attack" in Bond, *Fire and the Air War*, p. 167.

20. *ARP Tokyo*, p. 63; Daniels, "Tokyo Air Raid," pp. 125–26.

21. Daniels, "Tokyo Air Raid," pp. 125–26; Guillain, *Tokyo Burning*, pp. 184–86; Kato, *Lost War*, pp. 210–14; Emory, "Japanese Fire Departments," pp. 165, 167.

22. Havens, *Valley*, p. 179.

23. Guillain, *Tokyo Burning*, p. 187; USSBS, *Japanese Morale*, p. 37; USSBS, *The Effects of Bombing on Health and Medical Services in Japan* (n.p., 1947), pp. 149–51; Kato, *Lost War*, p. 214; "Special Report," Dec. 13, 1945.

24. "Special Report," Dec. 13, 1945; USSBS, *Health and Medical Services*, pp. 149–54; Guillain, *Tokyo Burning*, pp. 185–87; Kato, *Lost War*, p. 214.

25. Daniels, "Tokyo Air Raid," pp. 127–28; Havens, *Valley*, p. 181; Kato, *Lost War*, p. 215; *ARP Tokyo*, p. 83.

26. *ARP Tokyo*, p. 75; Havens, *Valley*, p. 168; Kato, *Lost War*, p. 215; Tillitse, "Bombs Rained," p. 85; "Special Report," Dec. 13, 1945; Daniels, "Tokyo Air Raid," p. 128.

27. *ARP Tokyo*, pp. 154, 158; Havens, *Valley*, p. 168; Tillitse, "Bombs Rained," p. 85.

28. Interview with Dr. Kazuo Kawai, Nov. 19, 1945, file 14 G-(36) 1 (a) documents 1 through 7. Special Interviews by Locality, Tokyo, USSBS, RG 243, NA; *ARP Tokyo*, pp. 160–61; Daniels, "Tokyo Air Raid," p. 127.

29. USSBS, *Japanese Morale*, pp. 18, 23–25, 32.

30. C&C 5: 636–643; Kato, *Lost War*, p. 17.

31. Joint Target Group, "General Analysis," Annex II, "Urban Area Attacks against Selected Industrial Concentrations," Apr. 28, 1945, file 142.6606-13, 15 Jan. 1945, AFSHRC.

32. LeMay, *Mission*, p. 373.

33. Norstad to LeMay, Apr. 3, 1945, box 133, LeMay Papers.

34. Combs for Norstad, Apr. 10, 1945, folder 11, box 101, RG 18, NA.

35. Ray S. Cline, *Washington Command Post: The Operations Division* (Washington, D.C., 1951), p. 339; minutes, meeting of JCS at the White House, June 18, 1945, CCS 334 Joint Chiefs of Staff (2-2-45); USSBS, Report, July 5, 1945, USSBS and JTG Conferences, file 319.1, RG 243, NA; USSBS, *Japanese Morale*, p. 4.

36. MacIsaac, *Strategic Bombing*, p. 99; memo, Robert A. Lovett for the Secretary of War, July 31, 1945, with accompanying "Report on USSBS and JTG Conferences," file Aircraft, Air Corps General, RG 107, NA; USSBS draft, n.d., and letter, Eaker to Arnold, n.d., file 383.8, Industrial Sites–Targets–Japanese, RG 243, NA.

37. Transcript of meeting of JTG–USSBS, entry 1, file .001, RG 243; Report accompanying Lovett for the Secretary of War, July 31, 1945, cited in note 36 above.

38. Minutes, first meeting, Target Committee, April 27, 1945, folder 5D2, box 3, Manhattan Project Top Secret files, 1942–1946, RG 77, NA.

39. Akira Iriye, *Power and Culture: The Japanese-American War, 1941–1945* (Cambridge, Mass., 1981), pp. 210–11; Commanding General 20th Air Force to Commanding General USASTAF, July 16, 1945, folder 12, box 101, RG 18, NA.

40. USSBS, *Japanese Morale*, pp. 33, 132–33; USSBS, *The Effects of Strategic Bombing on Japan's War Economy* (n.p., 1946), p. 38.

41. Quoted in Kato, *Lost War*, pp. 154–55.

42. Carter and Mueller, *Combat Chronology*, p. 670; Cunningham article in Fifth Air Force Advon, *Weekly Intelligence Review* 86 (July 15 to July 21, 1945), file 730.602-86, 15–21 July 1945, AFSHRC. For instances of unrestrained fighter attacks, including occasional strafing of civilians, see C&C 5: 696.

43. Walter S. Schoenberger, *Decision of Destiny* (Athens, Ohio, 1969), pp. 142–43; C&C 5: 705–6; Leslie R. Groves, *Now It Can Be Told: The Story of the Manhattan Project* (New York, 1962), pp. 267–68.

44. Memo for General L. R. Groves from Major J. A. Derry and Dr. N. F. Ramsey, May 12, 1945, folder 5D2, box 3, Manhattan Project Top Secret files, 1942–1946, RG 77, NA.

45. Martin J. Sherwin, *A World Destroyed: The Atomic Bomb and the Grand Alliance* (New York, 1977), pp. 207–8, 302.

46. Memo for Groves from Derry and Ramsey, May 12, 1945, cited in note 44; Arnold, *Global Mission*, p. 492.

47. "Kyoto," *Encyclopaedia Britannica* (Chicago, 1948) 3: 531; Office of the Assistant Chief of Staff, Intelligence, Kyoto 90.23 in "Air Objective Folder Japan," Sept. 22, 1944, file 1 d(18), USSBS, RG 245, NA; USSBS, *The Effects of Air Attack on Osaka-Kobe-Kyoto* (n.p., 1947), pp. 243, 246, 255, 262. Kyoto was hit by a few random bombings.

48. Minutes, first meeting, Target Committee, April 27, 1945, folder 5D2, box 3, Manhattan Project Top Secret files, 1942–1946, RG 77, NA; Combs to Norstad, Apr. 10, 1945, folder 11, box 101, RG 18, NA; USSBS, *Japanese Morale*, p. 36.

49. Target Description, Kyoto, July 2, 1945, folder 5D1, box 3, Manhattan Project Top Secret files, 1942–1946, RG 77, NA; Otis Cary, "The Sparing of Kyoto, Mr. Stimson's 'Pet City,'" *Japan Quarterly* 22 (Oct.–Dec. 1975): 337.

50. Groves, *Now*, pp. 273–76; memo for Groves from Derry and Ramsey, May 12, 1945, cited in note 44. The chief editorial writer for the *Nippon Times*

agreed that whom one bombed was very important. Dr. Kazuo Kawai told a USSBS interviewer in November 1945 that the March 10 Tokyo raid had not produced panic because "the people were not influential. If the raid had come in a 'better' section, the victims would have been able to spread more concern." Interview with Dr. Kazai, cited in n. 28 above.

51. Cary, "Kyoto," pp. 340, 342; Stimson Diary, June 1, 1945.

52. Arnold, *Global Mission*, pp. 492, 588–89; Cary, "Kyoto," p. 340; Groves, *Now*, p. 275; Schoenberger, *Decision*, p. 258; Stimson Diary, July 21, 1945.

53. Stimson Diary, July 24, 1945.

54. Gregg Herken, *The Winning Weapon: The Atomic Bomb in the Cold War, 1945–1950* (New York, 1981), p. 345; Alice Kimball Smith, *A Peril and a Hope: The Scientists' Movement in America, 1945–47* (Chicago, 1965), pp. 46, 560–72; Fletcher Knebel and Charles W. Bailey, "The Fight Over the A-Bomb," *Look* 27 (Aug. 13, 1963): 20–23; John J. McCloy, *The Challenge to American Foreign Policy* (Cambridge, Mass., 1953), pp. 40–42.

55. Robert J. C. Butow, *Japan's Decision to Surrender* (Stanford, 1954), pp. 243–44; Barton J. Bernstein, *Hiroshima and Nagasaki Reconsidered: The Atomic Bombings of Japan and the Origins of the Cold War* (Morristown, N.J., 1975), p. 17.

56. Iriye, *Power*, pp. 248, 263–64.

57. Spaatz took command of the newly organized United States Army Strategic Air Forces in the Pacific on July 18, 1945: Carter and Mueller, *Combat Chronology*, p. 677.

58. Interview with Spaatz by Noel F. Parrish and Alfred Goldberg, Feb. 21, 1962, AFSHRC. See also Coffey, *Hap*, p. 370, and Schoenberger, *Decision*, pp. 260–61. The directive, from Handy to Spaatz, is in July 1945 folder, box 21, Spaatz Papers.

59. USSBS, *Japanese Morale*, pp. 1–2, 194–95. The lower casualty figures are based largely on Japanese official reports known to contain large errors. The higher figures derive from a survey conducted by USSBS Morale Division Survey, which estimated a maximum sampling error for injuries and an unknown sampling error for deaths. For estimated effects of air operations on the Japanese economy, see USSBS, *Effects on Japan's War Economy*.

Chapter 8. The Bombing of Japan:
American Perceptions of the Moral Issues

1. Eaker interview with Goldberg and Hildreth, May 22, 1962, AFSHRC; LeMay's remarks are in *Air Power and Warfare*, ed. Alfred F. Hurley and Robert C. Ehrhart (Washington, D.C., 1979), pp. 200–201; Spaatz interview with Parrish and Goldberg, Feb. 21, 1962, AFSHRC; Spaatz interview by Goldberg, May 19, 1965, ibid.

2. Arnold for the Chief of Staff, May 28, 1945, with attached "Potentialities of New Developments in Warfare," file SAS400.12, box 117, Arnold Papers. The initials "LN" on this memo indicate that General Norstad helped prepare or supervised the preparation of this statement.

3. Wolfe interview by Robert Piper, June 1966, AFSHRC.

4. Spaatz interview, Feb. 21, 1962, ibid.

5. Spaatz interview, May 19, 1965, ibid.; Eaker interview, May 22, 1962, ibid.; Eaker to author, Jan. 11, 1969. Though morale had been an important objective of LeMay's incendiary bombing attacks, AAF leaders after the war did not attempt to justify the fire raids as a way of striking at Japanese military power by destroying civilian morale. Stimson, on the other hand, defended the use of the A-bomb as a morale weapon, as a way to influence the emperor and the Japanese people: Stimson, "Decision to Use the Atomic Bomb," pp. 101, 105, 106.

6. LeMay, Report of Operations 10 March 1945; idem, *Mission*, pp. 349, 384, 425. (Emphasis in original.)

7. LeMay, *Mission*, pp. 380, 384, 387–8.

8. Ibid., p. 388; Spaatz interview, May 19, 1965, AFSHRC.

9. McKelway, "A Reporter with the B-29s," p. 36; Haywood S. Hansell, Jr., *Air War against Japan* (Maxwell AFB, Ala., 1980), p. 92; LeMay, *Mission*, p. 381.

10. Taylor, "They Taught Tactics," p. 68; JSC 504 series, RG 218, NA; Stanley L. Falk, *Bataan: The March of Death* (New York, 1962).

11. Hansell interview by author, Oct. 1, 1980; LeMay *Mission*, p. 12; Spaatz interview, May 19, 1965; Eaker interview, May 22, 1962.

12. Falk, *Bataan*, p. 206; Arnold for the Chief of Staff, July 4, 1944, box 115, Arnold Papers; Arnold for the Chief of Staff, May 28, 1945, box 117, ibid. For Japanese bacteriological warfare experiments see John W. Powell, "Japan's Germ Warfare: The U.S. Cover-up of a War Crime," *Bulletin of Concerned Asian Scholars* 12 (Oct.–Dec. 1980): 2–15; and Michael Parks, "Germ Tests: Manchurian Mask Lifted," *Los Angeles Times*, Dec. 9, 1982.

13. Entry for June 16, 1945, Arnold Journals, 1945, June 6–24 folder, box 272, Arnold Papers.

14. Leslie R. Groves, *Now It Can Be Told: The Story of the Manhattan Project* (New York, 1962), p. 324.

15. Spaatz interview, May 19, 1965, AFSHRC; Eaker interview, May 22, 1962, ibid.; *Public Opinion Quarterly* 9 (Spring 1945): 94. Forty percent of the respondents to this poll would have treated the Japanese people, but not their leaders, leniently. Only 8 percent favored extremely harsh treatment for the German people. Nevertheless, Spaatz told air force interviewers that "we" would have dropped the A-bomb on Germany if it had been necessary to win the war: interview with Goldberg and Hildreth, Feb. 21, 1962, AFSHRC. In his May 1962 interview Eaker said the Allies would undoubtedly have dropped the bomb on the Germans if it had been available in 1942.

16. *Time* 43 (May 28, 1944): 68. For the origins of anti-Japanese sentiment in the United States, particularly on the West Coast, see Jacobus tenBroek, Edward N. Barnhart, and Floyd W. Matson, *Prejudice, War and the Constitution* (Berkeley and Los Angeles, 1954), pp. 11–96. There is also the question of whether air force leaders themselves were prejudiced against the Japanese as Asians, rather than vengeful toward the people of the nation that attacked the United States. The records examined for this study contain evidence of strong racial feelings in some of the AAF leaders, but no certain indication of hostility to Asians per se. For indications of attitudes of AAF leaders toward blacks, see, for example, Arnold Journal, April 18, 1945, box 272, Arnold Papers, and Noel F. Parrish interview, 1974, U.S. Air Force Academy Oral History Program, copy in AFSHRC.

17. Eaker interview, May 22, 1962; Wilson quotation from John Else et al., eds., *The Day after Trinity: J. Robert Oppenheimer and the Atomic Bomb*, transcript of PBS Broadcast, April 29, 1981 (Kent, Ohio, 1981), p. 10.

18. Else, *Day after Trinity*, pp. 14, 22.

19. Ibid., pp. 13–14; Bethe quoted in United States Atomic Energy Commission, *In the Matter of J. Robert Oppenheimer* . . . (Cambridge, Mass., 1971), p. 326.

20. J. Neyman to V. B. Rojansky, Jan. 15, 1945, box 195, NDRC division 11 records, NA; Neyman obituary, *Los Angeles Times*, Aug. 10, 1981, p. 16; Dyson quoted in Else, *Day after Trinity*, p. 30.

21. Louis F. Fieser, *The Scientific Method: A Personal Account of Unusual Projects in War and Peace* (New York, 1964), p. 14; *In the Matter of J. Robert Oppenheimer*, pp. 235–36. Fieser refers to "the crime of war" in *Scientific Method*, p. 153.

22. Zanetti, *Fire from the Air: The ABC of Incendiaries* (New York, 1941), pp. 48–49.

23. "Science Panel Recommendations on the Immediate Use of Nuclear Weapons," quoted in Sherwin, *World Destroyed*, pp. 304–5.

24. Arthur H. Compton, *Atomic Quest: A Personal Narrative* (New York, 1956), p. 242. Ewell to Bush, Oct. 12, 1944, file 373.2, Report of Operations, General, RG 18, NA.

25. Compton, *Atomic Quest*, p. 241; Vannevar Bush, *Pieces of the Action* (New York, 1970), p. 62.

26. Sherwin, *World Destroyed*, pp. 217–18.

27. Smith, *Peril*, pp. 46–47.

28. Knebel and Bailey, "Fight over the A-Bomb," p. 23; Bush, *Pieces*, pp. 623.

29. Smith, *Peril*, pp. 53–55, 560–72.

30. Compton, *Atomic Quest*, p. 236; Compton quoted in Knebel and Bailey, "Fight over the A-Bomb," p. 21.

31. Compton quoted in Knebel and Bailey, "Fight over the A-Bomb," pp. 20–21; Richard G. Hewlett and Oscar E. Anderson, Jr., *The New World, 1939–1946* (University Park, Pa., 1962), p. 355; Else, *Day after Trinity*, pp. 14, 22. Hewlett and Anderson interpret this letter to mean that Brewster thought existing nuclear materials should be used against Japan.

Nuclear scientists and high-level participants in the Manhattan Project knew that the bomb would produce dangerous radiation when it detonated as well as radioactive fallout that could affect people in the neighborhood of the target area. During a series of meetings in May 1945, the target committee, with J. Robert Oppenheimer present, proposed detonation heights ranging from 580 to 1,550 feet above the ground. During those meetings Oppenheimer informed the committee and General Groves of both the direct and indirect radioactive effects of the bomb and recommended that, solely for radiological reasons, no aircraft should come closer than two and a half miles to the point of detonation. Oppenheimer stated that radiation might reach the ground under any circumstances and would certainly reach it if there were rain, and he stated that it would be necessary to monitor radioactivity if the target area were "to be entered within some weeks of the primary detonation."

As far as I have been able to learn, until the bombs were detonated neither the opponents nor the proponents of dropping the bomb on Japanese cities appear to have devoted specific attention to the moral issue of exposing people in Japan to radiation. The scientists and military men and their civilian leaders may have felt that people exposed to direct radiation would be killed anyway by heat, blast, and flying objects. But that does not explain their lack of comment on the possible irradiation of Japanese outside the target area by fallout. As late as August 25 Groves and a Manhattan Project officer at Oak Ridge Hospital considered Japanese reports of radiation sickness to be propaganda. See Oppenheimer memorandum for Gen. Farrell, May 11, 1945, memoranda of telephone conversations of Aug. 25, 1944 between Groves and Lt. Col. Rea, folder 5G, and Memorandum for General Groves from Major J. A. Derry and Dr. N. F. Ramsey, May 12, 1945, folder 5D2, all in Manhattan Project Top Secret Files, 1942–1946, RG 77, NA.

32. W. A. Noyes, Jr., *Chemistry* (Boston, 1948), p. 479. For Noyes, see *American Men of Science* (10th ed.) 3: 3003.

33. McElroy, "The Work of the Fire Protection Engineers in Planning Fire Attacks" in Bond, *Fire and the Air War*, p. 135. (Italics in original.)

34. Minutes of COA meeting, Sept. 14, 1944, pp. 40ff., file 118.151–17, AFSHRC; minutes of COA meeting, Sept. 27, 1944, p. 72, file 118.151–18, AFSHRC.

35. Minutes of COA meeting, Sept. 27, 1944, cited in note 34, pp. 44, 73–75.

36. Perera, *Leaves*, 2: 110, 114, 190, 193; Perera to author, Jan. 4, 1979. A document in Perera's history of the Committee of Operations Analysts suggests that he favored urban fire raids. Perera and W. Barton Leach of the COA recommended on May 9, 1944, that the AAF attack urban industrial areas in March 1945, when wind and weather conditions would be most favorable for an incendiary raid (Perera and Leach for H. S. Hansell, Jr., frames 559–60 in appendix, COA History). Perhaps they were speaking for a COA consensus with which Perera disagreed.

37. Perera to author, Jan. 4, 1979. Perera thought the fire expert was Horatio Bond.

38. Ibid.; Perera, *Leaves* 2: 170.

39. Leahy, *I Was There: The Personal Story of the Chief of Staff to Presidents Roosevelt and Truman Based on His Notes and Diaries Made at the Time* (New York, 1950), p. 441.

40. "Biological Warfare," memorandum by the Chief of Staff, United States Army, enclosure A with JCS 625/7 [Jan. 13, 1944], file CCS385.2 (12-17-43), sec. 3, RG 218, NA; "Summary Status of Biological Warfare," Nov. 24, 1944, box 2, Secretary of War Safe file, RG 107, NA; L. S. Kuter for the Chief of Air Staff, Feb. 5, 1944, file 145.81–151, V2 reference folder, Feb. 1944, AFSHRC; AC/AS, A-2 Target Information Branch, Report of 11 Feb. 1944, file 122.43, Aug 1943–May 1944, ibid.

41. Leahy, *I Was There*, p. 440.

42. Smith, *Peril*, pp. 52–53; Sherwin, *World Destroyed*, pp. 307–8. It is not clear what Bard meant by the passage about "making representations" about Russia's position. He may have wished to threaten the Japanese government with the prospect of Soviet entry into the war, although it is also possible that he wanted to point out the shared interest the United States and Japan had in limiting Soviet expansion.

43. *The Forrestal Diaries*, ed. Walter Millis with E. S. Duffield (New York, 1951), p. 62.

44. Alice K. Smith, "Behind the Decision to Use the Atomic Bomb: Chicago 1944–45," *Bulletin of the Atomic Scientists* 14 (Sept. 1958): 297; Ernest J. King and Walter Muir Whitehill, *Fleet Admiral King: A Naval Record* (London, 1953), pp. 396n, 412; Diaries of William D. Leahy, microfilm reel 3, July 10, 1944, LC; minutes of JCS meeting, June 18, 1945, CCS 334 Joint Chiefs of Staff (2-3-45), RG 218, NA.

45. Minutes of JCS meeting, June 18, 1945, cited in note 44; Knebel and

Bailey, "Fight over the A-Bomb," p. 20; John P. Sunderland, "The Story Gen. Marshall told Me," *U.S. News & World Report* 47 (Nov. 2, 1959): 52; David E. Lilienthal, *The Atomic Energy Years, 1948–1950* (New York, 1964), pp. 198–99. In 1980 General Hansell wrote that one of the reasons for dropping the atomic bomb was to persuade the U.S. Army that an invasion was unnecessary, thus saving "great numbers of American lives that would be needlessly lost on the beaches and battlefields of the Japanese home islands." Nothing less than atomic bombs, Hansell declared, "would divert the single-minded determination of the U.S. Army" (Hansell, *Air War against Japan*, p. 92).

46. Sherwin, *World Destroyed*, p. 137; Arnold, *Global Mission*, p. 589.

47. Stimson, "The Decision to Use the Atomic Bomb," *Harper's Magazine* 194 (Feb. 1947): 99.

48. HLS[timson] to Dear Mr. President, Stimson Diary, May 16, 1945, June 6, 1945.

49. Memorandum of July 2, 1945, quoted in Stimson, "Decision," p. 103.

50. Ibid., pp. 106–7.

51. Ibid., pp. 103–4; Stimson Diary, July 24, 1945.

52. Herbert Feis, *Japan Subdued: The Atomic Bomb and the End of the War in the Pacific* (Princeton, 1961), pp. 176, 176n; Stimson Diary, June 19, 26, July 2, 1945. See Montgomery C. Meigs, "Managing Uncertainty: Vannevar Bush, James B. Conant and the Development of the Atomic Bomb, 1940–1945," (Ph.D. diss., University of Wisconsin, 1982), especially p. 255, for the reasons why the arguments for using the bomb in a long-term program to preserve peace probably seemed substantially less persuasive than the argument for dropping it on the Japanese to shorten the war. The comparison between killing Japanese with conventional bombs and with nuclear bombs comes as part of an interview with Harvey Bundy that Forrest C. Pogue quoted in a letter to the author, Dec. 13, 1983.

53. Dwight D. Eisenhower, *Crusade in Europe* (Garden City, N.Y., 1961), p. 470; Feis, *Japan Subdued*, p. 178n.

54. Stimson, "Decision," pp. 106–7.

55. Sherwin, *World Destroyed*, p. 198.

56. Stephen Early letter, *Fellowship* 10 (April 1944): 79.

57. Sherwin, *World Destroyed*, pp. 123, 131, 284. (Emphasis added).

58. Barton J. Bernstein, *Hiroshima and Nagasaki Reconsidered: The Atomic Bombings of Japan and the Origins of the Cold War, 1941–1945* (Morristown, N.J., 1975), pp. 4–5; Henry L. Stimson and McGeorge Bundy, *On Active Service in Peace and War* (New York, 1948), p. 613; Tully quoted in Schoenberger, *Decision of Destiny*, p. 45.

59. Truman to Samuel McCrea Cavert, Aug. 11, 1945, quoted in Bernstein, *Hiroshima and Nagasaki*, p. 3.

60. *Memoirs by Harry S. Truman: Year of Decisions* (New York, 1965), p. 462; Margaret Truman, *Harry S. Truman* (New York, 1974), p. 6.

61. Admiral Leahy to JCS, June 14, 1945, quoted in U.S. Department of Defense, *The Entry of the Soviet Union into the War against Japan: Military Plans, 1941–1945* (Washington, D.C., 1955), p. 76; John J. McCloy, *The Challenge to American Foreign Policy* (Cambridge, Mass., 1953), p. 42; minutes, JCS meeting, June 18, 1945, CCS 334 Joint Chiefs of Staff (2-3-45), RG 218, NA.

62. Minutes, JCS meeting, June 18, 1945, cited in note 61; Truman's speech of June 1, 1945, quoted in Schoenberger, *Decision of Destiny*, p. 202.

63. Schoenberger, *Decision of Destiny*, pp. 143–45; Robert Jungk, *Brighter than a Thousand Suns* (New York, 1958), p. 208.

64. *Off the Record: The Private Papers of Harry S. Truman*, ed. Robert H. Ferrell (New York, 1980), pp. 52–53.

65. Ibid., pp. 53–54, 55–56; Bernstein, *Hiroshima and Nagasaki*, p. 12.

66. *Off the Record*, pp. 55–56.

67. Quoted in Bernstein, *Hiroshima and Nagasaki*, p. 20.

68. Henry A. Wallace, *The Price of Vision: The Diary of Henry A. Wallace*, ed. John M. Blum (Boston, 1973), p. 474.

69. Groves, *Now*, p. 264.

Chapter 9. Reactions to the Moral Issue: Accounting for the Variations

1. Smith, *Peril*, pp. 3, 59–62; Groves, *Now*, p. 140; Hans Bethe, "Oppenheimer: 'Where He Was There Was Always Life and Excitement,'" *Science* 155 (Mar. 3, 1967): 1082.

2. Schoenberger, *Decision*, pp. 134–35, 142–43; Smith, *Peril*, pp. 48–49, 59.

3. *In the Matter of J. Robert Oppenheimer*, p. 34. Smith, *Peril*, notes (p. 63) that Oppenheimer was impressed by Stimson's deep understanding of the bomb's international implications.

4. "Air Terror Ruled Out by Stimson," *New York Herald Tribune*, Paris ed., Feb. 23, 1945; Barney Giles for Arnold, Mar. 7, 1945, box 223, Arnold Papers.

5. Stimson Diary, May 16, June 1, 1945; Statement by Col. Fisher of Arnold's office at meeting of AAF A-bomb target selection committee, Apr. 27, 1945, Manhattan Project Top Secret files, 1942–1946, folder 5D2, RG 77, NA.

6. Extracts of Griggs to E. L. Bowles, Oct. 17, 1944, with Bowles to Stimson, Nov. 21, 1944, Bowles file, box 2, formerly TS file, RG 107, NA; Morison, *Turmoil*, pp. 496, 535.

7. Carol S. Gruber, "Manhattan Project Maverick: The Case of Leo Szilard," *Prologue* 15 (Summer 1983): 73–74, 79; Smith, *Peril*, pp. 53–55; Else, *Day after Trinity*, p. 10.

8. Else, *Day after Trinity*, p. 14.

9. Compton, *Atomic Quest*, p. 238; Morison, *Turmoil*, pp. 520–21; Groves, *Now*, p. 265; Pogue to author, Dec. 13, 1983.

10. For a psychoanalyst's view of defense mechanisms, see Anna Freud, *The Ego and the Mechanisms of Defense* (New York, 1962). Samuel A. Stouffer et al., *The American Soldier*, vol. 2., *Combat and Its Aftermath* (Princeton, 1949), observes (p. 77) that a source of stress in battle is the "conflict of values . . . between previously accepted moral codes and combat imperatives," and that combat requires a sharp break with many moral precepts of peacetime society (pp. 85–86). Despite greater physical remoteness from the scene of killing, war leaders, including the people discussed here, had to cope with similar contradictions. In *Mission with LeMay* the head of the XXI Bomber Command shows a perceptive appreciation of the value of defense mechanisms to people who went on bombing missions. For the effects of distance, see James C. Thompson, Jr., "How Could Vietnam Happen? An Autopsy," *The Atlantic* 221 (April 1968): 51, and the account of Stanley Milgram's experiments in Lawrence S. Wrightsman and Kay Deaux, *Social Psychology in the 80's* (Monterey, California, 1981), pp. 389–92. General Power's statement (p. 131)

about his feelings during the March 9–10 Tokyo raid illustrates how hard it is for a military man to eliminate all emotional reaction to war.

11. For an analysis of this kind of cognitive inertia, see Irving L. Janis and Leon Mann, *Decision Making: A Psychological Analysis of Conflict, Choice, and Commitment* (New York, 1977), p. 283. David MacIsaac notes in *Strategic Bombing*, p. 107, that less than 22 percent of bomb tonnage dropped on Japan was aimed at specific industrial precision targets.

12. Transcript of USSBS-JTG meeting, p. 26, file .001, entry 1, Office of the Chairman, USSBS, RG 243, NA. For an analysis of why it helps civilian strategists to avoid moral questions when they work with military people, see Bernard Brodie, *War and Politics* (New York, 1973), p. 46.

13. Norstad to LeMay, Apr. 3, 1945, box 331, LeMay Papers; Cecil Combs for Norstad, Apr. 10, 1945, folder "Plans for Incendiary Attack II," box 101, RG 18, NA.

14. Memo by Hughes, July 5, 1944, file 519.4511-14, AFSHRC; B. W. Chidlaw to AFCAS, attn: General Hanley, file SAS 400.112, box 117, Arnold Papers; Rabinowitch quoted in Smith, *Peril*, p. 53.

15. Stimson Diary, June 6, 1945.

16. Lord Halifax to Prime Minister Churchill, quoted in Winston Churchill, *Triumph and Tragedy* (Boston, 1953), p. 481.

17. Department of Defense, *Entry of the Soviet Union*, p. 76; Minutes, meeting of Joint Chiefs of Staff, June 18, 1945, CCS 334 Joint Chiefs of Staff (2-2-45), RG 218, NA.

18. Irving L. Janis, *Victims of Groupthink: A Psychological Study of Foreign Policy Decisions and Fiascoes* (Boston, 1972), pp. 9, 13, 205. Subsequent research suggests that groupthink is even more common than Janis believed, and occurs in groups with low cohesion as well as in highly cohesive bodies: Wrightsman and Deaux, *Social Psychology*, p. 464. See also Phil Williams, *Crisis Management: Confrontation and Diplomacy in the Nuclear Age* (New York, 1976), ch. 5, for an analysis of other factors affecting the rationality of decision making.

19. Janis, *Victims*, pp. 5–7, 38–39, 41–43, 99.

20. Ibid., pp. 13, 147–53.

21. Ibid., p. 206.

22. Ibid., pp. 12, 38.

23. Ibid., pp. 116–17, 153–55; Robert F. Kennedy, *Thirteen Days: A Memoir of the Cuban Missile Crisis* (New York, 1969), pp. 38–39.

24. Perera to author, Jan. 4, 1979. The psychologist Alan Elms suggests another reason why the COA formed a highly cohesive group. Its members were generally very competent individuals with high status from the New York and Boston legal and banking communities, from Harvard, and from the Institute for Advanced Studies as well as from the armed forces. Elms notes in *Social Psychology and Social Relevance* (Boston, 1972), p. 141, that "a group whose members are seen as more attractive, more competent with regard to the issue at hand, or higher in status generally, is more likely to induce conformity."

25. Elms, *Social Psychology*, pp. 141–42.

26. Charles Hitch and Guido Perera were asked many years later about discussions that might have taken place between COA members off the record. They could not remember any, though that, of course, does not mean none occurred. Hitch to author, July 15, 1980; Perera to author, Jan. 4, 1979.

Chapter 10. Epilogue

1. E[ugene] R[abinowitch], "Five Years After," *Bulletin of the Atomic Scientists* 7 (Jan. 1951): 3; LeMay quoted in David Alan Rosenberg, "American Atomic Strategy and the Hydrogen Bomb Decision," *Journal of American History* 66 (June 1979): 67.

2. Kenneth W. Condit, *The History of the Joint Chiefs of Staff*, vol. 2, *The Joint Chiefs of Staff and National Policy* (Wilmington, Del., 1979), pp. 18, 22; Harry Borowski, *A Hollow Threat: Strategic Air Power and Containment before Korea* (Westport, Conn., 1982), pp. 94–96.

3. David Alan Rosenberg, "The Origins of Overkill: Nuclear Weapons and American Strategy, 1945–1960," *International Security* 7 (Spring 1982): 14–15; Borowski, *Threat*, pp. 104–5.

4. Rosenberg, "Overkill," p. 16; idem, "Hydrogen Bomb Decision," p. 72.

5. Rosenberg, "Overkill," pp. 15–16, 18; Borowski, *Threat*, p. 102; John T. Greenwood, "The Emergence of the Postwar Strategic Air Force, 1945–1953," in Hurley and Ehrhart, *Air Power and Warfare*, p. 223.

6. Rosenberg, "Hydrogen Bomb Decision," pp. 68–69; Condit, *Joint Chiefs* 2: 139; Lilienthal, *Atomic Energy Years*, p. 391.

7. Rosenberg, "Hydrogen Bomb Decision," p. 76; idem, "Overkill," pp. 17, 21–24; *Forrestal Diaries*, p. 487; Philip M. Stern, *The Oppenheimer Case: Security on Trial* (New York, 1969), p. 166.

8. David Alan Rosenberg, "American Postwar Air Doctrine and Organization: The Navy Experience," in Hurley and Ehrhart, *Air Power and Warfare*, pp. 253–54; Greenwood, "Emergence," p. 226. Gallery's memorandum was leaked through Drew Pearson in March 1948.

9. MacIsaac, *Strategic Bombing*, pp. 112, 206; Rosenberg, "Postwar Air Doctrine," p. 254.

10. Rosenberg, "Postwar Air Doctrine," pp. 255, 260.

11. Rosenberg, "Hydrogen Bomb Decision," p. 70; idem, "Postwar Air Doctrine," pp. 253, 274.

12. "An Admiral Talks Back to the Airmen," *Saturday Evening Post* 221 (June 25, 1949): 25, 136–38.

13. Borowski, *Threat*, p. 155.

14. Paul Y. Hammond, "Super Carriers and B-36 Bombers: Appropriations, Strategy and Politics," in *American Civil-Military Decisions*, ed. Harold Stein (Birmingham, Ala., 1963), p. 488; U.S. Congress, House, Committee on Armed Services, *The National Defense Program—Unification and Strategy*, Hearings . . . , 81st cong., 1st sess. (Washington, D.C., 1950) (hereafter Unification Hearings), pp. 51, 81, 102, 103, 106.

15. Unification Hearings, pp. 184–86, 189.

16. Hammond, "Super Carriers," p. 498.

17. Unification Hearings, pp. 434, 436.

18. Ibid., pp. 522, 525–26.

19. Condit, *Joint Chiefs* 2: 350; Rosenberg, "Overkill," p. 30; idem, "Postwar Air Doctrine," p. 266.

20. General Eaker was one of the skeptics. Eaker interview with Goldberg and Hildreth, May 22, 1962, AFSHRC.

21. Rosenberg, "Postwar Air Doctrine," p. 258.

22. Smith, *Peril*, pp. 78-79.

23. Rosenberg, "Hydrogen Bomb Decision," p. 79; Herbert York, *The Advisors: Oppenheimer, Teller, and the Superbomb* (San Francisco, 1976), pp. 41, 45, 156-57. Glenn T. Seaborg, another GAC member, was out of the country; he had written Oppenheimer that he did not have enough information to say the hydrogen bomb program should not be accelerated (*In the Matter of J. Robert Oppenheimer*, p. 238).

24. *In the Matter of J. Robert Oppenheimer*, pp. 508, 513.

25. York, *Advisors*, pp. 158-59.

26. JCS reply to GAC report, Jan. 13, 1950, excerpted in Thomas Etzold and John L. Gaddis, eds., *Containment: Documents on American Policy and Strategy* (New York, 1978), pp. 368-73; Rosenberg, "Hydrogen Bomb Decision," pp. 82-83.

27. Lilienthal, *Atomic Energy Years*, p. 632.

28. Michael S. Sherry, *Preparing for the Next War: American Plans for Postwar Defense, 1941-45* (New Haven, 1977), pp. 195, 200-201, 213; Rosenberg, "Overkill," p. 17.

29. Sherry, *Preparing*, p. 202; Greenwood, "Emergence," p. 221.

30. Brodie conversation with author, Sept. 1977.

31. Excerpts from NSC 68, Apr. 14, 1960, in Etzold and Gaddis, *Containment*, pp. 416, 419-20, 429-30.

32. Hanson W. Baldwin, "War of Prevention," *New York Times*, Sept. 1, 1950; "Matthews Favors War for Peace," ibid., Aug. 26, 1950; "Aggressors for Peace" (editorial), ibid., Aug. 27, 1950; ibid., Sept. 3, 1950.

33. Orvil A. Anderson, "Air Warfare and Morality," *Air University Quarterly Review* 3 (Winter 1949): 9-13; Nathan F. Twining, *Neither Liberty nor Safety: A Hard Look at U.S. Military Policy and Strategy* (New York, 1966), p. 19.

34. Anderson quoted in John H. Scrivner, Jr., "Pioneer into Space: A Biography of Major General Orvil Arson Anderson" (Ph.D. diss., University of Oklahoma, 1971), p. 351.

35. Austin Stevens, "General Removed over War Speech," *New York Times*, Sept. 2, 1950; Walter H. Waggoner, "U.S. Disowns Matthews' Talk of Waging War to Get Peace," ibid., Aug. 27, 1950; Scrivner, "Anderson," pp. 351, 352-54. President Truman reported that Matthews told him he had heard so many admirals and other high navy officials "talk" preventive war that he had repeated the phrase without realizing how far it departed from the president's policy. Truman, *Years of Trial and Hope*, p. 436.

36. David Alan Rosenberg, "'A Smoking Radiating Ruin at the End of Two Hours': Documents on American Plans for Nuclear War with the Soviet Union, 1954-1955," *International Security* 6 (Winter 1981/82): 27.

37. Rosenberg, "Overkill," pp. 26-27.

38. Eisenhower memo to John Foster Dulles, Sept. 8, 1953, quoted ibid., p. 33.

39. Ibid., p. 34.

40. Robert H. Ferrell, ed., *The Eisenhower Diaries* (New York, 1981), pp. 311-12.

41. U.S. Congress, Senate, Joint Committee on Armed Services and Foreign Relations, *Military Situation in the Far East: Hearings to Conduct an Inquiry into the Military Situation in the Far East and the Facts surrounding the Relief of General of the Army Douglas MacArthur from his Assignment in that Area*, 4 vols., 82nd cong., 1st sess. (Washington, D.C., 1951), p. 1,245.

42. John E. Wiltz, "The MacArthur Hearings of 1951: The Secret Testi-

mony," *Military Affairs* 39 (Dec. 1975): 168–70; Robert F. Futrell, *The United States Air Force in Korea, 1950–1953* (Washington, D.C., 1983), pp. 241-42; Memorandum of discussion, Dept. of State, JCS meeting, Mar. 27, 1953, in U.S., Department of State, *Foreign Relations of the United States: 1952–1954*, vol. 15, *Korea*, p. 817.

43. Memo of discussion, NSC meeting, Mar. 31, 1953, in Dept. of State, *Foreign Relations of the United States: 1952–1954*, vol. 15, *Korea*, pp. 826–27; minutes of NSC meeting, May 13, 1954, ibid., p. 1,014; "Might Be Worth It, Eisenhower Felt," *New York Times*, June 8, 1984.

44. Glenn H. Snyder, "The 'New Look' of 1953," in Warner R. Schilling, Paul Y. Hammond, and Glenn H. Snyder, *Strategy, Politics and Defense Budgets* (New York, 1962), p. 437; Samuel F. Wells, Jr., "The Origins of Massive Retaliation," *Political Science Quarterly* 96 (Spring 1981): 34; Rosenberg, "Overkill," p. 34.

45. Rosenberg, "Smoking Radiating Ruin," pp. 25, 28.

46. Wells, "Massive Retaliation," pp. 35–36; Rosenberg, "Overkill," pp. 35, 37, 41.

47. Futrell, *Ideas*, p. 362.

48. Ibid., pp. 550–51, 570–72; Rosenberg, "Overkill," p. 57.

49. Futrell, *Ideas*, pp. 569, 571.

50. Rosenberg, "Overkill," pp. 62–63.

51. Robert S. McNamara, Memorandum for the President, Nov. 21, 1962, quoted in Robert Scheer, "Interview with McNamara," *Los Angeles Times*, Apr. 8, 1982.

52. John W. Finney, "Pentagon Raises Atom Toll Count," *New York Times*, Sept. 17, 1975; USSBS, *Overall Report (European War)* (Sept. 30, 1945), p. 72; idem, *Japanese Morale*, p. 194.

53. Futrell, *Ideas*, p. 667; Rosenberg, "Overkill," p. 68.

54. See, for example, "1954 Study by the Joint Chiefs on Possible U.S. Intervention," "1961 Rusk-McNamara Report to Kennedy on South Vietnam," and "McNaughton Draft for McNamara on 'Proposed Course of Action,'" in Neil Sheehan et al., eds., *The Pentagon Papers* (New York, 1971), pp. 44, 150, 432; 1964 Air Force Policy Letter for Commanders in Futrell, *Ideas*, p. 804.

55. Ira C. Eaker, "Some Observations on Air Power," in Hurley and Ehrhart, *Air Power and Warfare*, p. 358.

56. Rosenberg, "Smoking Radiating Ruin," p. 27; Curtis E. LeMay with Dale O. Smith, *America Is in Danger* (New York, 1968), pp. 262–63.

57. LeMay, *America*, p. 309.

58. Twining, *Liberty*, pp. 19, 170, 174.

59. Eaker, "Observations," p. 358.

60. LeMay, *America*, pp. 308–9.

61. Twining, *Liberty*, p. 195.

62. Ibid., p. 110.

63. Spaatz interview with Goldberg and Parrish, Feb. 21, 1962, AFSHRC.

64. Futrell, *Ideas*, pp. 392–93.

65. Robert S. McNamara, draft memorandum for the President, Oct. 14, 1966, excerpt in Steven Cohen, ed., *Vietnam: Anthology and Guide to a Television History* (New York, 1983), p. 139.

66. Rosenberg, "Overkill," p. 18; idem, "Smoking Radiating Ruin," pp. 30–31.

67. Bernard Brodie, *War and Politics* (New York, 1973), pp. 46–47; *In the Matter of J. Robert Oppenheimer*, p. 6.

68. Twining, *Liberty,* p. 104. See U.S. Marine Corps, *Small Wars Manual* (Washington, D.C., 1940), pp. 31–32.

69. Notably in *Strategy and the Missile Age* (Princeton, 1959), pp. 235–37.

70. Lilienthal, *Atomic Energy Years,* p. 271.

71. LeMay, *America,* pp. 33–34.

Essay on Sources

Like the other American military services, the Army Air Forces employed professional scholars to compile historical records and to write detailed official histories. These scholars received access to an enormous mass of written documents and interviewed participants in the air war while it was taking place and afterward. Yet AAF leaders treated them warily. They sometimes denied the historians sensitive information and tried to control the records from which history would be written so that the final product would reflect favorably on their service. Thus General Eaker wrote the assistant chief of air staff for intelligence early in 1944 that no criticism of the conduct of the war ought to appear in official correspondence without clearance from the "war chiefs." There was "a mass of historians at both ends watching all this correspondence," Eaker warned, "and these things cannot but creep into the official record unless we are all on guard."*

The following October, when the British were promoting an air offensive against German civilian morale, General Kuter informed General Spaatz that he was not to allow Bruce C. Hopper, an official historian at USSTAF, to see any document from the Air Ministry containing minutes that indicated "contention or disagreement." This order followed from an official AAF policy, promulgated October 18, 1944, denying all official historians of the U.S. armed forces access to information discussed by the Joint Chiefs of Staff, the Combined Chiefs of Staff, and their planning agencies which included "personal or political controversy."†

At the end of the war the air force encouraged a group of professional scholars, led by Wesley Frank Craven and James L. Cate, to prepare a multivolume quasi-official history, *The Army Air Forces in World War II*. It permitted them to see large quantities of documents, some of which contained information about morally sensitive aspects of the American bombing offensive. Yet the Craven and Cate history devotes limited space to moral problems of the air war, though it discusses technical and operational matters in meticulous detail. It never examines the moral question systematically and it occasionally buries in a mass of data bits of information which might signal an alert reader that some important moral

---

*Eaker to Clayton Bissell, Jan. 8, 1944, container 18, Eaker Papers, Library of Congress.
†Kuter to Spaatz, Oct. 27, 1944, Frederick L. Anderson Diary, Oct. 27, 1944, Anderson Papers, Hoover Institution Archives.

question was being passed over. Thus in the middle of the second paragraph on page 698 of volume 5 it states without elaboration that possibly the most spectacular Far East Air Forces actions against Kyushu were "incendiary attacks upon urban targets, ostensibly to destroy industrial plants."

Why did Craven and Cate fail to explore such matters systematically? One answer is that the historians, like the military arm whose history they were writing, concerned themselves chiefly with the enormous practical tasks the AAF accomplished. But there are other reasons. According to John E. Fagg, who wrote the sections that discuss THUNDERCLAP, the Dresden raid, and Operation CLARION, he and his colleagues lacked access to all the documents which subsequently became available, for instance the letter about Dresden on which Arnold wrote that war must be somewhat ruthless and inhuman. Furthermore, Fagg observed that while the AAF history was being written, "we were still basking in the great victory of the war and aware that the account had to be cleared before publication" and that "[h]ence the conclusions and intimations here and there were not as sharp" as those I had drawn elsewhere.* Finally, he suggested that the personal qualities of the AAF leaders impressed the "official" historians very strongly and very favorably. "In those pre-Vietnam days," he wrote in 1981, "we . . . had great confidence in our leaders, regarding them as men of exceptional intelligence, honor, and integrity."†

Professor Craven felt much the same way. "Working as I did," he explained, "with high ranking officers of the AAF who understood our professional problem and gave us tremendous support, I learned to respect the professional soldier for his intelligence and for his patriotism, if I may put it that way."‡ In the 1940s and 1950s neither the air force nor its historians were ready to examine thoroughly in a published work the sensitive painful moral questions that arose in the air war.

Nevertheless, the air force made it possible for other scholars to do so by transferring its records to its own depositories and to the National Archives and opening them to researchers. Those records and the personal files that AAF generals made available to scholars are among the most important of the primary source collections used to write this book.

PRIMARY SOURCES IN LIBRARIES AND DEPOSITORIES

Albert F. Simpson Historical Research Center, Maxwell Air Force Base, Alabama
   Army Air Forces Planning and Operational Records
   Oral History Interviews with Ira C. Eaker, Carl Spaatz, and Kenneth Wolfe
   Papers of Charles P. Cabell, Guido R. Perera, and David M. Schlatter
   Air Corps Tactical School Texts and Lectures

Columbia Oral History Collections, Butler Library, Columbia University, New York City
   Interviews with Charles P. Cabell, James Doolittle, Ira C. Eaker, Robert A. Lovett, and Carl Spaatz

---

*Ronald Schaffer, "American Military Ethics in World War II: The Bombing of German Civilians," *Journal of American History* 47 (Sept. 1980): 318–334.

†John E. Fagg to author, Sept. 8, 1981.
‡Frank Craven to author, Sept. 27, 1977.

Dwight D. Eisenhower Library, Abilene, Kansas
    Pre-Presidential File

Hoover Institution Archives, Stanford, California
    Papers of Frederick L. Anderson

Library of Congress, Washington, D.C.
    Papers of Henry H. Arnold, Vannevar Bush, Ira C. Eaker, Curtis LeMay,
William D. Leahy, Elwood R. Quesada, and Carl Spaatz

National Archives, Washington, D.C.
    Record Group 18   Headquarters, Army Air Forces
    Record Group 77   Chief of Engineers
    Record Group 107   Office of the Secretary of War
    Record Group 165   War Department General and Special Staffs
    Record Group 218   U.S. Joint Chiefs of Staff
    Record Group 226   Office of Strategic Services
    Record Group 227   Office of Scientific Research and Development, Na-
tional Defense Research Committee
    Record Group 239   American Commission for the Protection and Salvage
of Artistic and Historic Monuments in War Areas
    Record Group 243   United States Strategic Bombing Survey
    Record Group 319   The Army Staff
    Record Group 331   Allied Operational and Occupation Headquarters,
World War II
    Papers of Lauris Norstad (Housed in National Archives Modern Military
Records Division)

Franklin D. Roosevelt Library, Hyde Park, N.Y.
    Map Room File
    Official File

U.S. Air Force Academy Library
    Papers of Laurence S. Kuter

Yale University Library
    Papers and Diary of Henry Stimson (microfilm copies used)

INTERVIEWS BY THE AUTHOR

    James Doolittle, Aug. 24, 1979
    Haywood S. Hansell, Jr., Oct. 1, 1980
    Mr. and Mrs. Mamoru Iga, July 18, 1983
    James G. McDonald, June 12, 1978

OTHER SELECTED PUBLISHED WORKS AND DISSERTATIONS

Chapter 1
Despite the richness of primary sources and the candor with which several air
leaders answered questions of oral historians, not a single definitive biography of

a World War II AAF general has appeared. The closest thus far is Thomas M. Coffey's fluently written *Hap: The Story of the U.S. Air Force and the Man Who Built It, General Henry H. "Hap" Arnold* (New York: Viking Press, 1982). Coffey's work provides intimate details of the AAF chief's personal life and admirable though brief discussions of the professional issues he faced during World War II. But it does not show how Arnold felt about the tremendous power he wielded. Thus Coffey misses a crucial element of this commander's inner life. General Arnold's *Global Mission* (New York: Harper & Brothers, 1949) is a detailed guide to the air force chief's activities and to some of his thoughts. It should be supplemented by Coffey's *Hap* and by two articles that General Kuter wrote about his chief several years after the war: "The General vs. the Establishment: General H. H. Arnold and the Air Staff," *Aerospace Historian* 22 (Winter 1974): 185–89, and "How Hap Arnold Built the AAF," *Air Force* 56 (Sept. 1973): 88–93.

With his usual bluntness, General LeMay tells exactly how he remembered feeling when he and his flyers destroyed enemy targets. *Mission with LeMay: My Story* (Garden City, N.Y.: Doubleday, 1965), which the general wrote with Mac-Kinlay Kantor, is one of the finest sources for historians of generalship in the age of the strategic bomber. Other useful studies of AAF leaders include Lowell Thomas and Edward Jablonski, *Doolittle: A Biography* (Garden City, N.Y.: Doubleday, 1976); Alfred Goldberg, "General Carl A. Spaatz," in *The War Lords: Military Commanders of the Twentieth Century*, ed. Michael Carver (Boston: Little, Brown, 1976); and a series of articles by General Haywood S. Hansell, Jr.: "Brig. Gen. Kenneth N. Walker, Prophet of Strategic Air Power," *Air Force* 61 (November 1978): 92–94; "Gen. Muir S. Fairchild: Strategist, Statesman, Educator," *Air Force* 62 (January 1979): 72–74; "The High Command: Then and Now," *Strategic Review* 1 (Summer 1973): 44–52; and "Gen. Laurence S. Kuter," *Air Force* 63 (June 1980): 95–97.

For Franklin Roosevelt's views on war in general and air war in particular, see James MacGregor Burns, *Roosevelt: The Soldier of Freedom* (New York: Harcourt Brace Jovanovich, 1970) and Robert Dallek, *Franklin D. Roosevelt and American Foreign Policy, 1932–1945* (New York: Oxford University Press, 1979). Forrest C. Pogue's *George C. Marshall* (three volumes thus far, New York: Viking Press, 1963–73) is the standard biography. Dr. Pogue kindly provided the author with information from a part of the Marshall collection which is presently closed to outside historians. The best published sources of information about Henry L. Stimson are Elting E. Morison, *Turmoil and Tradition: A Study of the Life and Times of Henry L. Stimson* (New York: Atheneum, 1964) and Henry L. Stimson and McGeorge Bundy, *On Active Service in Peace and War* (New York: Harper & Row, 1948).

Chapter 2

For prewar American air force bombing doctrine see, in addition to the manuals and lectures cited in footnotes, [Thomas H. Greer et al.,] *The Development of Air Doctrine in the Army Air Corps, 1917–1941*, USAF Historical Studies No. 89 (Maxwell Air Force Base, Ala.: USAF Historical Division, Air University, 1955); Robert F. Futrell, *Ideas, Concepts, Doctrine: A History of Basic Thinking in the United States Air Force, 1907–1964*, 2 vols. (Maxwell Air Force Base, Ala.: Air University, 1971), and Haywood S. Hansell, Jr., *The Air Plan That Defeated Hitler* (Atlanta: Higgins-McArthur/ Longino & Porter, 1972). Giulio Douhet's major works, translated by Dino Ferrari, appear in *The Command of the Air* (New York: Coward-McCann, 1942). The

Office of Air Force History reprinted this seminal work in 1983. The best
published study of William "Billy" Mitchell is Alfred F. Hurley, *Billy Mitchell,
Crusader for Air Power* (Bloomington, Ind.: Indiana University Press, 1975). For the
relative importance in American air force thinking of Douhet, Mitchell, and other
early air-power theorists, see, in addition to the works of Futrell and Greer,
Raymond R. Flugel, "United States Air Power Doctrine: A Study of the Influence
of William Mitchell and Giulio Douhet at the Air Corps Tactical School, 1921-
1935" (Ph. D. diss., University of Oklahoma, 1965).

Chapter 3

Charles Webster and Noble Frankland, *The Strategic Air Offensive against Germany,
1939-1945*, 4 vols. (London: Her Majesty's Stationery Office, 1961) is the well-
documented British official history. It should be supplemented by three critical
works about RAF bombing of German cities: Max Hastings, *Bomber Command* (New
York: Dial Press/James Wade, 1979); Martin Middlebrook, *The Battle of Hamburg:
Allied Bomber Forces against a German City in 1943* (New York: Scribner's, 1981); and
David Irving, *The Destruction of Dresden* (New York: Ballantine Books, 1965). Thomas
M. Coffey analyses the early struggles of American air generals to prove their
bombing theory and to preserve a separate strategic bombing force in *Decision over
Schweinfurt: The U.S. Eighth Air Force Battle for Daylight Bombing* (New York: David
McKay, 1977). One of the protagonists in the transportation bombing contro-
versy presents his position in Solly Zuckerman, *From Apes to Warlords* (New York:
Harper & Row, 1978) and is countered by Walt W. Rostow, *Pre-Invasion Bombing
Strategy: General Eisenhower's Decision of March 25, 1944* (Austin: University of Texas
Press, 1981). The British prime minister's account of the events discussed in this
chapter appears in Winston S. Churchill, *Closing the Ring* (Boston: Houghton
Mifflin, 1951), the fifth volume in his history of the Second World War.
    Efforts by the Roberts commission and other U.S. public and private agencies
to preserve and rehabilitate the treasures of Italy and other places attacked by the
American armed forces are described in *Report of the American Commission for the
Protection and Salvage of Artistic and Historic Monuments in War Areas* (Washington, D.C.:
Government Printing Office, 1946). An eyewitness to some of these efforts
presents a vivid, sometimes touching account in Frederick Hartt, *Florentine Art under
Fire* (Princeton, N.J.: Princeton University Press, 1949), while Gerald Haines, in
"'Who Gives a Damn about Medieval Walls,'" *Prologue* 8 (Summer, 1976): 97-106,
compares the large aims of the preservationists with their much smaller accom-
plishments. In *Salerno to Cassino* (Washington, D.C.: Office of the Chief of Military
History, 1969), a thorough, clearly written history of a major part of the Italian
campaign, Martin Blumenson carefully weighs the responsibility of various individuals and agencies for the bombing of Monte Cassino Abbey. David Hapgood
and David Richardson present additional information about the Cassino episode,
including testimony of monks who were inside the abbey, in *Monte Cassino* (New
York: Congdon & Weed, 1984). For the way an American officer on a mountainside below the abbey felt about its demolition, see Harold L. Bond, *Return to Cassino:
A Memoir of the Fight for Rome* (Garden City, N.Y.: Doubleday, 1964). For the political
and military context of Anglo-American terror bombing in one Balkan country,
see Marshall L. Miller, *Bulgaria during the Second World War* (Stanford: Stanford
University Press, 1975).

Chapter 4

One of the most realistic depictions of the inner struggles of an AAF field commander in the war against Germany is *Twelve O'Clock High*, a motion picture written by two AAF veterans, Sy Bartlett and Bierne Lay. For the arguments against obliteration bombing see—in addition to Vera Brittain's "Massacre by Bombing," *Fellowship* 10 (March 1944): 50–64—an essay by the American Jesuit theologian, Prof. John C. Ford, "The Morality of Obliteration Bombing," which first appeared in a 1944 issue of *Theological Studies* and is excerpted in *War and Morality*, ed. Richard Wasserstrom (Belmont, Ca.: Wadsworth, 1970), pp. 15–41. The best analysis of U.S. public attitudes toward Germany is Richard W. Steele, "American Popular Opinion and the War against Germany: The Issue of Negotiated Peace, 1942," *Journal of American History* 45 (Dec. 1978): 704–23.

Chapter 5

Volume 3 of Craven and Cate's history of the AAF, Webster and Franklin's official history of the strategic air offensive, and Max Hastings's *Bomber Command* provide a view of the path the Allied air forces took to CLARION, THUNDERCLAP, and Dresden. David Irving's analysis, *The Destruction of Dresden*, reignited the controversy that began when the AAF and RAF undertook their climactic raids on the eastern German cities. For critical evaluations of Irving's work, see Melden E. Smith, Jr., "The Bombing of Dresden Reconsidered" (Ph.D. diss., Boston University, 1971), which places great emphasis on the Soviet desire to have those cities bombed, and Ronald Schaffer, "Sur le bombardement de Dresde," *Revue d'histoire de la Deuxième Guerre Mondiale*, no. 62 (April, 1966), pp. 75–77.

Chapter 6

James P. Baxter III, *Scientists against Time* (Boston: Little, Brown, 1948) presents an overview of American scientific contributions to the war. For the development of incendiary weapons and techniques, see J. Enrique Zanetti, *Fire from the Air: ABC of Incendiaries* (New York: Columbia University Press, 1941); Leo P. Brophy and George J. B. Fisher, *The Chemical Warfare Service: Organizing for War* (Washington, D.C.: Office of the Chief of Military History, 1959); the chapter on "Incendiary Bombs" by E. P. Stevenson in *Chemistry: A History of the Chemistry Components of the National Defense Research Committee, 1940–1946*, ed. W. A. Noyes, Jr. (Boston: Little, Brown, 1948); and especially the essays in *Fire and the Air War*, ed. Horatio Bond (Reprint, Manhattan, Kans.: Military Affairs/Aerospace Historian, 1974).

The first chief of the XXI Bomber Command examines the Pacific Air War in Haywood S. Hansell, Jr., *Air War against Japan* (Maxwell Air Force Base, Ala.: Air Power Research Institute, 1980). Other accounts by American eyewitnesses include LeMay and Kantor, *Mission with LeMay*; St. Clair McKelway, "A Reporter with the B-29's: III. The Cigar, the Three Wings, and the Low-Level Attacks," *New Yorker* 21 (June 23, 1945): 26–39; and the memoir by Kevin Herbert, *Maximum Effort: The B-29's against Japan* (Manhattan, Kans.: Sunflower University Press, 1983). Herbert, a professor of classics, served as a Superfortress tail gunner. For the vivid recollections of a French journalist who was in the target area, see Robert Guillain's elegantly written *I Saw Tokyo Burning: An Eyewitness Narrative from Pearl Harbor to Hiroshima*, trans. William Byron (Garden City, N.Y.: Doubleday, 1981).

Chapter 7

Published accounts of the March 9–10 Tokyo raid include, in addition to the works of McKelway, Guillain, and LeMay and Kantor, Lars Tillitse, "When Bombs Rained on Us in Tokyo," *Saturday Evening Post* 218 (Jan. 12, 1946): 34, 82, 85; Masuo Kato, *The Lost War: A Japanese Reporter's Inside Story* (New York: Alfred A. Knopf, 1946); and Gordon Daniels, "The Great Tokyo Air Raid, 9–10 March 1945," in *Modern Japan: Aspects of History, Literature and Society*, ed. W. G. Beasley (Berkeley and Los Angeles: University of California Press, 1975). There are two illuminating chapters on this subject in Bond, *Fire and the Air War:* Robert Nathans, "Making the Fires That Beat Japan," and Forrest J. Sanborn, "Fire Protection Lessons of the Japanese Attacks." The United States Strategic Bombing Survey published a series of reports on the fire raids, including *Field Report Covering Air-Raid Protection and Allied Subjects: Tokyo* (Washington, D.C., 1947); *The Effects of Strategic Bombing on Japanese Morale* (Washington, D.C., 1947); *The Effects of Strategic Bombing on Japan's War Economy* (Washington, D.C., 1946); and *The Effects of Bombing on Health and Medical Services in Japan* (Washington, D.C., 1947). David MacIsaac, *Strategic Bombing in World War II: The Story of the United States Strategic Bombing Survey* (New York: Garland, 1976) is the standard history of that agency.

Of the many works on the development and use of the atomic bomb, the author found particularly useful for this chapter the recollections of Leslie R. Groves, *Now It Can Be Told: The Story of the Manhattan Project* (New York and Evanston: Harper & Row, 1962); Walter S. Schoenberger, *Decision of Destiny* (Athens, Ohio: Ohio University Press, 1969); and Martin J. Sherwin, *A World Destroyed: The Atomic Bomb and the Grand Alliance* (New York: Random House, 1977), which includes several key technical and diplomatic documents. A detailed, well-written official history of the American A-bomb project appears in Richard G. Hewlett and Oscar E. Anderson, Jr., *The New World, 1939–1946* (University Park: Pennsylvania State University Press, 1962), which is the first volume of *A History of the United States Atomic Energy Commission*. Otis Cary offers a persuasive explanation of why the U.S. government chose not to destroy Kyoto in "The Sparing of Kyoto, Mr. Stimson's 'Pet City,'" *Japan Quarterly* 22 (Oct.–Dec. 1975): 337–347.

Chapter 8

Military men presented their explanations for using the A-bomb in LeMay and Kantor, *Mission with LeMay*; Groves, *Now It Can Be Told*; H. H. Arnold, *Global Mission* (New York: Harper & Brothers, 1949); and in John P. Sunderland, "The Story Gen. Marshall Told Me," *U.S. News and World Report* 47 (Nov. 2, 1959): 50–56. The secretary of war offered his rationale for dropping it on Hiroshima and Nagasaki in Henry L. Stimson, "The Decision to Use the Atomic Bomb," *Harper's Magazine* 194 (Feb. 1947): 97–107. In *I Was There* (New York: Whittlesey House, 1950), Admiral William D. Leahy explains why he felt it need not have been dropped.

President Truman presented his public account of the A-bomb decision in *Year of Decisions* (New York: New American Library, 1965), the first volume of his memoirs—and offered his private views in *Off the Record: The Private Papers of Harry S. Truman*, ed. Robert H. Ferrell (New York: Harper & Row, 1980). Sherwin, *A World Destroyed*; Schoenberger, *Decision of Destiny*; and Barton J. Bernstein, *Hiroshima and Nagasaki Reconsidered: The Atomic Bombings of the Japan and the Origins of the Cold War, 1941–1945* (Morristown, N.J.: General Learning Press, 1975) discuss the decision to use the bomb as part of the evolving conflict between the United States and the

USSR. In 1955 the U.S. Department of Defense published several crucial documents concerning the military and diplomatic context in which the decision was made to drop the bomb in *The Entry of the Soviet Union into the War against Japan: Military Plans, 1941–1945.*

A lucid discussion of the moral issue appears in Robert C. Batchelder's *The Irreversible Decision, 1939–1950* (Boston: Houghton Mifflin, 1961), which examines alternatives to dropping the bomb on human targets and the reasons why those alternatives were not chosen. For problems the unconditional surrender doctrine raised for American and especially for Japanese leaders, see Anne Armstrong, *Unconditional Surrender: The Impact of the Casablanca Policy upon World War II* (New Brunswick, N.J.: Rutgers University Press, 1961); Robert J. C. Butow, *Japan's Decision to Surrender* (Stanford: Stanford University Press, 1954); and Akira Iriye, *Power and Culture: The Japanese-American War, 1941–1945* (Cambridge: Harvard University Press, 1981).

Alice K. Smith explains how nuclear scientists felt about the moral and military implications of their work in "Behind the Decision to Use the Atomic Bomb: Chicago, 1944–45," *Bulletin of the Atomic Scientists* 14 (October 1958): 288–312, and *A Peril and a Hope: The Scientists' Movement in America, 1945–1947* (Chicago: University of Chicago Press, 1965). This volume includes in an appendix the Franck report issued by Chicago Metallurgical Laboratory scientists on June 11, 1945. In "Manhattan Project Maverick: The Case of Leo Szilard," *Prologue* 15 (Summer 1983): 73–87, Carol S. Gruber describes the conflicts between an outspoken Met Lab scientist who thought it was morally wrong to drop the bomb on Japanese civilians and higher-ups in the Manhattan Project. The director of the Chicago laboratory, Arthur H. Compton, recalls his thoughts about using the A-bomb on a live target in *Atomic Quest: A Personal Narrative* (New York: Oxford University Press, 1956). Other participants in the A-bomb project recalled how they felt about the moral issue in a 1981 television documentary by Jon Else, David Peoples, and Janet Peoples, *The Day after Trinity: J. Robert Oppenheimer and the Atomic Bomb* (Transcript: PTV Publications, Kent, Ohio). Oppenheimer recalls how he felt about the moral question during the war in United States Atomic Energy Commission, *In the Matter of J. Robert Oppenheimer: Transcript of Hearing before Personnel Security Board and Texts of Principal Documents and Letters* (Cambridge, Mass.: MIT Press, 1971).

Chapter 9

The key work here is Irving Janis, *Victims of Groupthink: A Psychological Study of Foreign Policy Decisions and Fiascoes* (Boston: Houghton Mifflin, 1972). An expanded version of this study appeared in 1983 as *Groupthink: Psychological Studies of Policy Decisions and Fiascoes* (Boston: Houghton Mifflin). Lawrence S. Wrightsman, Kay Deaux et al. summarize recent research in group behavior in *Social Psychology in the 80's* (Monterey, Ca.: Brooks/Cole, 1981). In *The Ego and the Mechanism of Defense*, trans. Cecil Barnes (New York: International Universities Press, 1962) Anna Freud describes psychological processes that protect people from the stress arising from exposure to morally sensitive activities.

Chapter 10

Anyone interested in the development of U.S. nuclear strategy should read a series of pioneering articles by David Alan Rosenberg based on extensive archival

research: "American Postwar Air Doctrine and Organization: The Navy Expe-
rience," in *Air Power and Warfare*, ed. Alfred F. Hurley and Robert C. Ehrhart
(Washington, D.C.: Office of Air Force History, 1979); "American Strategy and
the Hydrogen Bomb Decision," *Journal of American History* 66 (June 1979): 71–84;
"The Origins of Overkill: Nuclear Weapons and American Strategy, 1945–1960,"
International Security 7 (Spring 1983): 3–71; "'A Smoking Radiating Ruin at the End
of Two Hours': Documents on American Plans for Nuclear War with the Soviet
Union, 1954–1955," *International Security* 6 (Winter 1981–82): 3–38; and "U.S. Nu-
clear Stockpile, 1945 to 1950," *Bulletin of the Atomic Scientists* 38 (May 1982): 25–30.

Kenneth W. Condit traces crucial postwar military decisions in *The History of
the Joint Chiefs of Staff*, vol. 2, *The Joint Chiefs of Staff and National Policy* (Wilmington,
Del., 1979). Documents on this subject can also be found in a collection by
Thomas Etzold and John L. Gaddis, *Containment: Documents on American Policy and
Strategy* (New York: Columbia University Press, 1978). On the relative military
strengths of the United States and the Soviet Union after World War II, see Harry
R. Borowski, *A Hollow Threat: Strategic Air Power and Containment before Korea* (Westport,
Conn.: Greenwood Press, 1982). This book should be read in conjunction with
Melvyn P. Leffler, "The American Conception of National Security and the
Beginnings of the Cold War, 1945–48," *American Historical Review* 89 (April 1984):
346–81, which considers the crucial question of Soviet intentions and suggests
that American planners may have misperceived Soviet threats to U.S. interests.
For the development of the postwar U.S. Air Force and its strategic doctrine see
Futrell, *Ideas, Concepts, Doctrine*, and John T. Greenwood, "The Emergence of the
Postwar Strategic Air Force, 1945–1953," in Hurley and Ehrhart, *Air Power and
Warfare*.

Paul Y. Hammond analyzes the revolt of the admirals in "Super Carriers and
B-36 Bombers: Appropriations Strategy and Politics," part of *American Civil-
Military Decisions*, ed. Harold Stein (Birmingham, Ala.: University of Alabama
Press, 1963). Greenwood, in "The Emergence of the Postwar Strategic Air Force,"
shows how the air admirals changed their position on nuclear warfare and
presents an explanation of why they did so. The admirals' attack on the morality
of strategic bombing appears in U.S. Congress, House, Committee on Armed
Services, *The National Defense Program—Unification and Strategy*, Hearings . . . , 81st
Cong., 1st sess. (Washington, D.C., 1950).

For the debate on the hydrogen bomb, see Rosenberg, "Hydrogen Bomb
Decision"; Herbert York, *The Advisors: Oppenheimer, Teller, and the Superbomb* (San
Francisco: W. H. Freeman, 1976), which reprints the General Advisory Commit-
tee memoranda opposing immediate construction of the bomb; and *In the Matter of
J. Robert Oppenheimer*. Orvil A. Anderson discussed "Air Warfare and Morality" in
Air University Quarterly Review 3 (Winter 1949): 9–13. John H. Scrivner, Jr., describes
the events leading to General Anderson's suspension in "Pioneer into Space: A
Biography of Major General Orvil Arson Anderson" (Ph.D. diss., University of
Oklahoma, 1971). The views of President Eisenhower on using hydrogen and
fission bombs in Korea and elsewhere can be found in the U.S. State Department
publication, *Foreign Relations of the United States, 1952–1954*, vol. 15, *Korea* (Washington: U.S. Government Printing Office, 1984). Two analyses of Eisenhower's
nuclear policy and the reasons behind it are Glenn H. Snyder, "The 'New Look' of
1953," in Warner R. Schilling, Paul Y. Hammond, and Glenn H. Snyder, *Strategy,
Politics and Defense Budgets* (New York: Columbia University Press, 1962) and Samuel

F. Wells, Jr., "The Origins of Massive Retaliation," *Political Science Quarterly* 96 (Spring 1981): 31–52.

For postwar views of U.S. Air Force generals, see LeMay and Kantor, *Mission with LeMay*; LeMay with Dale O. Smith, *America Is in Danger* (New York: Funk & Wagnalls, 1968); Nathan F. Twining, *Neither Liberty nor Safety: A Hard Look at U.S. Military Policy and Strategy* (New York: Holt, Rinehart & Winston, 1966); and the remarks of Generals Eaker and LeMay in Hurley and Ehrhart, *Air Power and Warfare.*

Those who wish to explore the philosophical problem of morality in warfare may consult, in addition to Batchelder's *The Irreversible Decision* and Wasserstrom's collection, *War and Morality*, the following books and articles: Michael Howard, *War and the Liberal Conscience* (New Brunswick, N.J.: Rutgers University Press, 1978); Peter Karsten, *Law, Soldiers and Combat* (Westport, Conn.: Greenwood Press, 1978); Malham M. Wakin's book of readings, *War, Morality, and the Military Profession* (Boulder: Westview Press, 1979); Michael Walzer, *Just and Unjust Wars: A Moral Argument with Historical Illustrations* (New York: Basic Books, 1977); and a series of articles on war and morality in *Philosophy and Public Affairs*, including Robert K. Fullinwider, "War and Innocence" 5 (Fall 1975): 90–97 and George Mavrodes, "Conventions and the Morality of War" 4 (Winter 1975): 117–31.

Finally, since 1980 *The United States Air Force Academy Journal of Professional Military Ethics* has published several theoretical and practical articles on that subject, including Charles W. Hudlin, "Morality and the Military Profession: Some Problems and Tentative Solutions" 3 (Dec. 1982): 14–23, and Kenneth H. Wenker, "Military Necessity and Morality" 4 (Sept. 1983): 29–34. These articles indicate directly and indirectly the nature of current Air Force thinking about the kinds of issues discussed in this book.

Index

AAF (Army Air Forces): reasons for change in bombing practices of, 103-4
AAF intelligence (A-2): and incendiary bombing data, 109, 112
AAF leaders, 8-16; age of, 9; seeming amorality of, 149-51; bonds between, 16-17; attitude of, towards death, 17-18; fatalism of, 17; hardening of, 17-18; and moral issue, 149-55; social origins of, 8
Absolutist view of war, 215
Air Corps Tactical School (ACTS): 10, 23, 24, 29, 32, 107, 153; and bombing civilians, 27-28; and breaking Japanese civilian morale; 31 and moral issue, 30-31
Aircraft types: B-17 bomber, 29, 38, 40, 46, 49, 64, 65, 66, 85, 97, 103, 115; B-24 bomber, 50; B-26 bomber, 42; B-29 bomber, 119, 120, 121, 123, 124, 125, 126, 127, 128, 129, 130, 131, 137, 141, 142, 150, 191; B-36 bomber, 195-96; Messerschmitt 109 fighter, 65
Air force, American: official names of, 4
Air force planning, 10, 13
Air force public relations, 9, 10-12, 26, 37-38, 52, 78, 84, 91-100, 102
Air force units: Fifth Air Force, 140, 142; Seventh Air Force, 8, 140; VII Fighter Command, 140; Eighth Air Force, 10, 13, 36, 37, 38, 39, 64-67, 73, 87, 94, 96, 109; VIII Bomber Command, 10; Ninth Air Force, 8, 94; Twelfth Air Force, 10, 13; Fifteenth Air Force, 10, 44, 50, 52, 57, 59, 68, 73, 84, 87; XIX Tactical Air Command, 89; Twentieth Air Force, 113, 121, 122, 123, 140, 143, 145, 180, 183; XXI Bomber Command, 8, 121, 124, 125, 128, 138, 140, 141, 144, 151, 152, 180; XXI Bomber Command, 73rd

wing, 128, 131-32; XXI Bomber Command, 313th wing, 128, 131-32; XXI Bomber Command, 314th wing 128, 131-32; XXI Bomber Command 509th Composite Group, 143, 147; Mediterranean Allied Air Forces (MAAF), 10, 49, 50, 52; Mediterranean Allied Strategic Air Force, 8; Northwest African Air Forces, 13, 54; United States Army Strategic Air Forces, 13; United States Strategic Air Forces (USSTAF), 13, 72, 73, 86, 88, 90, 181, 188
Air Ministry: and morale bombing, 80
Air power: F.L. Anderson feels, can defeat Germany, 106, 38
Air power, supremacy of: AAF generals wish to demonstrate, 52, 66, 90, 93
Air war doctrine (U.S.): and air force public relations, 26; and Clausewitz, 24-25; and Douhet, 23-24; and economic theory, 28-30; and Liddell Hart, 24; and W. L. Mitchell, 24-27; and Trenchard, 14; before Pearl Harbor, 27-34; and selective bombing, 29-30; and World War I, 20
Alamogordo, N. M., 169
Alexander, Henry, 139, 140
Allport, Gordon: and morale bombing, 90, 122
American Commission for the Protection and Salvage of Artistic and Historic Monuments in Europe. *See* Roberts Commission
American Defense Harvard Group: role of, in preservation program, 48
American ideals, 4, 26, 81, 141-42, 165, 204
American omnipotence: AAF leaders and, 215-16